An Illustrated History of the

North Yorkshire Moors Railway

An
Illustrated History
of the

North Yorkshire Moors Railway

Philip Benham

An imprint of
Ian Allan Publishing

First Published 2008

ISBN 978 0 86093 622 0

Published by Ian Allan Publishing

an imprint of Ian Allan Publishing Ltd, Hersham, Surrey KT12 4RG
Printed in England by Ian Allan Printing Ltd, Hersham,
Surrey KT12 4RG

Code: 0810/B2

Visit the Ian Allan Publishing website at www.ianallanpublishing.co.uk

Front cover: **On the warm summer evening of 24 July 1958, Thompson Class L1 2-6-4T No 67766 heads towards Ruswarp with the 19.50 Whitby to Middlesbrough train.** *Michael Mensing*

Back cover (bottom): **'K4' class 2-6-0 No 61994 *The Great Marquess* passes under the Larpool viaduct with the 14.00 Whitby to Pickering on 2 August 2007.** *Author*

Back cover (top): **Extract from the North Eastern Railway system map for 1922.**

Half title page: **Preserved Class K4 2-6-0 No 3442 *The Great Marquess* and Class K1 2-6-0 No 62005 head the 'Whitby Moors' railtour across Larpool Viaduct, Whitby, on 'closure day', 6 March 1965.** *Gavin Morrison*

Title page: **Pickering station from the Castle in the early 20th century.** *Sydney Smith, Beck Isle Museum*

Below: **Class A8 4-6-2T No 69861 stands at Whitby Town on 14 April 1958 with the 18.50 to Malton.** *Mike Feather*

Contents

Introduction

When the locomotives Nos 3442 *The Great Marquess* and 62005 double-headed away from the seaside town of Whitby on 6 March 1965, everyone thought this would be the last steam train across the moors to Pickering. The British Railways of Doctor Beeching had done its worst, and Whitby's once extensive rail network was reduced to a whimper. And yet, some 42 years later on 20 October 2007, those same two locomotives retraced their tracks with a North Yorkshire Moors Railway train from Whitby to Pickering; for the railway had not been destined to die after all.

Not only is the current North Yorkshire Moors Railway (NYMR) one of the premier 'heritage' railways, but it is also one of the oldest. In fact, few lines have such historic roots stretching way back to the very earliest days of railways, when no less a figure than George Stephenson proposed a railway to Pickering as his favoured option to link the port of Whitby with the outside world. And so it was that the Whitby & Pickering Railway was born, opening for business from Whitby to Grosmont in 1835, and through to Pickering the following year. Initially horses were the staple motive power, hauling passengers in what were in effect stagecoaches on rails with a rope-worked incline used to lift the line out of the Esk Valley up onto the North York Moors at Goathland. Taken over by the railway entrepreneur George Hudson's York & North Midland Railway in 1845, steam traction arrived over the next two years, with the line soon to become part of the emerging empire of the North Eastern Railway upon the latter's creation in 1854.

A decade later the rope incline was replaced by a new diversionary route, designed for locomotive operations. By 1885 four railway routes had been opened to Whitby, but, with good southern connections via Malton, the line through Pickering and Grosmont became established as the 'main-line' route to Whitby. During the first half of the 20th century railway life went on much as before, with the line seeing its busiest days in Edwardian times, but storm clouds were gathering, and the huge economic and social changes following the Second World War were to take their toll. Like so much of Britain's railway network, the growth of road transport put the railways to Whitby under great pressure. The line north along the coast to Loftus shut in 1958; then in 1963 the infamous Beeching Report recommended closure of the remaining three routes to the town. In the event one was reprieved, the Esk Valley line to Middlesbrough via Battersby. But south of Grosmont, most of the original Whitby & Pickering line closed on 8 March 1965 when train services were withdrawn between Whitby, Pickering and Malton, together with those on the route to Scarborough.

Talk of preservation soon followed in the hope that part of the region's historic railway could be saved. A society was formed

Now owned by John Cameron, 'K4' No 61994 *The Great Marquess* double-heads the North Eastern Locomotive Preservation Group's 'K1' No 62005 away from Goathland to recreate the 'Whitby Moors' railtour from 1965 heading from Whitby to Pickering at Moorgates on 20 October 2007. *Peter Van Campenhoot*

in 1967 to reopen at least a section of the line south from Grosmont, and, after much hard work, Easter 1973 saw public services recommence throughout from Grosmont to Pickering. Today the NYMR has been operating for more than a third of a century and has become the busiest of Britain's heritage railways, a fitting tribute to the vision of the founders and the dedication of the NYMR's volunteers and employees over the past 40 years. Around 320,000 passengers a year travel through the majestic North York Moors National Park between Pickering and Grosmont. From 2007 many have continued onwards to Whitby with its sandy beaches, historic abbey and other attractions, for the railway has now extended its operations over the tracks of Network Rail, and once again steam trains run regularly between Whitby and Pickering.

Much has been written about the Whitby & Pickering Railway over the years. Indeed, a book about the railway was published in its very first year (*The Scenery of the Whitby and Pickering Railway* by Henry Belcher, 1836), surely a first for any railway. In the early years of the last century, G. W. J. Potter wrote *A History of the Whitby and Pickering Railway*, while more recently David Joy and the late Ken Hoole have also written extensively. John Hunt, Martin Bairstow and others have produced a number of excellent photographic surveys and features covering the NYMR in their books. But many of these publications are now out of print, and it is nearly 40 years since the last book solely devoted to the history of the railway was published. With steam trains running once again over the whole of the original Whitby & Pickering Railway route, this is an appropriate time for a new look at the subject.

As the title implies, the book takes as its starting point the routes over which NYMR trains now run. While largely this means the old Whitby & Pickering Railway, such trains also operate from time to time over the Grosmont to Battersby Junction section of Network Rail's Esk Valley line from Middlesbrough. To put these routes into context, the now closed lines around the town of Whitby and through to Malton also get brief coverage.

It is hoped that this account will appeal both to railway enthusiasts and those interested visitors to the North Yorkshire Moors Railway who would like to know more about this remarkable line.

Acknowledgements and Author's Notes

I have been overwhelmed by the support and assistance received from so many people during the writing of this book. Friends and colleagues on the NYMR have all been extremely helpful, both with information and the loan of valuable documents and photographs. I am particularly grateful to John Bruce, David Clarke, Dave Fenney, David Idle, Neal McDonald, Tammy and Phil Naylor, David Sibley, and Nigel Trotter for the loan of precious historical and reference material. Murray Brown, Chairman of the North Yorkshire Moors Historical Railway Trust, and Neal Clarke, Chairman of North Yorkshire Moors Railway Enterprises (the railway's operational arm) and other fellow directors have all been hugely supportive. Michael Pitts, who was one of the railway's founders, has provided much valuable background information from those early preservation days, while Keith Ware and Mark Sissons have been most helpful in guiding me through the NYMR archives.

There are, however, several NYMR people I wish to mention especially. The first is sadly no longer with us. John Boyes was the NYMR Signalling & Telegraph Engineer throughout the railway's preservation period, until he died suddenly on a train at Levisham in December 2006. He was also a prolific photographer in his younger days, and it is fitting that a number of his photographs appear in the book. John Hunt has been one of the foremost photographers of the NYMR scene for many years. As a writer himself about the NYMR, he has been extremely generous in making his vast collection of photographs available to me. The NYMR archivist for many years has been Graham Reussner, who possesses an unrivalled knowledge of the railway's development and all things NYMR. Not only has he guided me through the history of the railways in this part of North Yorkshire, but his many historical articles in the NYMR house magazine, *Moorsline*, have been invaluable sources of reference. If this book has any historical merit, much of the credit must go to Graham. Any inaccuracies, however, are mine and mine alone. I am also indebted to both Graham and David Idle for independently checking the text.

There are many others who have given their help and assistance. Christiane Kroebel, librarian for Whitby Museum and the Whitby Literary & Philosophical Society, provided access to original material from the earliest days of the Whitby & Pickering Railway; including copies of George Stephenson's report on the proposed railway, and many other essential documents and pictures (the Whitby Literary & Philosophical Society was at the centre of plans for the first railway more than 175 years ago). Roger Dowson and Gordon Clitheroe from the Beck Isle Museum, Pickering, have supplied several photographs from the museum's collection. John Addyman provided important information including photographs of the 1930s flood in the Esk Valley, and Sam Wood supplied details of the 1930s cruise trains. Richard Pulleyn most kindly produced the signalling plans and reviewed the section on signalling, while Frank Dean provided details about the Royal Train working and freight services to Pickering following the passenger closures.

Michael Blakemore, editor/publisher of *Backtrack* magazine, supplied many photographs from the Pendragon Press archives, and put me in contact with several people who have been of great assistance. One of these was John Minnis, who lent his collection of photographs taken by G. W. J. Potter. It was also a privilege to correspond with David Joy, author of *The Whitby & Pickering Railway*, published in 1969, and to borrow some of the material he collated nearly 40 years ago. Martin Bairstow, who has written two excellent books on the railways around Whitby, supplied details about the introduction of Camping Coaches and use of Sentinel railcars.

One of the pleasures of this project has been making acquaintance with many photographers whose names I have seen in print over the years but have never met. All have been immensely helpful. Michael Mensing, for example, generously supplied a complete set of his superb photographs taken in 1957 and 1958, leaving me with the incredibly hard task of deciding what to exclude. Peter Ward provided both his own excellent photographs taken in 1950, and several other historically important images dating back to NER days. Maurice Burns, Richard Casserley, Peter Cookson, John Edgington, Mike Feather, Alec Ford, Gavin Morrison, David Sutcliffe, Tony Ross, Brian Rutherford, Neville Stead and Alf Williamson have kindly made available material from their collections. Thanks are also due to Alan Thompson of the J. W. Armstrong Trust, Ron White of Colour-Rail, and Brian Stephenson of Rail Archive Stephenson, and finally to Michael Stewart for the superb selection of tickets.

Much information about the early life of the Whitby & Pickering Railway is contained in G. W. J. Potter's book *A History of the Whitby & Pickering Railway*, first published in 1906. Potter, who worked in Whitby, was evidently a contributor to *The Railway Magazine*, and in the summer of 1899 was planning an article about the railway. He wrote to George Gibb, General Manager of the North Eastern Railway, requesting information. Mr Gibb replied promising assistance, and instructed Philip Burtt, Superintendent of the Line, to gather the information together. Considerable effort went into compiling a brief on the W&PR's history, including interviewing active and retired NER staff who had worked on the railway in its early days. Mr Burtt seems to have personally visited these staff with his clerk, Harry Butcher, who recorded their recollections. Further historical notes were also compiled by George Graham, another NER staff member. Much of this material was used by Potter when writing his book. I am grateful to the National Archives at Kew for being able to refer to these notes.

No book that touches upon the North Eastern Railway is likely to make much progress without reference to the works of that pre-eminent authority on North Eastern matters, the late Ken Hoole. I warmly acknowledge the value obtained from his prolific writings, and the help given by Madi Grout at the Ken Hoole Study Centre at Darlington Railway Museum and members of the North Eastern Railway Association, a body whose research and publications are keeping alive knowledge of this historically important and progressive railway.

The development of the NYMR has been due to the efforts of so many people that to mention even just the key individuals is impracticable. The names of the 12 founders are inscribed on a plaque in Pickering station booking hall. Although many are no longer with us, it is pleasing to record that Tom Salmon, at whose home the first meeting to discuss reopening was held, Charlie Hart and Michael Pitts are still involved with the railway in 2008.

My last words of appreciation must go to my wife Lesley and son Alastair. Not only have they had to put up with a husband and father shut away in the study for days on end, but Lesley has also undertaken much of the preparation work on the manuscript. I could not have written this book without their encouragement, support and patience.

In a historical work such as this, despite the drive for total accuracy it is difficult to achieve with absolute confidence, while some information, such as dates for signal box closures, proved elusive. I would be extremely grateful for any further information, via the publisher, that would enable any inaccuracies and gaps to be remedied.

For the sake of simplicity, the 24-hour clock has been used throughout, except in quoted speech.

Philip Benham
Welburn
North Yorkshire
April 2008

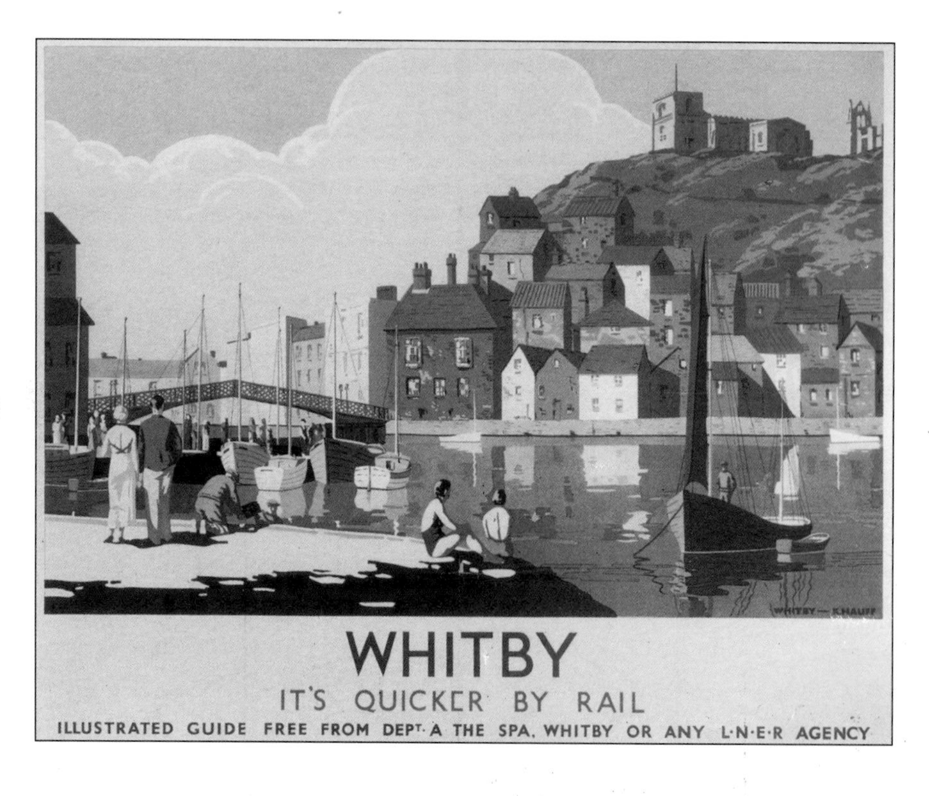

1

A Railway from Whitby to Pickering: The Horse-Drawn Days (1830-1845)

The ancient and picturesque town of Whitby nestles at the mouth of the River Esk between the sea and the moors. To the south the hills rise rapidly in the form of the North Yorkshire Moors, reaching around 1,500 feet at the highest point, while to the west stand the Cleveland Hills. The River Esk breaks forth from this terrain through two main tributaries that converge a few miles upstream from the coast. From the south the River Murk Esk descends rapidly from the moorland hills in a series of waterfalls and rapids down a steep and rocky ravine. The main river arrives a little more gently from the western moors along the pastoral but still rocky terrain of the Esk Valley. Although one of the oldest of northern seaports, over the centuries Whitby's land-locked position has hindered communications, and even today the town remains a relatively remote community.

Whitby can trace its history back at least to the seventh century with the founding of a monastery called Streanæshealhan in AD 657, later to become Whitby Abbey. Through its first abbess, St Hilda, the abbey and town soon became an ecclesiastical centre of great importance at a time when the church was the focus of most organised life. In AD 664 the Synod of Whitby settled how the dates for Easter are calculated, and established the Church of Rome as supreme in Britain, a position that was to hold for more than 800 years. Destroyed by the Vikings in the ninth century, the first abbey was rebuilt from 1078, only to be closed down by Henry VIII. Today the spectacular ruins, visible for miles around, still dominate the town.

In more recent times Whitby prospered as a centre for the production of alum. Extracted from local rock, alum was an important substance with a range of uses from leather curing and dyeing to medicine. The port benefited from the need to transport alum away to market, and bring in coal for the production process. The town also became a centre for whaling and fishing, with a thriving boat-building industry developing to meet the needs of the whalers. But although Whitby was well placed for seafaring, inland communications were another matter. Not until 1759 was the first turnpike road established across the moors to Pickering, at last providing an inland link of sorts to the south, but the journey remained long and difficult through the steep and high terrain. A 'diligence', an early form of stagecoach, started operating to York in 1788, being replaced by a more substantial stagecoach service in 1795, eventually running three times a week. A weekly link to Stockton started in 1814 at a fare of 14 shillings outside and 20 shillings inside, by which time Whitby could also be reached by stagecoach from Scarborough.

By the 1820s the future for Whitby's economy was not looking too healthy. Whaling was now in decline, and with it shipbuilding, while the local alum reserves were becoming worked out. True, with the Industrial Revolution in full swing, other potential opportunities were arising, as demands grew for new minerals available in the area, such as whinstone (a hard rock much prized as a roadstone) and limestone. Iron ore in the Esk Valley offered a chance of iron production, attracting fresh imports of coal through the port. But for Whitby to benefit, the slow and infrequent inland transport links needed improving fast. Incredible as it may seem, a canal had been proposed in 1793, based on plans to ascend over the North Yorkshire Moors to Pickering. This would have involved no fewer than 44 locks at the northern end, with a further 36 in the southern descent to Pickering, resulting in a journey time between the two towns of more than 18 hours. Rejected as impracticable, and probably too expensive, something more realistic was needed – but time was ticking by.

The business community in Whitby had not been slow to recognise the benefits of railways. Nineteen local residents had subscribed £8,500 towards the building of the Stockton & Darlington Railway in 1818, out of the original £120,000 share capital. By 1826 correspondence in the local *Whitby Repository* was talking up the advantages of a 'railroad' to link Whitby with the outside world. In 1830 John Hugill, who worked for Whitby's 'Lord of the Manor', produced a pamphlet strongly promoting the case for a railway, and arguing that this should go south to Pickering and Malton. He contrasted the benefits that Liverpool had already derived from good transport links, although the Liverpool & Manchester Railway did not open until September of that same year.

By now quite a lively debate was under way within Whitby, and there were several alternative views, including some who still argued for a canal. Political change was also on the horizon at this time, with moves afoot for Whitby to be made a borough. Inevitably ideas for a railway became drawn into these discussions. Local businessman, banker and Tory, Robert Campion, was particularly keen to see one established. On the other hand, Richard Moorsom, a prominent Whig and prime mover behind the drive for enfranchisement, was thought to be more lukewarm towards the railway project.

Campion's preference was for a link with Stockton, the terminus, of course, of the pioneering Stockton & Darlington Railway. In the latter half of 1830 he organised a survey into a projected railway to Stockton, while recognising the potential for branches through the North York Moors to Pickering and either Helmsley or Kirbymoorside. Engineer Thomas Storey reported on the proposal to the Whitby Literary and Philosophical Society (a body still very active today) at the town Museum on 2 March 1831. Storey gave a positive assessment suggesting two possible routes between Stockton and Whitby, concluding his report with the words: 'I am quite of the opinion that the speculation will be found advantageous to those who may embark upon it, and confer great and lasting benefits on the districts through and adjoining which it passes.' Two months later, on 6 May, Campion chaired a meeting at the Angel Inn, resulting in a subscription and a Committee being set up to fund a proper survey by Storey.

Members of the Committee were other prominent local businessmen and industrialists. Between them they represented Whitby's commercial interests, with a strong emphasis on shipping. Campion's many interests included potash production and shipping, as well as banking; Joseph Barker was a timber and iron merchant; Henry Belcher was a solicitor; John Chapman was a sail-maker and ship-owner; Henry Simpson was involved in banking, shipping and rope-making; and Gideon Smales was engaged in timber linked to shipbuilding.

George Stephenson, in an engraving published in 1849, the year after his death, by Thomas Lewis Atkinson. *National Portrait Gallery*

Subsequently some doubts must have set in among the committee, not helped when Storey 'modified' his estimate to twice the cost. There were also those who still argued strongly for Pickering rather than Stockton. In December 1831 a pamphlet entitled 'Thoughts on a Railway from Whitby into the Interior' went on sale in Whitby simply signed 'A Townsman'. This came down in favour of Pickering, arguing, with some foresight, that 'at no distant period' links would follow to Malton, York and Leeds. A return of 6-7% could be expected, and the author stated:

'I have not the least hesitation in expressing my decided opinion that a Railway from here to Pickering, or the neighbourhood, with a branch on the line already surveyed, as far as Lealholmbridge, would be both a great and immediate benefit to our town; and tend not only to the increase of our present branches of trade, but open new channels for the employment of the dormant capital and industry of Whitby.'

The following year, the pioneer of the Stockton & Darlington Railway, George Stephenson, was invited to report on the relative merits of both the Stockton and Pickering options. His authoritative report was presented on 5 July 1832, effectively clinching it for the Pickering route. On both commercial and engineering grounds, Stephenson was convinced that this was the preferred destination for a Whitby railway. He was particularly exercised by the extra power required to surmount the highest point on the Stockton route, which he calculated would make the journey of 35 miles the equivalent of 57 miles. Consequently he did not believe that such a line could adequately compete against a combination of rail to Middlesbrough and 'the water communication of vessels thence to Whitby'. By contrast, Stephenson saw huge potential for the Pickering route (presumably the gradients were discounted because of the intended haulage of trains up to the moors by rope-worked incline) and had 'little hesitation in saying that an estimate of probable revenue amounting to the sum of £10,500 which has been submitted to me, and which has been prepared I believe with much care, is considerably underrated.' Calculations were given to justify a likely income of £6,000 a year from coal imported through Whitby for the Pickering and Malton areas, projected to be at least 40,000 tons. Lime was seen as another lucrative source of revenue, with estimated annual carryings of 96,000 tons expected to yield £7,200. Add to this the potential for carrying whinstone, timber and other products and it is clear that Stephenson was convinced.

Turning to the engineering aspects, Stephenson's report is less detailed, although he does give a comprehensive breakdown of the anticipated cost per mile. The line would proceed from Whitby along the Esk Valley to Grosmont (or Growmond in the spelling of the day), where it would enter the Goathland Valley. Passing up a steep plane, 'the rise of which for about one mile in length is abrupt' the route would then continue through Newton Dale to Pickering. Stephenson believed that, apart from the incline mentioned, the whole route 'appears to be very favourable'. Based on his calculations of £2,000 per mile, he considered that the 24-mile line could be built for £48,000. Stephenson's concluding paragraph is worth quoting in full:

'In conclusion, I will merely remark, that, after taking a general view of the merits of the scheme, it appears to me to be deserving of the most cordial support of all parties; of the inhabitants of Whitby, from its insuring both to the town and harbour of increased activity of trade: - of the landowners, from its affording them the opportunity of converting an immense barren tract into fertile land: — of the inhabitants of Pickering, and all the towns and villages of the Northern District of Yorkshire, from its enabling them to obtain coal (far superior to that with which they are at present supplied) as well as other commodities imported into Whitby, at a considerably lower price: and, lastly if the public and the capitalists, from the prospect (amounting, I conceive to certainty) that the revenue arising from the use of the Whitby and Pickering Railway, will amply remunerate the proprietors for the money invested.'

A further meeting at the Angel Inn on 12 September 1832 followed consideration of Stephenson's report by a sub-committee. This committee produced another positive assessment, including projected annual revenue of £13,354; mostly from freight with just £1,252 coming from passengers. It was concluded that the line could be built for less than £80,000 and should generate a 10% rate of return to shareholders. Buoyed with enthusiasm, a share list was opened with £30,000 subscribed at the meeting, and within weeks a prospectus had been issued and the momentum gathered pace. Effectively the Whitby & Pickering Railway (W&PR) was born.

Whitby had also just achieved its goal to become a borough. At the election in December 1832 to select the town's first Member of Parliament, Robert Moorsom, the Whig politician who had done so much to bring this about, was defeated by the Conservative, Aaron Chapman. Perhaps Moorsom's lack of enthusiasm for the railway had counted against him, even though his election manifesto had professed support for railways in general.

On 14 February 1833 the Bill for the railway was laid before the House of Commons. It proceeded remarkably swiftly with little opposition, receiving the Royal Assent less than three months later on 6 May 1833 (at the same time, incidentally, as those for the Grand Junction and London & Birmingham railways – exalted company indeed.). The Act authorising the Whitby & Pickering Railway had a number of interesting features. Authority was given to divert the course of the River Esk, and certain other water courses, to ease construction. The line was to be of a gauge not less than 4ft 8½ in and no more than 5ft 1in, but provision was made for the use of 'Outram' rails. These consisted of cast-iron plates supported on stone blocks, with an inner flange so that the wheels ran in a trough (hence the term 'platelayer' to describe the men who laid them). In the event conventional rails of the early fish-bellied type were used in 15-foot lengths weighing 40lb per yard, laid on diagonally placed stone blocks, and the gauge was set at 4ft 8½ in. There were also some contradictions in the drafting of the Act, most famously with Section 114 authorising the use of 'locomotive engines', only for Section 134 to prohibit them.

Meanwhile a pamphlet entitled 'The Whitby & Pickering Railway: its probable traffic and revenue', by one William Thompson, had produced slightly more cautious revenue figures of £8,787 from carriage of the main commodities, with estimated annual operating costs of £3,000. Nevertheless, a satisfactory dividend of 7.5% would still be payable against the £80,000 authorised share capital. Mr Thompson subsequently became station master at Whitby. A few dissenting voices thought the projections were still too optimistic, including one from Pickering, who predicted a loss of at least £175 a year. But these did little to dampen enthusiasm for the project and in any case the die was now cast.

WHITBY & PICKERING
RAILWAY
COACHES.

The Public are respectfully informed that the Railway Coaches commence running, Daily, on Monday the 6th Inst., at the following hours, between Whitby and Pickering; and that Passengers proceeding to Malton and York, will immediately be forwarded from Pickering, at the usual Fares.

FROM WHITBY TO PICKERING,
Every Morning at ½ past 6 o'clock, and every Evening at 5 o'clock

FROM PICKERING TO WHITBY,
Every Morning (except Sundays) at ½ past 10 o'clock, and on Sundays at 7 o'clock.
Every Evening, after the arrival of the York Coach, at 5 o'clock.

FROM WHITBY TO BECKHOLE AND TUNNEL,
Every Day at ½ past 1 o'clock.

FROM TUNNEL TO WHITBY,
Every Evening at 7 o'clock.

FARES THROUGH.

	s. d.		s. d.
Inside per First Class Coach -	3 6	Top - - - - -	2 6
Front and Back Cabriolets -	3 0	Second Class Coach - -	2 6

SHORT FARES.

FIRST CLASS.	Inside. Cab. Top. s. d. s. d. s. d.	FIRST CLASS.	Inside. Cab. Top s. d s. d. s. d.
From Whitby to Ruswarp Bridge	0 6—0 6—0 6	From Pickering to Raindale	1 6—1 3—1 0
Do. Sleights Bridge......	0 9—0 8—0 6	Do. Incline Station House	2 0—1 9—1 6
Do. Tunnel Inn	1 6—1 3—1 0	Do. Beckhole	2 3—2 0—1 9
Do. Beckhole	2 0—1 9—1 6	Do. Tunnel Inn........	2 6—2 3—2 0
Do. Incline Station House	2 6—2 3—2 0	Do. Sleights Bridge....	3 0—2 6—2 3

☞ Second Class Coaches same Fare as Top of First Class.

Parcels to be Booked 20 Minutes before the Time of Departure.

REGULATIONS.

BOOKING.—In order to insure punctuality in the times of starting, no Persons will be admitted through the outer door of the Railway Stations, later than five minutes before the appointed time of starting, unless previously booked; and Passengers too late to take their seats, or otherwise prevented going, may receive back half the fare paid, if claimed not later than the day after that for which the places were taken.

LUGGAGE.—The weight allowed for each Passenger is 42lbs, beyond which a charge will be made at the rate of 4s per cwt.

GUARDS.—No Gratuity is allowed to be taken by any Guard, Coachman, Porter, or other Servant of the Company.

SMOKING.—No Smoking will be permitted in any of the First Class Carriages, even with the consent of the Passengers present.

MERCHANDIZE.—A train for Merchandize will leave Whitby and Pickering immediately after the starting of the first Coaches.

Persons having Goods to send, are requested to give information thereof at the Railway Office, on the day before, if possible.

THOMAS CLARK,
TREASURER.

Railway Office, Whitby, June 1st, 1836.

HORNE AND RICHARDSON, PRINTERS, WHITBY.

Above: **Handbill advertising the opening of the Whitby & Pickering Railway.** *Whitby Museum*

The first directors' meeting of the Whitby & Pickering Railway Company took place on 30 May 1833, with Robert Campion elected as chairman, and Thomas Fishburn as deputy chairman. Despite his personal preference for Stockton, he seems to have set this aside and put his energies fully into the Pickering decision. Thereafter, with Stephenson as superintending engineer, the first construction contract was soon let for the section from Whitby to Sleights. Tenders were invited for the supply of materials, with rails being particularly critical as supplies were tight. Contracts were let to:

Capponfield Ironworks near Birmingham;
Bradley and Foster, Stourbridge;
Nantyglo Ironworks, Blaenau Gwent, South Wales; and
Bedlington Ironworks, Northumberland.

At the northern end most material arrived by water through Whitby, and at Pickering via the Derwent Navigation to Malton and thence by ox-cart.

Work began on 10 September 1833 with cutting of the first sod by Campion at Boghall, Whitby, west of the river estuary on the site of the former Fishburn & Brodrick shipyard. A substantial early task was the diversion of the River Esk between Whitby and Ruswarp, thus avoiding two swing bridges on the tidal lower reaches of the river used by shipping. From Ruswarp, bridges could not be avoided, with the first of many also being the longest, at 312 feet. Despite some problems due to a combination of poor ground conditions and the need to cut through some rocky outcrops, good progress was made, while by December contracts were in place enabling work to proceed from the Pickering end of the route. At Grosmont a short tunnel was needed through a hilly outcrop known as Lease Rigg, to access the Vale of Goathland and allow the line to progress towards Beck Hole. The community that grew up immediately to the north was initially known as Tunnel, until becoming assimilated into the overall village of Grosmont.

At Beck Hole the Eller and West Becks merge into the River Murk Esk, and consideration had been given to accessing the high moors via a long tunnel after taking a route paralleling West Beck to the west of Goathland village, but in the event a rope-worked incline, almost a mile long from Beck Hole up to Goathland, was chosen instead. Beyond Goathland, the summit of the line was reached some 12 miles from Whitby, having climbed to a height of 532 feet. This was near Fen Bog, a location where the unstable ground conditions caused a major headache, as the route entered the spectacular but remote

Right: **A section of original W&PR track on display at Pickering station. Note the 'fish-bellied' rail section.** *Author*

NEW COACH.

THE Public are respectfully informed that the QUEEN, a Four-Inside Coach, has commenced running from SCARBORO' to PICKERING and HELMSLEY, Daily, (Sundays excepted.) The QUEEN leaves the GEORGE INN, SCARBORO', at SEVEN o'Clock in the Morning, reaching the BLACK SWAN INN, PICKERING, at HALF-PAST NINE o'Clock, in time for the RAILWAY COACH TO WHITBY; and, after the arrival of the Railway Coach FROM Whitby, it proceeds to the NEW INN, HELMSLEY, arriving there at TWELVE o'Clock.

At THREE o'Clock in the Afternoon, the same Coach leaves Helmsley for Pickering, at which place it arrives in time for the Railway Coach TO Whitby, remaining at Pickering until the Arrival of the Railway Coach FROM Whitby, and proceeds to Scarboro', arriving there at TEN o'clock.

N. B. Only Two Coachmen and no Guard.

Pickering, July 19th, 1836.

Above left: **Newspaper advertisement of 19 July 1836 for the stagecoach *Queen*, which connected with the railway at Pickering to serve Scarborough and Helmsley.** *NYMR Archive*

Above: **'Tunnel Inn Bridge & The Premier Railway Carriage'. This 1836 oil painting by an unknown artist shows a W&PR horse train at Grosmont. Tunnel Inn is on the left and the first Grosmont tunnel to the right.** *Whitby Museum*

Newton Dale. Stephenson resorted to the same technique employed at Chat Moss when building the Liverpool & Manchester Railway. This involved stabilising the land by 'pile-driving' fir trees into the bog and overlaying them with sheaves of heather bound in sheep skin, together with more timber and moss. To this day Fen Bog presents one of the biggest challenges in maintaining the permanent way. Similar problems were encountered further south, with much clearance of stones and loose earth necessary as the line made its sinuous way through Newton Dale's rocky glacial valley and on to Pickering. The overall distance from Whitby to Pickering was slightly less than 24 miles.

All these engineering problems played havoc with Stephenson's original cost estimates. Difficulties were also occurring in other areas. A dispute about rails with Capponfield Iron Company dragged on unhelpfully – indeed, problems with rail supply seem to have been ongoing almost until the line was finished. In the directors' report of 12 May 1834 to the half-yearly meeting we read: 'In all public works there is a variety of expenses not to be foreseen, and under the heads of contingencies a considerable sum is always allowed.' A truism if ever there was one. Even so, it was hoped that services could commence from Whitby towards Grosmont within two months, an estimate that was to prove sadly optimistic. These were the heady days leading up to the Railway Mania, with many railways being proposed across the country. It would seem that George Stephenson's personal involvement with the W&PR became less and less as he became much in demand elsewhere. Increasingly, supervision of the construction work was in the hands of his 24-year-old assistant Frederick Swanwick, and by 1835 the directors' minute books are showing frustration at the infrequent attendance on the railway of both men. Cash flow was becoming a big problem, as construction costs and the price of iron rose dramatically, but with no income yet flowing. Track-laying costs more than doubled to £4,400 a mile, and the final cost of constructing the railway came in at £105,600, considerably more than the original £80,000 estimate. This was a burden that would dog the railway throughout its independent existence.

By the middle of 1835, however, the line was complete between Whitby and the Tunnel Inn at Grosmont (today's Station Tavern). Although consideration may have been given initially to steam traction, the plans for the railway had gone forward on the basis of horse power alone. And so it was that on 15 May 1835 the directors had a run out in the appropriately named horse-drawn coach *Premier*. It was planned to start public coach services on 29 May, and fares were set in preparation. These ranged from 9d (inside) and 6d (outside) in the First Class coach for journeys as far as Sleights Bridge, through to 1s 5d (outside) and 1s 0d (inside) as far as Beck Hole, even though the coach would terminate initially at Tunnel Inn. Second Class fares were the same as the First Class outside fares, although the railway had yet to take delivery of any Second Class coaches. In the event the opening was delayed until 8 June, with the directors' minute book reporting, 'the Company's First Class Coach Premier left Whitby at 2 o'clock in the afternoon, returning about 8 o'clock'. Thus, without much apparent fuss, the railway was in business.

Some 6,000 passengers made the journey in the first three months. The popularity of the new service was seen just a few weeks later in July 1835 when *The Yorkshire Gazette* reported that a special coach had made 16 trips to Ruswarp Fair, and 1,000 passengers were carried, some making more than one trip just for the novelty value. By mid-August the line was complete as far as Beck Hole. It appears that coach services on this section remained by arrangement, although by now another, Second Class, coach had been delivered. Other accounts suggest that services also subsequently ran between Pickering and Raindale prior to the main opening; however, hard evidence to support this is difficult to find.

Completion of the railway depended on the commissioning of the line's most remarkable engineering feature, the incline plane between Beck Hole and Goathland (known then as Goadland). This was 1,500 feet long with a gradient averaging 1 in 15, but reaching 1 in 11 at its steepest point. Coaches or wagons were attached to a rope wound around a 10-foot-diameter horizontal drum located at the top station, before making a stately ascent through an avenue of trees in 4½ minutes. The description of the incline drive is interesting. Made of hemp, the rope was apparently 5¾ inches in diameter (though by 1864 the diameter is quoted as being 4½ inches with the rope made up of six stranded wires, each with a hemp core), running on a series of 10-inch pulley wheels (174 in total) with their holding frames set at 24-foot intervals in stone blocks. As sections of the incline were curved, some of these wheels were angled, with additional wooden friction rollers provided (2 feet long by 6 inches in diameter) to allow for play in the rope. A basic communication system was provided between top and bottom of the incline using wire connected levers. More detail is not known, but apparently it was called 'the token'. Initially, balancing power on the descent came from a 4-ton rail-mounted water tank topped up from two reservoirs. Water was discharged into the river at Beck Hole with a nearby farmer contracted to haul the tank back up by horse; a white flag being hung out to indicate when his services were required. Perhaps, not surprisingly, this primitive system was discontinued in due course when the York & North Midland Railway installed a stationary steam engine, and replaced the water tank vehicle by a van on each train fitted with brakes that clasped the rails.

Although horses were used for the remaining stretches of the line, it became the practice to couple two coaches together for descent by gravity on the steeper sections, particularly southwards from the summit near Fen Bog and north from Beck Hole to Grosmont. Such multiple passenger coach 'trains' were possibly excursions that ran occasionally in the early 1840s. On the gravity runs, when working goods trains, the horses were rewarded for their exertions by a ride in a dandy cart coupled to the train. Two horses were needed for the steeper uphill sections.

Spring 1836 finally saw the railway approaching completion, and the countdown to opening began in earnest. Nevertheless the directors were advised on 6 April by Frederick Swanwick that the line needed 'more righting before it could conveniently be used for Coach travelling'. Accordingly, it was decided to delay opening until 25 May, although goods traffic could be sent by arrangement. Subsequently this date was changed to Thursday 26 May to avoid a clash with Kirby Fair near Pickering. On 22 April passenger fares were set for the complete journey at 3s 6d (inside) and 2s 6d (outside), and the directors felt confident enough to instruct the company treasurer and engineer to make arrangements for the opening, to be celebrated 'with éclat' and to report back. They did on 6 May, proposing special fares of 5s 0d for a First Class coach and 3s 6d for a Second Class coach, whether inside or out. Tickets were to go on sale first to shareholders from 9 May, then to the general public from the 16th to the 19th. Four tickets each were put at the disposal of the directors. The coaches were to leave Whitby at 08.00, returning from Pickering at 14.00, following a public breakfast at the Black Swan Inn.

Accounts say that Thursday 26 May 1836 dawned brilliantly and the towns of Whitby and Pickering were *en fête*. Church bells were rung from 07.00 and around an hour later a procession, led by four constables and railway workers, set off from the Angel Inn, Whitby, to the station accompanied by the Whitby Brass Band. Allocated seats had been arranged, with eight coaches (some reports suggest nine) provided to include space for those who turned up on the day. All in all around 150 people joined the coaches, including the Whitby Brass Band on the last one. With the passengers seated, a bell was rung for the horses to be brought out and attached to each coach. Departure time had been set for 08.00 with a planned arrival in Pickering around 11.00, although it must be assumed that the cavalcade actually left late if the account of the procession only leaving the Angel Inn at around this time is correct. Under the supervision of the two engineers, Frederick Swanwick and his assistant Mr Harding, a bell was again rung and each horse and coach set off, their speed controlled by guards on the coaches using flags (white for 'go on'; red for 'go slow'; and blue for 'stop'). All did not go quite according to plan. *The Whitby Gazette* reported that within a short distance from Whitby the new coach *Lady Hilda* had derailed two or three times, with passengers having to transfer to the remaining coaches.

Stops were made at Tunnel Inn, to observe the lime kilns then under construction, and at Lease Rigg, where a flag-bedecked wagon of stone was observed descending the inclined plane from the quarry. At Beck Hole the coaches were attached three at a time to the incline rope for the climb to Goathland and, to the accompaniment of the band, in the words of Thomas Clark, the railway's treasurer, 'glided up the steep ascent with a pleasing, rapid and easy pace'. At the top of the incline the coaches were greeted by a cheering crowd and volleys of gunfire. New teams of horses then took over for the continued climb over the line's summit to a point where the gradient began to fall significantly. From here, with the horses removed once more, the coaches descended by gravity towards Pickering. Fresh horses finally hauled them the last stretch into town. Arrival was around 1¼ hours late, no doubt due to the late start from Whitby and the *Lady Hilda* derailments.

In Pickering the delayed arrival does not seem to have dampened spirits among the vast crowd covering the hillsides. Accounts vary on numbers, with Thomas Clark estimating 7,000, while a local newspaper, the *York Courant,* put the figure at nearer 20,000. Church bells had been ringing since 09.00, and with several cannon opposite the castle firing at intervals and five bands, the spectators were not lost for noise and entertainment. Sighting of the first coach *Premier* at around 12.15 was the trigger for all the bands to strike up, with the Whitby band joining in from their coach. The passengers and well-wishers made their way in procession from the station to the Black Swan Inn, where around 300 sat down for the celebratory 'breakfast'. The cavalcade returned to Whitby without incident, remarkable perhaps since the journey down the incline had included a demonstration not only of the emergency braking system, but also release of the rope to show that the train would not derail. Complete with passengers, it appar-

The Whitby & Pickering Railway Weigh House at Whitby (from *The Scenery of the Whitby and Pickering Railway* by Henry Belcher, 1836). *Whitby Museum*

ently accelerated to around 20 miles per hour free-wheeling to a stand some way beyond the foot of the incline. The coaches arrived back at Whitby around 17.00 with the festivities, centred on the Angel Inn and another banquet, continuing long into the night. Summarising the event many years later, the North Eastern Railway's George Graham wrote: 'All were delighted with the ceremonial opening of the fifth railway in England.'

The W&PR now settled down to making a living. As anticipated, the railway triggered the opening of a number of quarries along the route. The Whitby Stone Company had already commenced operations in 1834 and was soon exporting 10,000 tons a year through Whitby to London, together with ironstone to Birtley Iron Company in Middlesbrough. The Grosmont Limestone Company started up in 1836 and the Wylam Iron Company in 1839. In fact, developments in the lower Esk and Murk Esk valleys were to continue apace through much of the 19th century.

In terms of passengers, 8,000 were carried in July and August 1836 alone, and as well as the connection to York, a new road service, using the stagecoach *Queen*, was providing links from Pickering to Scarborough and Helmsley. The dramatic benefits are well illustrated by the story of a sea captain arriving at Whitby from the Baltic. Finding orders requesting him to make his way to Liverpool, he took the W&P to Pickering, and the connecting stagecoach to York. Here he boarded a train for Manchester (connecting by coach over the incomplete part of the Leeds & Manchester Railway) and completed his journey to Liverpool. The journey had taken a matter of hours rather than the several days that would have applied just a few years earlier. The railway's value as a lifeline was also demonstrated in the line's first winter. When heavy snow closed roads in the region the railway continued to run with only limited delays.

Already there were signs of a developing tourist market, helped by the publication during 1836 of a book by Henry Belcher, possibly commissioned by the railway. Belcher, as we have seen, was a local solicitor, also acting as clerk and solicitor to the railway company. Entitled *The Scenery of the Whitby & Pickering Railway*, the book highlighted the scenic attractions of the area with lavish illustrations by George Dodgson and others.

Sadly, despite this activity the company's finances failed to prosper, in large part due to the burden of debt left by the increased cost of construction. In the summer of 1835 the

company had investigated obtaining a government loan, but managed to borrow more than £20,000 from a number of private sources instead. Now, late in 1836, the company was again in trouble with debts of £13,000. A further call on existing shareholders was judged unrealistic as the shares were already trading at a 50% discount. Leasing the operation of the line to another company was also considered. But instead it was decided in early 1837 to seek powers to raise additional capital of £30,000, the Royal Assent being given on 5 May.

Meanwhile the line was becoming an established reality within the local community. Among the more interesting events during this period was the running of special carriages for the laying of the foundation stone of St Matthew's Church, Grosmont, on 16 September 1840. As with the railway, Henry Belcher was a leading light in this project, and upon his death in 1854 a memorial stained glass window was inserted in his honour.

Back in 1834 during one of his, by then, rather infrequent visits, George Stephenson had met the up-and-coming railway entrepreneur George Hudson. Although the meeting was quite by chance, the two Georges clearly liked each other and began a business relationship that would serve them both well over the next few years. This was the start of an interest in Whitby for George Hudson that would last the rest of his life. As an aside, the Stephenson family were also to have a long acquaintance with Whitby. Upon the retirement of the town's first MP, Aaron Chapman, in 1847, George's son Robert took over the seat, retaining it until his death in 1859.

As long ago as 1834 Robert Campion and fellow directors, together with George Stephenson, had attended a meeting in York to lobby for the proposed York & Leeds Railway to be extended to Pickering and thus create a link through to Whitby. At the time George Hudson, who was at this meeting, was still some years away from the height of his powers, and his sights were set on establishing York's railway links to the south and London. Had the Campion team's advances paid off, it is interesting to speculate on how Whitby's development might have been affected; would Whitby have become a major port to rival Hull? Perhaps not, since Hull was already a growing port before being reached by rail in 1840, but the direction of Whitby's economic expansion would almost certainly have been different.

CHEAP, SAFE, & EXPEDITIOUS TRAVELLING.

WH TBY & PICKERING RAILWAY

I' E Public are respectfully informed that the RAILWAY COACHES, during the SUMMER MONTHS, will start from Whitby and Pickering, at the following Hours, viz.—

From WHITBY to PICKERING, every Morning at 7 o'Clock, and every Evening, at 5 o'Clock.

From PICKERING to WHITBY, every Morning at Half-past 8 o'Clock and every Evening, after the arrival of the York Coach (about Half-past 5 o'Clock).

(Sundays excepted.)

FARES.—INSIDE, 3s. 6d.—CAB, 3s.—TOP, 2s. 6d.

N. B. No Gratuity allowed to be taken by Guard, Coachman, Porter, or other Servant of the Company.

PASSENGERS may be Booked at York, at the BLACK SWAN and TAVERN COACH OFFICES, to proceed to Whitby by the NEPTUNE COACH, which leaves York every Day, (Sundays excepted) at 2 o'Clock in the Afternoon; and Passengers leaving Whitby by the 7 o'Clock Coach will be forwarded to York to arrive in time for the Coaches proceeding to Sheffield, Hull, Leeds Manchester, Liverpool, and London.

Trucks and Cribs for the conveyance of Carriages and Horses may be had on notice.

WHITBY & PICKERING RAILWAY.

Lately published by Messrs. LONGMAN and Co., and to be had of all Booksellers,

ILLUSTRATIONS of the SCENERY on the LINE of the WHITBY and PICKERING RAILWAY, rom Drawings by G. DODGSON; with a short Description of the District and Undertaking, by HENRY BELCHER.

Large-paper Copies .. .. 15s.
Small ditto .. .. 10s.

Left: **Newspaper advertisement for what is thought to be the 1837 summer W&PR service, and Henry Belcher's book *The Scenery of the Whitby and Pickering Railway*.** *Graham Reussner Collection*

Left: **Cutting in Eskdale (from *The Scenery of the Whitby and Pickering Railway* by Henry Belcher, 1836).** *Whitby Museum*

Right: **Entrance to Newton Dale. An engraving by George Haydock Dodgson (from *The Scenery of the Whitby and Pickering Railway* by Henry Belcher, 1836).** *Whitby Museum*

Below: **South Dale, Newton Dale. An engraving by George Haydock Dodgson (from *The Scenery of the Whitby and Pickering Railway* by Henry Belcher, 1836).** *Whitby Museum*

Below right: **George Hudson, in the original portrait by John Andrews of 1845. A copy was made in 1984 and hung in the Board Room of the former NER Headquarters in York, by then BR Eastern Region's Headquarters Offices.** *British Railways Board*

The year 1840 had also seen plans laid for a railway from York to Scarborough with a branch to Pickering, as an extension of the York & North Midland Railway (Y&NM) of which George Hudson was chairman. Once again, however, Hudson's mind was to be attracted elsewhere. With plans for a railway north from York to Newcastle in difficulty, Hudson had seized the chance to gain control of events, with a view to developing an East Coast route towards Scotland. Scarborough, and with it a link to the W&PR, had been forced to take a back seat for a few more years. By 1843 Hudson's railway empire was at its zenith, and expanding rapidly. With his dream of a through route from London to Newcastle and Scotland close to being delivered, he could finally turn his attention to the Scarborough line. The earlier plans were resurrected and laid before Parliament. Royal Assent for the Y&NM's line from York to Scarborough and the Pickering branch came a year later on 4 July 1844.

Even by the 1840s the W&PR was not meeting traffic expectations, with revenue failing to reach even half the levels predicted by the railway's original promoters (see Appendix 3). By this time the directors were looking seriously at an amalgamation. Once again thoughts had turned to the Stockton & Darlington, but in the end, with a railway connection to the outside world via Pickering now in the offing, it was to be Hudson's Y&NM.

A link up made sense, but no doubt George Hudson's powers of persuasion also played a part. The purchase price of £80,000 was some £25,000 below the costs borne by the long-suffering W&PR shareholders on the line's construction, never mind the additional £30,000 of capital raised from them since. In reality, however, this reflected considerably more than the railway's current value. Some years later, during the Committee of Investigation into George Hudson's financial affairs, there was much criticism that the Y&NM had paid considerably over the odds for the W&PR, which 'at the time of the negotiation ... was scarcely paying the expenses of working it'. A more realistic market valuation of £30,000 was suggested. Referring to the purchase, this report summed up the situation bluntly: 'Your Committee cannot sufficiently condemn the most improvident bargain, and the unjustified extravagance in the subsequent outlay.'

But this was all in the future, as the Act authorising purchase of the W&PR by the Y&NM, including powers to rebuild the line for steam traction, gained Royal Assent on 30 June 1845. The independent days were over.

2

Nineteenth-Century Development: in the Empire of the North Eastern (1845-1922)

Just a week after the Act authorising purchase of the Whitby & Pickering by the York & North Midland, the first train steamed into Scarborough with the opening of the Y&NM's line from York on 7 July 1845. The branch from Rillington Junction, near Malton, to Pickering appears to have opened on the same day; this date being referred to four years later in the 1849 report by a committee of inquiry examining the affairs of the Y&NM and George Hudson. This may, however, have been only for freight since, in his authoritative 1906 book, G. W. J. Potter states October as the month in which passenger services started running to Pickering.

The Act authorising purchase of the W&PR also included new money-raising powers of up to £180,000 to fund the upgrade of the line. Certainly drastic action was needed, for the railway's financial position had reached a truly parlous state at the time of the takeover. During the period 1 September 1845 to 5 July 1846, the old Whitby & Pickering (albeit now part of the Y&NM) paid the lowest passenger duty to the government of any railway in the land at £1 19s 6¾d, equivalent to less than a pound a week in actual passenger receipts (compare this with the highest, the London & Birmingham, which paid more than £25,300). It may be that these results were affected by the line rebuilding then under way, but they were still grim.

Fortunately the Y&NM was not slow in implementing its modernisation programme. A contract was let in February 1846 to Messrs Tredwell & Co for £95,573 to rebuild the line. The scale of the work was extensive; several new bridges of iron or stone replaced the old timber structures over the River Esk; new stations were built, including both Pickering and Whitby; track was re-laid and doubled; and Grosmont Tunnel was replaced with one of much larger diameter to cater for two tracks.

Steam was permitted to work north of Pickering to Levisham from 1 September 1846 on a single track only, but it was to be Friday 4 June 1847 before the first steam locomotive entered Whitby. Inspection by the Board of Trade inspector, Captain R. E. Coddington, took place on the following day. He reported that the Goathland incline and its new stationary engine 'were in complete working order' and recognised the urgent desire of the Y&NM to complete the transition from horse to steam, but it appears that he was not totally satisfied when he wrote:

'Under the peculiar circumstances of this line and the difficulties attending the alteration to one kind of moving power while another kind is in daily operation I beg to recommend that the Company be permitted to use the 2nd line of Rails between Pickering and Leavisham (sic) and to open the portion between Whitby and the foot of the incline with a Locomotive so as to enable them to get rid of the horses now upon the latter but that they be restrained from using Locomotive power upon the centre interval from the incline to Leavisham until the line is in a more complete state.'

It seems that the Y&NM chose to focus on getting the necessary work done rather than use the limited permission granted. Barely three weeks later, on 29 June, Captain Coddington was back accompanied by 'Mr Cabry the Locomotive Superintendent, Mr Birkenshaw Jn. the Resident Engineer and Mr Low the Contractor'. This time he said, 'I am of the opinion that the line may be opened with safety on the 1st Inst according to the wish of the Company,' but he went on to express concern about 'the severity of the gradients

Above: **Map of Whitby in the 1840s by Francis Pickernell. The Whitby & Pickering Railway can be seen in the centre of the map running vertically to terminate near Esk House (from a 'Book of Whitby', Roslin Barker).** *David Clark Collection*

Left: **'Whitby from the Railway', published in 1848 (from a print described as 'drawn from nature on stone' by Edward Cockburn, and dedicated to Robert Stephenson, the town's MP at the time). The view is downstream towards Whitby with the rebuilt railway line and a York & North Midland Railway train depicted on the left.** *Whitby Museum*

Right: **Station track layouts at Grosmont and Pickering in 1849.** *NYMR (Moorsline magazine)*

Below right: **Station track layouts at Beck Hole and Goathland (Incline Top) in 1849.** *NYMR (Moorsline magazine)*

Below: **Looking north along the trackbed of the original railway at the foot of the incline at Beck Hole. Following the opening of the new deviation route, the truncated Beck Hole branch terminated a short distance north of 'Incline Cottage' (now a private residence) visible in the centre of the photograph. This building may have been used as a booking office.** *Author*

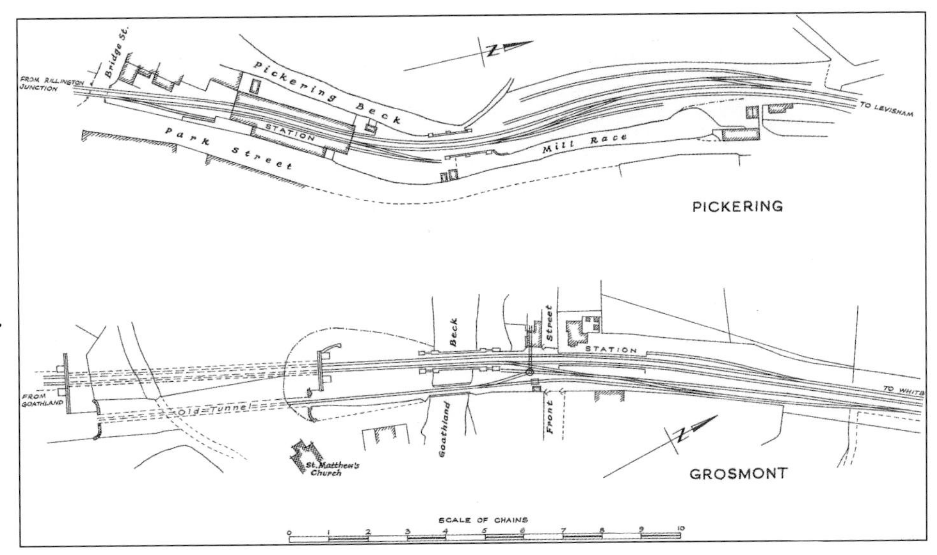

and the sharpness of the curves'. In his opinion speed should not exceed 20mph at least until drivers had 'become thoroughly acquainted with the line'. Steam-hauled services commenced on 1 July 1847 throughout what was essentially a new double-track railway; only the old rope incline remained between Beck Hole and Goathland.

On the new route between Rillington and Pickering, intermediate stations were built at Low Marishes, High Marishes and Black Bull (later Kirby). Low Marishes and Black Bull closed very soon after opening, although Kirby, at least, appears to have had a second lease of life in the 1850s before closing again to passengers in 1858 (a siding remained in use until after the Second World War). High Marishes had assumed the name Marishes Road by 1852. Further north, between Pickering and Whitby, stations were established at Levisham, Goathland (Bank Top), Grosmont, Sleights and Ruswarp, with passengers also able to join and alight from trains at Beck Hole.

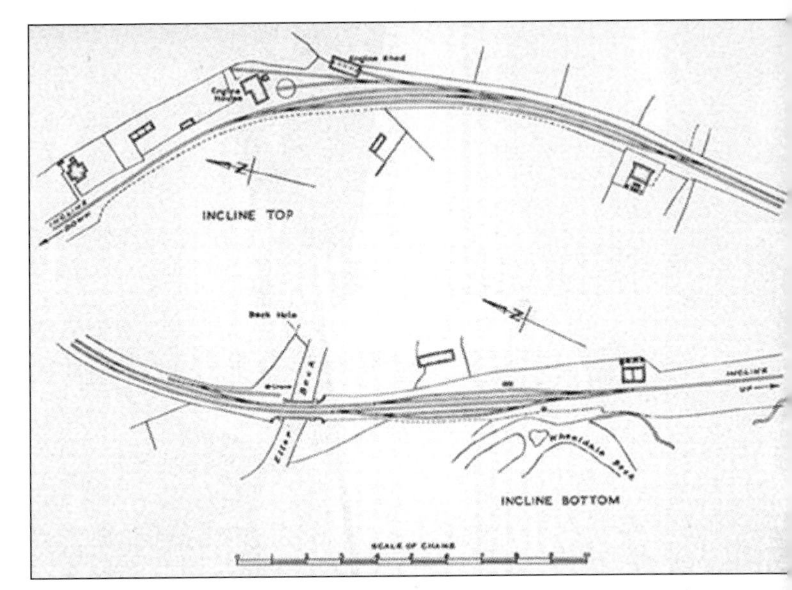

Despite the continued inconvenience of the Goathland incline, Whitby was now well and truly on the railway map. George Hudson wasted little time in capitalising on this, with plans to turn Whitby into a fashionable resort. He bought land on the hills west of the main town, appropriately known as West Cliff, forming the Whitby Building Company to develop the district. The Royal Hotel and a number of other boarding and guest houses were built, together with a road, still called the Khyber Pass, giving access down to the harbour. The names George Street and Hudson Street are other current reminders of his influence in the area. Unfortunately for Hudson, doubts about his financial practices caused a dramatic fall from grace in the late 1840s. Although the development plans were put on hold, Whitby's prospects and that of the railway fared rather better.

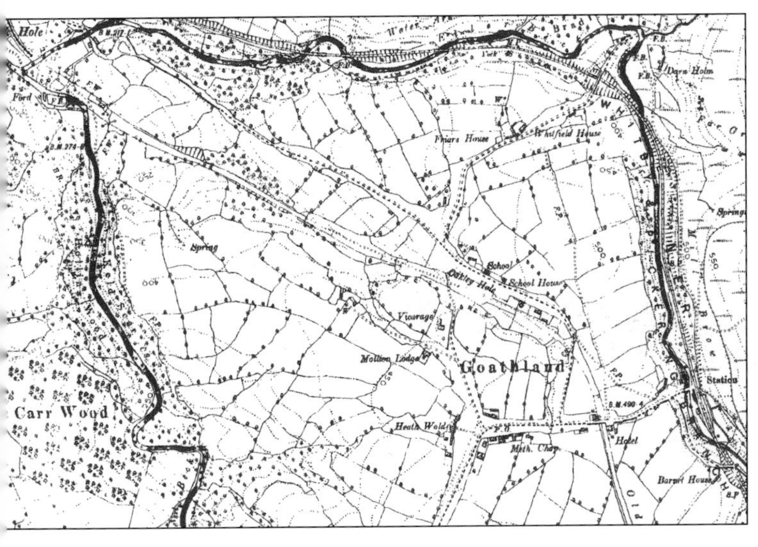

Left: **Extract from 1895 OS map of Goathland. The track of the old W&PR, including the incline, can be traced from the bottom right-hand corner of the map running roughly north-west to reach the terminus of the truncated Beck Hole branch in the top left-hand corner. The new line follows the course of the river, running due north, then west. Note also the track of the Sil Howe tramway east of Goathland station, heading north then east around the 550-foot contour line.** *Crown copyright, Landmark Information Group Ltd*

Left: **A view of Whitby from Larpool around 1860, with the railway prominent on the west bank (from an engraving by J. Stephenson).** *Whitby Museum*

Below: **A view near Goathland Summit, where the 1865 deviation route met the original course of the railway, seen on the right.** *Ken Hoole Study Centre*

One of the mineral deposits available in the area was a black stone called 'jet'. Partly through Queen Victoria's choice of jet as a symbol of mourning following the death of Prince Albert, this substance was to become highly desirable as a 19th-century fashion item. 'Whitby jet' helped to popularise the town and enhance its status as a tourist destination.

1854 was to see further change. On 31 July Royal Assent was given for the amalgamation of the Y&NM with the Leeds Northern, the York, Newcastle & Berwick and the little Malton & Driffield Junction railways. Henceforth the Whitby to Malton line would be part of the North Eastern Railway (NER), a company whose empire would come to dominate North East England as one of the most prosperous in the land, with more than 1,700 route miles of track.

Three weeks earlier, authorisation was given for a totally new railway for Whitby. The Whitby & Pickering Extension Act had authorised a line west from Grosmont through the Esk Valley to Castleton as long ago as 1846, but this was just before George Hudson's nemesis, and the scheme was never progressed. Now the North Yorkshire & Cleveland Railway (NY&C) was authorised to run from Picton (on the Leeds Northern's Northallerton to Stockton route) to Grosmont. At last Robert Campion's vision of more than 20 years before, of a railway to link Whitby with Stockton, would be realised. Heading east to skirt the northern fringes of the North York Moors, the line was to climb to a summit on Kildale Moor before dropping down into Eskdale at Castleton. Thereafter the route followed the River Esk through several villages including Danby, Lealholm and Glaisdale to the junction at Grosmont.

Progress on the NY&C east from Picton was slow. The market town of Stokesley was reached on 3 March 1857, with the line extending first to Ingleby (near Battersby), then to Kildale by April 1858. With attention focused on opening up the substantial ironstone deposits in the hills to the south (which were to culminate with the construction of the Rosedale Railway), perhaps the eastwards extension through a largely rural area with limited commercial potential seemed less important. Whatever the reason, it was another three years before Castleton, the next community of any size, was reached on 1 April 1861. Worked from the outset by the NER, the NY&C had been taken over in 1859 by its larger neighbour. Even so, completion along the Esk Valley to link up with the old Whitby & Pickering line took the NER a further four years, and another parliamentary bill, before Grosmont was finally reached on 2 October 1865. A branch from the new line at Battersby was opened to a junction at Ormesby (on the Middlesbrough & Guisborough Railway) for freight in 1864, with passenger operations commencing on

1 April 1868. Today this forms the northern leg of Whitby's surviving Esk Valley branch line to Middlesbrough.

Meanwhile, on the original Whitby & Pickering route the rope-worked incline at Goathland was an increasing source of frustration to the NER, and no doubt to its passengers. The incline added at least 20 minutes to every journey, and there were concerns about safety, concerns that were to prove sadly prophetic. At the NER's half-yearly meeting on 10 August 1860, the Company Chairman, Harry Stephen Meysey Thompson, argued the case for a deviation line to eliminate the incline at an estimated cost of £50,000. Perhaps it was not entirely a coincidence that Thompson – one of George Hudson's arch-enemies, incidentally – was MP for Whitby at the time. Evidently he believed that the resort attractions of Whitby were being held back, for the meeting records state that:

'The advantage derived by developing the traffic on the Scarboro Railway had been so great that he thought it would be desirable to make an endeavour to bring out the Whitby traffic, which could not be affected without the incline were done away with.'

Thus on 11 July 1861 the parliamentary bill authorising construction by the NER of the final stage of the NY&C route between Castleton and Grosmont also included powers to construct a new line from a point just south of the tunnel at Grosmont for a distance of 4½ miles, joining the old formation near Goathland Summit. Tenders were invited for construction of the new line in June 1862, with Thomas Nelson awarded the contract at a tendered price of £56,000. (The same contractor was also engaged for the NY&C completion.) Work on the deviation was under way by autumn of the same year but, even at this relatively advanced date in railway building, the project was to prove challenging. No fewer than eight bridges were required over the Murk Esk and Eller Beck, two farms had to be relocated, and the new line climbed on a 1 in 49 gradient continuously to Goathland

Right: **Goathland station around the turn of the 20th century.** *J. F. Mallon Collection, NYMR Archive*

station, before easing to between 1 in 90 and 1 in 178 on the last 1½ miles towards Goathland Summit. East of Goathland village a new station was built, initially called Goathland Mill but later shortened to Goathland. The new route was opened on 1 July 1865, but before then the worries about safety were to be vindicated with tragic results.

In fact, there were three notable accidents around Goathland in the five years prior to the opening of the deviation route. The first occurred at Fen Bog on 6 August 1859, when the 12.30 Whitby to Pickering train derailed completely. Contemporary accounts suggest that the train crew had to be rescued from the bog by passengers. While some sources blame buckled track in the summer heat, both NER records and the Board of Trade enquiry state the cause to have been a dislodged wooden key used to hold the rails in place within a special 'joint chair' that in turn held two adjoining rails together. Apparently, despite the track upgrade in the 1840s, some elements of the original design had remained, including the absence of fishplates used to fasten consecutive rails together. With the key dislodged there was nothing to hold the rails secure and the leading wheels of the locomotive were easily derailed. The NER was in the process of upgrading the track but the work programme had yet to reach Fen Bog.

The other two accidents involved vehicles running away on the rope-worked incline. The first occurred on 12 October 1861 when the rope hauling a goods train up to Bank Top broke. The wagons careered down the incline, smashing into a train at its foot. Although there were no fatalities on this occasion, it was by no means the first time that the rope had broken. Accident records show two such incidents in 1836 alone, the very first year of operations, one involving a passenger coach. Now, 28 years later, the railway's luck was about to run out.

On the evening of 10 February 1864 the final train from Malton, consisting of five four-wheeled coaches, had arrived at Bank Top. In accordance with normal practice the engine ran round the coaches and propelled them onto the incline, where they were coupled to a special six-wheeled 'incline brake van' equipped with two sledge brakes that acted on the rails. This van, attached to the wire rope, then led the train down the slope. On this occasion, shortly after leaving Bank Top, the rope broke, leaving the 40 tons of train to run away out of control. After passing through Beck Hole station the van and leading coaches derailed on a curve about 200 yards further on. Two commercial travellers were crushed to death in the wreckage of the second vehicle, a 'First Class' coach that landed upside down, and 13 others were injured. It appears that snow and ice may also have made the brakes on the incline brake van ineffective.

Captain Henry Whatley Tyler conducted the Board of Trade inquiry into the accident. Some accounts have suggested that the coaches hit the 'incline brake van', either when buffering up or because they had not been coupled to it, with the force of the impact causing the rope to fail. More than 30 years later the train's driver, William Pickering, recollected that 'the speed at which the carriages started from the top of the incline was too great, and they ran with great force against the braked van causing the rope to break.' Nevertheless, Captain Tyler did not buy this theory, being convinced that the rope 'was not subjected to any greater violence than might have been expected, or than it ought to have been capable of sustaining without any risk of actual fracture'. He concluded that 'the wires were sufficiently worn at the point of fracture to account for its having failed, as it evidently did, without any strain greater than anticipated having been brought to bear upon it.'

The rope had been in use for 27 months since the last breakage and, according to the NER, a new one had been due for installation within a few days. The end furthest from the winding drum experienced the most friction and the practice had developed of turning the rope to even wear, and cutting off the ends when badly worn. Captain Tyler was highly critical of the lack of any effective supervision over this arrangement, which was left to the discretion of the engineman in charge of the winding engine. Referring to the 1861 accident, he also strongly criticised the NER for having 'permitted two ropes to break, one after the other, in the course of ordinary traffic', and the company's failure to implement his previous recommendation that telegraphic communication should be established between the top and bottom of the incline. It must be presumed that the 'token' from the line's opening was no longer in use, as communication was described as being by 'tightening or jerking the rope'.

The coroner's jury also criticised the condition of the rope, and expressed 'surprise that it was not regularly examined by a superior officer'. All in all it was a grim occurrence, which spurred the NER to complete the deviation work as quickly as possible, while action was also quickly taken to replace the rope with a much stronger one of 'copper wire' for the remaining 18 months of operation. The train guard, Joseph Sedman, was awarded 60 guineas, raised by public subscription, for his bravery in sticking to his post in the stricken train.

With the opening of the new deviation line, the old route via the Goathland incline was abandoned south of Beck Hole. Orders for removal of the equipment and track were issued in 1868 and 1870. A short branch 1 mile 69 chains long was retained to the foot of the old incline at Beck Hole from Deviation Junction, the location where the old and new formations diverged on the south side of Grosmont Tunnel. The branch continued to supply the isolated communities along this remote stretch of the Esk Valley, together with a number of sidings (the NER Sectional Appendix for 1895 lists four such sidings, of which Dowson's Garth and Beck Hole were 'Public Delivery Sidings').

But the incline's days were not quite over, for in 1872 the trackbed was commandeered for an unusual exercise. The Leeds-based locomotive manufacturer, Manning, Wardle & Co, was looking for somewhere to test one of three 3ft 7⁵⁄₁₆ in-gauge Fell locomotives being built for the Cantagallo Railway in Brazil. This railway, being built to open up a major coffee-growing region, needed locomotives capable of operating through mountainous

Above: **A Fell locomotive built by Manning, Wardle for the Cantagallo Railway of Brazil, one of which was tested on the formation of Goathland incline in 1872.**
Ken Hoole Study Centre

Left: **Tunnel Village, Grosmont, and Hay's Ironstone Mine around 1874. Tunnel Inn is on the extreme right, with the ironworks to the left of the railway.**
Tammy Naylor Collection

Below: **Grosmont around 1889, showing the ironworks blast furnaces, with a Fletcher 0-6-0 at the Malton platforms. The signal cabin was replaced in 1907. Note the brick platform shelter on the Esk Valley line platform in the middle distance, one of the few features in the scene still recognisable today.** *Frank Sutcliffe, NYMR Collection*

terrain with sharply curved track and gradients of 1 in 13. In 1863 James Barraclough Fell had developed a system to allow adhesion operation on steep inclines, using a centre rail gripped by pairs of horizontal wheels on the locomotive to assist both adhesion and braking. (The Snaefell Railway in the Isle of Man uses this system solely for emergency braking purposes.)

The NER Board agreed, subject to what today would be called an indemnity from Manning, Wardle against risk of accident. Track was laid on the incline over a 750-yard section, incorporating the centre rail and two sharp curves laid in 'S' formation. The test engine arrived at Goathland in early May 1872, and an initial 'light engine' run was made on Wednesday 8 May. The main trial took place on Friday and Saturday 21 and 22 June 1872 and was clearly a high-profile event, being attended by Messrs Manning, Wardle and Fell, as well as the NER Locomotive Superintendent, Edward Fletcher. Driving the locomotive was Thomas Morton, who was about to take up the post of Locomotive Superintendent for the Cantagallo Railway. The trial was judged a success, with the engine lifting a train conveying 30 passengers and four loaded wagons, weighing 40 tons in all, up the gradient in 3½ minutes. This apparently prompted some wag to comment that the NER need never have abandoned the old incline. The locomotive left Goathland for Brazil three weeks later on 13 July 1871, thus finally drawing to a close rail operations on the old Whitby & Pickering incline.

Just as the initial opening of the W&PR had led to new industry in the area, the much-improved line, now linked to the rest of the growing national railway network, provided a further boost to the local economy. For much of the remaining years of the 19th century new quarrying, iron-smelting and related processing activities were much in evidence, particularly between Grosmont and Goathland. Many would wax and wane in a few years, only to be replaced by new developments.

Among the more substantial industrial sites along this stretch of the Murk Esk valley were the ironworks at Grosmont and Beck Hole. Although ironstone had been worked for centuries, it was the building of the railway that led to the discovery of iron ore where the line bridged the Murk Esk and entered Grosmont Tunnel. Following the Whitby Stone Company's 1836 sample consignment to Birtley Iron Company, ironstone mining had started in earnest. Ironically, mining at Grosmont was suspended in 1842, but appears to have been restarted at a later date. In any event this did not stop development of an ironworks, and by 1862 there were two blast furnaces at Grosmont, extended to three by 1875. During this period the North Eastern Railway declined an offer to buy the ironstone beneath the railway, except under the Murk Esk river bridge where the rights now reside with today's NYMR. By 1891 the site was up for sale, with a slag processing plant coming to occupy the site for a time. Brick and tile works also existed alongside the railway immediately north of Grosmont station, continuing to be active until the 1950s, mineral activity also led to the construction of seven railway sidings between Grosmont and Sleights.

With other iron ore deposits in the vicinity, Beck Hole also saw both mining and an ironworks. Despite employing 180 men in 1860, the latter appears to have been plagued by technical problems, including a landslip that buried the local mine entrance, and production ceased only four years later. Ironstone mining faired slightly better, but seems to have ended around 1876 when the owning company, the South Cleveland Ironworks, went into liquidation.

Other types of stone quarried around the Esk Valley continued to benefit from the railway. Around Lease Rigg quarrying for both sandstone and whinstone brought good business for the railway. The Whitby Stone Company's stone to London went by rail and sea through Whitby and whinstone from the quarry at Lease Rigg, on the west side of the Murk Esk valley, continued to develop through the late 19th century. Output

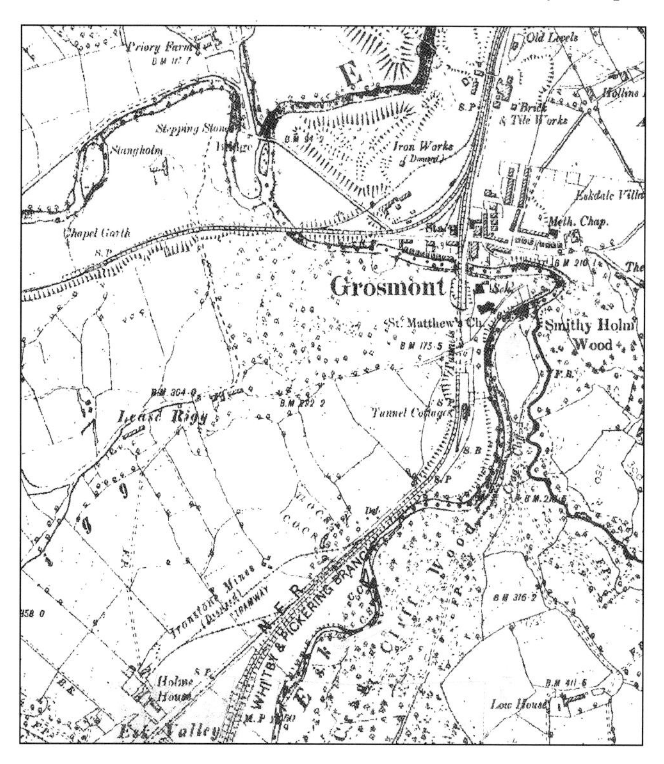

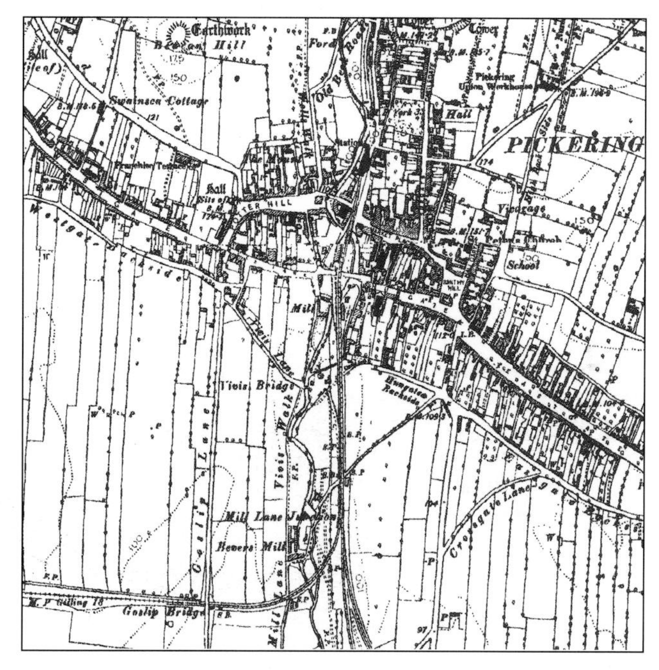

Above right: **Extract from the 1895 OS map of Grosmont. Note the ironworks and other industry around the station, and the start of the Beck Hole branch through the Esk Valley in the bottom left-hand corner.** *Crown copyright, Landmark Information Group Ltd*

Right: **Extract from the 1893 OS map of Pickering. The Whitby branch runs from south to north. dissecting the map, with the three-way junction at Mill Lane prominent towards the bottom. The one-time signal box at Goslip Bridge is marked, where the Gilling line changes from double to single track.** *Crown copyright, Landmark Information Group Ltd*

doubled from 10,000 to 20,000 tons between 1873 and 1905, with the vast majority of the stone despatched via the railway. Whinstone remained an important commodity well into the 20th century. Extensive lime kilns had also been established at Grosmont as soon as the W&PR had opened in 1836, with stone from Lockton, near Levisham, brought in by rail.

Many of the mines and quarries had their own narrow gauge tramways to convey the stone to processing sites and loading points for onward transport by rail, and a number associated with drift mining involved rope-worked inclined planes. Near Esk Valley cottages a standard gauge horse-worked siding passed under the viaduct connecting with a narrow gauge incline. Later a second tramway ran through a tunnel to open up a lower level of the mine. One of the most extensive of these mine tramways, although not built until rather later, used a combination of horse-drawn and gravity operation to bring stone from the whinstone dyke that runs across the moorland north and east of Goathland. This was constructed initially around 1875, after the 'deviation route' had opened, following agreement with the Duchy of Lancaster to convey stone to a steam-driven crushing plant and rail loading point alongside the new Goathland station. It was expanded in 1899 to a length of about a mile when a new drift mine was opened high up on the Moors at Sil Howe, from which the tramway took its name. Believed to have had a gauge of 3 feet, the line included a tunnel into the mine, and gravity operation was employed for loaded wagons descending to Goathland. Initially horses, stabled at Barnet House, hauled the empty wagons back to the mine but in the 1930s old motor cars were apparently used, their wheels straddling the narrow-gauge track. Initially these were two solid-tyred Trojans, later being replaced by a Wolseley. The railway ceased operations in the late 1940s, with the mine closing in 1951.

The NY&C line also triggered several mineral feeder lines to serve various mines and quarries. The already mentioned Rosedale branch was the most significant, running from Battersby up the rope-worked Ingleby incline, then extending some 10 miles south to the West and East Rosedale ironstone workings in the heart of the North Yorkshire Moors. (Although outside the scope of this book, an excellent photographic exhibition about this line can be found at the Beck Isle Museum in Pickering.) Further east, at Commondale, a branch five-eighths of a mile long served a brickworks, while at Glaisdale, just a few miles from those at Grosmont and Beck Hole, a third ironworks started production in 1866. Unfortunately, after changing hands several times ownership passed to the South Cleveland Ironworks, whose 1876 liquidation brought activity to an end. The operation seems to have been dogged by supply problems, with the local stone of inadequate quality or quantity. Attempts to import ironstone through Whitby proved uneconomic, and a planned rail link to bring Cleveland stone in to Glaisdale, the Cleveland Extension Railway, was never completed.

Above: **Goathland around 1904, showing the stone loading plant and sidings. Note the rail wagon high up on the Sil Howe tramway, and the men on the right who appear to be rescuing an errant truck!** *G. W. J. Potter, John Minnis Collection*

Above right: **The Saintoft tramway some time in the 1950s, with a loaded stone train en route to the exchange sidings at New Bridge.** *Beck Isle Museum*

Bottom right: **The building of the 915-foot-long Larpool Viaduct in the 1880s for the Scarborough & Whitby Railway, Whitby's last railway line.** *Frank Sutcliffe, Ken Hoole Study Centre*

On the old Whitby & Pickering route, south of the watershed at Fen Bog a number of railway sidings sprang up to serve the quarries and mines. Altogether there were no fewer than 23 freight sidings between Pickering and Goathland at various times in the line's history. These included Walker Pit near Skelton Tower, the only ironstone mine in Newton Dale. Although this never materialised as intended, traces of the mine can still be found and the mine chimney was standing until recent times. Traces of an old trackbed and loading dock exist, together with the remains of a tramway incline that served a stone quarry. At Farworth (or Farwath), midway between Pickering and Levisham, a small stone quarry had its own siding, which was still shown in use in the last LNER Sectional Appendix issued in 1947.

On this section of line, however, the forwarding of timber, much in demand for pit props, was also important. Records show 11 timber sidings all told, although many only lasted a few years, the time needed to fell all suitable trees in the immediate vicinity. Generally these consisted of two sidings, one long one for the timber wagons, and a shorter one for a rail-mounted loading crane. The NER would install the sidings in return for payment by the owner of an annual percentage for the material handled and the cost of any staff wages.

Two sidings had a broader role as 'Public Delivery Sidings' and lasted longer than many others. Raindale was situated about a mile north of Levisham adjacent to Raindale Mill (a traditional corn mill now rebuilt at the Castle Museum, York), serving both the mill and adjoining hamlet. Newton Dale Siding was further north, controlled by the signal box of the same name. Finally, beyond the period of this chapter, in 1926 a siding was provided at Ellerbeck, near Goathland Summit, primarily to handle road materials for North Riding County Council. Eventually all three closed, although Ellerbeck lasted until 1960.

Limestone quarrying and lime processing around Pickering gave rise to three sets of sidings in the mile north of the station to New Bridge, one consisting of a short spur line running behind today's signal box to serve New Bridge quarry. As early as 1840 *The Yorkshire Gazette* was advertising the sale of the rail-connected 'Capital Limestone Quarry', thought to have been near High Mill. Certainly by 1865 there were two sidings at New Bridge, one of which was to last until the line was closed to freight traffic by British Railways in 1966. Sandstone was also handled through New Bridge, after deposits of silica sand had been found at Saintoft, a short distance from the railway, early in the 20th century. In 1919 a 2-foot-gauge railway was constructed by the Pickering Sand Co to transport sandstone the 2½ miles from two quarry sites at Saintoft to the exchange sidings at New Bridge, where a brickworks was established for a time in the 1920s. Although this closed during the Depression in 1932, the despatch of sandstone continued, as did the Saintoft tramway. Always locomotive-worked, a petrol-driven engine, supplied for the start of operations, was supplemented in 1928 by a Kerr Stuart 0-4-0 saddle tank named *Forward*. The internal-combustion engine returned in 1936 when first one, then two Ruston diesels were acquired. The Saintoft tramway finally ceased operations on 13 October 1961.

The last quarter of the 19th century saw completion of the remaining railway lines linked to the original Whitby & Pickering route. West of Pickering a line had arrived across rural Ryedale from Gilling and Kirbymoorside on 1 April 1875. At Gilling a junction with the Thirsk and Malton branch allowed access to the East Coast Main Line at Pilmoor, south of Thirsk, thus opening up an alternative route to York. The trials and tribulations of this particular enterprise are outside the scope of this book, but it was to remain a rural backwater throughout its life. Initially the line was planned to access Pickering from the north-east, with one option involving a tunnel through the foothills of the Moors at Wrelton. In the event a southerly approach was adopted via a junction with the Rillington to Whitby line at Mill Lane on the outskirts of Pickering.

The opening of the Goathland deviation in July 1865 had also seen a north-to-east curve brought into use at Rillington to enable trains to run through between Scarborough, Pickering and Whitby. The NER had hoped that this would help open up the holiday market by providing a route for regular and excursion traffic between Scarborough, Yorkshire's principal holiday resort, and the Moors. It cannot have been a success, however, as records suggest that the curve was closed in little over a year, many years before the coastal route was opened from Whitby to Scarborough. But this short-lived experiment was not the end of through trains between Pickering and Scarborough. On 1 May 1882 the NER opened the Forge Valley line from Pickering to Seamer, just a few miles from Scarborough on the line from York. Like the line from Gilling, the single-track Forge Valley line joined the line from Rillington at Mill Lane Junction.

To the north around Whitby there were two important lines that would radically change the town's landscape. Both involved routes along the coast but, apart from the Esk Valley, the terrain allowed no alternatives. First of these was the Whitby, Redcar & Middlesbrough Union (WRMU), a railway that had been attempting to forge a route along the rocky northern coastline through Loftus since 1866. Eventually the line was finished by the NER and opened throughout to Whitby on 3 December 1883, curving through 180 degrees around Airy Hill to a junction with the route from Grosmont at Bog Hall. During construction, coastal erosion had destroyed the original chosen course, necessitating re-routing between Kettleness and Sandsend, on the outskirts of Whitby. Independent, but leased to the NER from 1875, the WRMU was amalgamated with the NER in 1889. With three tunnels, five viaducts and steep gradients, the line was always difficult to operate and maintain; eventually this would prove to be its downfall, resulting in the route being the first of Whitby's lines to close.

Meanwhile, attempts to link Whitby with Scarborough had proved equally challenging. Although the Scarborough & Whitby Railway (S&W) was formed in 1871, it took 14 years and the financial help of a wealthy landowner, W. H. Hammond of Raven Hall, Ravenscar, before the line was opened for traffic on 16 July 1885. The S&W marked its arrival at Whitby in dramatic fashion

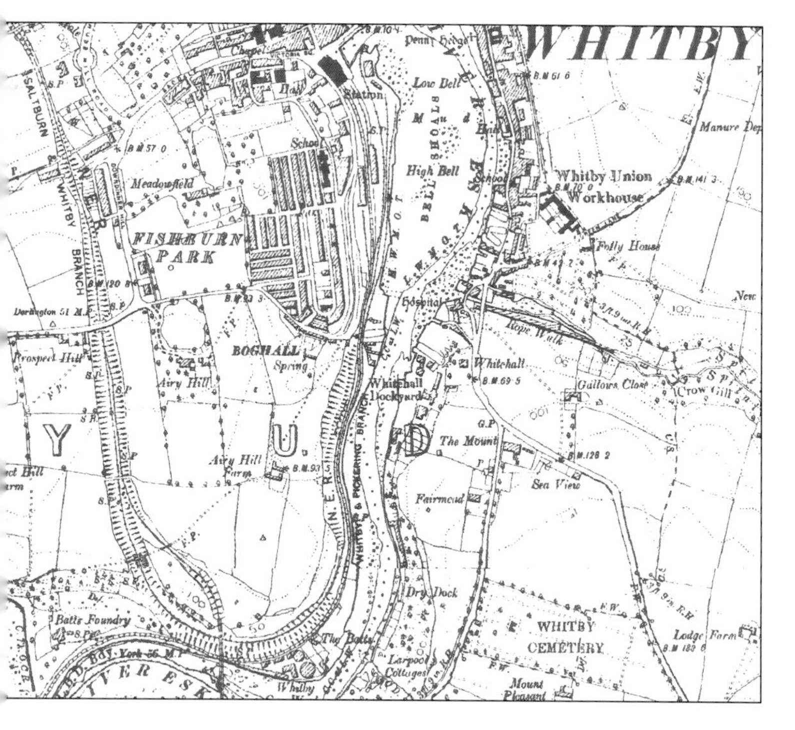

via the 915-foot-long Larpool Viaduct, spanning the River Esk and both the existing railways from Pickering and Loftus; before joining the latter at Prospect Hill Junction. Although an independent railway, it was worked from the outset by the NER in return for 50% of gross receipts. Unfortunately, the relationship between owner and operator seems to have been marked by acrimony throughout. This only ended in 1898, when the NER bought out the S&W for £261,633 – well under half the £649,813 cost of construction. Creation of what was in effect an east-to-west route across Whitby led to a new station at West Cliff high above the town, and not far from George Hudson's 1840s property developments.

One of the relatively few serious accidents in the region occurred early in the 20th century. On 7 August 1901, during the peak summer holiday week, several holiday extras were running to and from Whitby. A late-running freight from Whitby had been shunted at Grosmont to make way for one of these excursions and an engineer's special. Too long to be accommodated in the sidings, the rear portion was left on the down line a short distance north of the signal box. Having signalled and passed the excursion from Whitby forward towards Battersby (then the branch route), the Grosmont signalman reset the junction for the main route from Pickering to Whitby. The signalman

Above: Extract from the 1895 OS map of Whitby, showing the railway routes converging on the town. Larpool Viaduct is at the bottom of the map, and Whitby West Cliff station on 'The Saltburn & Whitby branch' is just off the map area to the north. Further land reclamation for sidings at Bog Hall is still to follow. *Crown copyright, Landmark Information Group Ltd*

Right: A view of Whitby around 1890 from Larpool. The line from Bog Hall Junction to Prospect Hill Junction climbs around Airy Hill away from the Malton route in the left-hand foreground, with the 1835 Whitby & Pickering Railway Weigh House prominent alongside the track. *Whitby Museum*

Left: Whitby engine shed, goods yard and carriage sidings, looking towards the station around 1907. There is no shortage of locomotives, with a long line stabled on the opposite side of the double-track running line from the engine shed, where Class A and G1 locomotives are prominent. The hand-operated crane used for coaling became the subject of a strike in 1910, which was to involve the NER Chief Mechanical Engineer, Vincent Raven. Eventually a steam crane was provided. *R. S. Carpenter, NYMR Collection*

Left: **Class A 2-4-2T No 469 is on the goods yard outlet road in front of Grosmont's new signal box (constructed in 1907) with a line-up of local staff.** *Pendragon Collection, Stanley Ashton Collection*

Below: **Inspection Saloon locomotive No 957, converted from a 'BTP' tank engine, at Prospect Hill Junction around 1910. The Saloon is probably working between Middlesbrough and Scarborough, a regular route for the unique No 957 with such a special.** *Pendragon Collection*

AUTOCAR AND TRAIN SERVICE, 1st JULY TO 30th SEPTEMBER, 1912.

	WEEKDAYS.														
			A									B			
	a.m.	a.m.	a.m.	a.m.	a.m.	a.m.	a.m.	a.m.	p.m.	p.m.	p.m.	p.m.	p.m.	p.m.	p.m.
GOATHLAND ....dep.	—	7 46	—	—	10 27	10 40	11 39	11 52	—	—	—	—	2 43	—	3 6
Glaisdale .... „	—	—	8 7	9 2	—	—	—	—	12 9	12 52	—	2 3	—	2 56	—
Egton .... „	—	—	8 12	9 6	—	—	—	—	12 14	12 56	—	....	—	3 0	—
Beckhole .... „	—	—	—	—	—	—	—	—	—	—	1 35	—	—	—	—
Grosmont .... „	6 3	7 55	8 16	9 12	....	10 49	....	12 0	12 19	1 1	1 45	2 10	2 52	3 5	3 13
Sleights .... „	..	8 5	..	9 21	..	10 58	..	12 9	12 29	1 10	1 54	..	3 1	3 14	..
Ruswarp .... „	....	8 9	....	9 25	....	11 2	....	12 13	12 33	1 14	1 58	....	3 5	3 18	....
WHITBY ....arr.	6 18	8 16	8 35	9 33	10 51	11 8	12 2	12 19	12 40	1 20	2 4	2 27	3 12	3 24	3 30

	WEEKDAYS—*continued.*														SUN.	
										C						
	p.m	p.m	p.m	p.m	p.m	p.m	p.m	p.m.	p.m.	p.m.	p.m.	p.m.	p.m.	p.m.	a.m.	a.m.
GOATHLAND ....dep.	—	—	3 54	—	—	—	5 36	—	—	—	7 47	8 36	—	10 37	....	9 15
Glaisdale .... „	—	3 38	—	—	—	—	—	5 42	6 8	7 18	—	—	9 48	—	—	—
Egton .... „	—	3 42	—	—	—	—	—	5 47	....	7 22	—	—	9 53	—	—	—
Beckhole .... „	3 20	—	—	4 12	4 51	5 25	—	—	—	—	—	—	—	—	—	—
Grosmont .... „	3 30	3 47	4 1	4 22	5 1	5 35	5 44	5 54	6 14	7 27	7 54	8 43	9 58	10 44	6 3	9 22
Sleights .... „	3 39	3 56	4 11	4 31	5 10	5 44	..	6 4	6 22	7 36	8 2	8 53	10 8	10 53	..	9 32
Ruswarp .... „	3 43	4 0	4 15	4 35	5 14	5 48	5 59	6 8	....	7 40	....	8 57	10 12	10 57	....	9 36
WHITBY ....arr.	3 50	4 7	4 22	4 41	5 20	5 54	6 6	6 15	6 30	7 47	8 10	9 4	10 19	11 3	6 18	9 43

	WEEKDAYS.														
	a.m.	a.m.	a.m.	a.m.	a.m.	a.m.	a.m.	a.m.	p.m	p.m.	p.m.	p.m.	p.m.	p.m.	p.m.
WHITBY ....dep.	7 0	7 30	7 40	9 0	9 40	10 11	11 0	11 11	12 13	1 0	1 32	1 58	2 20	2 35	3 8
Ruswarp .... „	7 5	7 35	..	9 5	9 45	10 16	11 5	..	12 18	1 5	..	2 3	2 25	2 40	3 13
Sleights .... „	7 10	7 39	7 48	9 9	9 50	10 21	11 10	....	12 22	1 10	●	2 8	2 30	2 45	3 18
Grosmont .... „	7 20	7 48	7 58	9 18	9 59	10 30	11 19	11 26	12 31	1 19	1 50	2 18	2 39	2 54	3 27
Beckhole .... „	—	—	—	—	—	—	—	—	—	1 29	—	—	—	3 4	—
Egton .... „	7 25	—	8 2	—	—	10 35	—	11 31	—	—	1 55	—	2 44	—	3 32
Glaisdale .... „	7 30	—	8 6	—	—	10 40	—	11 35	—	—	2 3	—	2 48	—	3 37
GOATHLAND ....arr.	—	7 58	—	9 28	10 9	—	11 29	—	12 41	—	—	2 27	—	—	—

	WEEKDAYS—*continued.*													SUN.	
								C		B	D				
	p.m.	p.m.	p.m.	p.m.	p.m.	p.m.	p.m.	p.m.	p.m.	p.m.	p.m.			a.m.	p.m.
WHITBY ....dep.	3 30	4 0	4 15	4 50	5 35	6 15	7 8	7 55	9 10	9 45	10 20	—	—	7 5	6 2
Ruswarp .... „	3 35	..	4 20	4 55	5 40	6 20	f	8 0	....	9 50	10 25	—	—	7 10	6 7
Sleights .... „	3 40	....	4 25	5 0	5 45	6 24	7 16	8 5	9 18	9 55	10 30	—	—	7 14	6 11
Grosmont .... „	3 49	4 14	4 34	5 9	5 56	6 33	7 25	8 15	....	10 5	10 39	—	—	7 23	6 20
Beckhole .... „	3 59	—	4 44	5 19	—	—	—	—	—	—	—	—	—	—	—
Egton .... „	—	—	—	—	6 1	—	—	8 20	—	10 11	—	—	—	—	—
Glaisdale .... „	—	—	—	—	6 6	—	—	8 25	—	10 17	—	—	—	—	—
GOATHLAND ....arr.	—	4 24	—	—	—	6 43	7 35	—	9 34	—	—	—	—	7 33	6 30

A—Saturdays only. B—Saturdays only; will not run beyond Grosmont after 7th September. C—Will not run after 14th September. D—Wednesdays only. ●—Stops when required to take up. f—Stops when required from 16th to 30th September.

Left: **The Summer 1912 North Eastern Railway timetable for Whitby-based tourist 'auto-car' services.** *John Bruce Collection*

Below: **A lengthy down freight train hauled by what appears to be a Class W tank engine approaches Levisham probably around the time of the First World War.** *Sidney Smith, Beck Isle Museum*

accepted from Deviation Junction, the next box to the south another excursion from Leeds bound for Whitby. Fortunately the driver of this train, comprising 12 four-wheeled coaches headed by McDonnell '38' class 4-4-0 No 112, had shut off steam approaching Grosmont, and passed through the station at around 15 to 20mph. Less fortunately, he was momentarily distracted by a shouted question from the station master, since about 150 yards ahead were the wagons of the freight train, entirely forgotten by the signalman. A shouted last minute warning from the fireman enabled the brakes to be applied, but collision was inevitable. Damage was relatively minor, being confined to the leading wagon, the buffer-beam of the locomotive and some couplings. Injuries were similarly minor, being confined to cuts and bruises to the footplate crew and one passenger. At the subsequent inquiry the inspecting office, Lt-Col Von Donop, placed responsibility on the signalman for failing to comply with signalling regulations that would have prevented his error.

The start of the new century and the Edwardian era also saw the most prosperous years for all the railway routes through the North York Moors to Whitby. The Victorian period, with its huge industrial and technological expansion, was just over, for the moment the country was at peace, and a new technology-based middle class had money. People wanted to travel, and the area's combination of coastal and moorland scenery was highly attractive to a developing tourism market. True, some of the staple freight traffic, such as ironstone, was less active, but carriage of minerals, timber and general merchandise still remained strong.

A symbol of this generally buoyant position was the introduction of summer passenger services on the Beck Hole branch.

Right: **Beck Hole station between 1908 and 1912, with a 'BTP' tank and single-coach 'auto-car', and several members of staff posing for the photograph.**
Tammy Naylor Collection

Below: **Whitby station on 30 April 1914 before landfill extended the waterfront away from the station.**
Ken Hoole Study Centre

Below right: **Fletcher 'BTP' 0-4-4T No 498 at Whitby, marshalled in the centre of an 'auto-car' push-pull train around 1920.**
W. Leslie Good, Peter Ward Collection

NORTH EASTERN RAILWAY.

HOLIDAY

CONTRACT TICKETS

enabling the holders to travel WHEN, WHERE, AND AS OFTEN AS THEY LIKE over the lines covered, can be obtained (between 1st May and 30th September).

WHITBY & DISTRICT.

Holiday Ticket No.		One Week. 1st Class	One Week. 3rd Class	A Fortnight. 1st Class	A Fortnight. 3rd Class
1	Whitby, Sandsend, Hinderwell (for Runswick Bay), Staithes, Saltburn and Redcar	11/6	7/-	21/-	12/-
2	Whitby, Sandsend, Hinderwell (for Runswick Bay), Staithes and Saltburn ... Robin Hood's Bay, Ravenscar, Hayburn Wyke and Scarborough	14/-	9/-	25/-	16/-
3	Whitby, Robin Hood's Bay, Ravenscar, Hayburn Wyke, Scarborough, Filey, Speeton, Bempton, Flamborough and Bridlington	14/-	8/6	25/-	15/6
4	Whitby, Ruswarp, Sleights, Grosmont, Goathland, Levisham, Pickering, Thornton Dale, Snainton, Forge Valley, Ganton, Malton, Scarborough, Hayburn Wyke, Ravenscar and Robin Hood's Bay	21/-	14/6	37/6	26/-
14	Whitby, Robin Hood's Bay, Sandsend, Hinderwell (for Runswick Bay) and Staithes Ruswarp, Sleights, Grosmont, Beckhole, Egton, Glaisdale and Castleton ...	13/-	8/-	23/-	14/-

(No Half-fares for Children.)

Apply at any of the Booking Offices concerned, or to the Passenger Manager, North Eastern Railway, York.

HOLIDAY CONTRACT TICKETS covering other portions of the N.E.R. system are also issued, for particulars of which see the Company's Tourist Programme, &c.

York, June, 1911.

Petty & Sons, Ltd., Whitehall Printeries, Leeds.

Left: **A 1911 NER Excursion fares leaflet (Holiday Contract Tickets).**
Chris Cubitt Collection

Steam 'auto-cars' (or 'rail-motors') had been introduced to the Whitby area in 1905. Consisting of a tank locomotive and one, later two, coaches, with driving controls in the leading vehicle, the combination operated in push-pull mode without the need for engines to run-round their trains when reversing direction. This greater flexibility was ideal for the dead-end Beck Hole branch, and in 1908 a small wooden station and platform was constructed for a summer 'auto-car' service targeted at tourists. Some refurbishment of the branch was also needed, with the District Superintendent reporting that the total cost of all the work, including the station, was £739. Trains started running on 1 July 1908, and continued from Whitby to Beck Hole during July, August and September each year until 1914. The outbreak of the First World War caused immediate suspension of the trains on 21 September 1914, and they were destined never to return.

The reality of war came to the railway in Whitby early in the conflict. On the morning of 16 December 1914 several German warships shelled the North East coast of England in the first enemy attack on mainland Britain. The battle cruisers *Derfflinger* and *Von der Tann* attacked Scarborough and Whitby, where some 200 shells were fired at the port. Damage was caused to the stables, Bog Hall signal box, the weigh office, and goods warehouse, while a shell blew a hole in the cattle dock. An NER rulleyman (in charge of delivery horses) was killed by flying glass while attempting to pacify his horse. Minor damage also occurred at Prospect Hill.

The war had one other significant and long-lasting consequence for the route from Pickering to Whitby. The upgrading of the old horse-worked railway had included conversion throughout to double track. In 1916 it appears that there was an urgent need to supply track materials to feed the demands of the war in France. Singling between Pickering (New Bridge) and Levisham was one of a number of schemes identified to release materials, the intention being that the government would pay for restoration after the war. Contemporary accounts suggest that the work was instituted at very short notice, with the signalmen being given only nine days' notice to learn the electric token signalling regulations required for single-line operation. The work took place on Sunday 31 December 1916 under an engineering possession taken at 06.54. Remarkably, by 15.45 the same day the up line had apparently been taken out of use and the new electric token instruments both installed and tested. A further consequence was the loss of the intermediate signal box at Farworth. There are suggestions that the material was sunk in the English Channel on the way to France; however, it also appears that at least some never left England at all. As a result, after the war the government refused to pay the full amount for reinstatement, and after some prevarication the LNER finally decided in 1926 to leave the line single.

3

Twentieth Century: 'Forward' to Decline (1922-1965)

The 1921 Railways Act grouped all but a handful of minor railways in Britain into four new regionally based companies. Thus all NER routes became part of the London & North Eastern Railway (LNER) on 1 January 1923. Geographically the second largest of the 'Big Four', the LNER was destined to serve many of the areas most severely affected by the economic slump that was to drag on through much of the 1920s and 1930s. The LNER's new coat of arms proudly proclaimed the motto 'Forward', but despite a flair for publicity, epitomised by its high-speed expresses on the East Coast Main Line, the LNER was to struggle financially throughout its 25-year life. Not once did the company manage to reach the 'Standard Revenue' set for it under the 1921 Act, and the LNER had the lowest net revenue per route mile of all the companies.

So, from being owned by one of the country's most prosperous railways, the lines to Whitby were now part of the most impecunious of the four main line companies. How did this affect them? At first, outwardly at least, very little seemed to change. Trains and services carried on much as before, with timetables and facilities little changed. But a comparison of traffic trends at local stations between the halcyon Edwardian years and the LNER years shows a steady fall in passengers, and although goods traffic picked up well in the 1920s, here too decline is evident by the depression years of the 1930s (see Appendix 4). There are also some clues that belt-tightening was having an effect quite early on in the LNER period.

A case in point is the already discussed failure to reinstate the double track between New Bridge and Levisham. More detailed examination reveals that the LNER had intended to carry out the work, with a decision to go ahead minuted at the Traffic Committee held on 4 October 1923. A cost of £19,369 was quoted and it was hoped to complete the re-doubling before the 1924 summer season. In the event this did not happen, and it appears that by 1925 the LNER was faced by a claim from the Department of Transport for repayment of compensation received before 1923 by the NER (and other railways). This related to costs incurred, and the value of materials used, during the First World War. Other records indicate that at least £6,000 worth of the materials recovered from the singling scheme had not gone to the war effort. But why had the work not been completed as planned in 1924, some time before the compensation issue appears to have surfaced? The work seems to have been started but was then stopped in 1925. £6,000 is the equivalent of £150,000 today – a sizeable sum to be sure, but for an enterprise the size of the LNER surely not that insurmountable? Could it be that the company already needed to make economies? In any event, on 29 July 1926 the Traffic Committee decided that, '...under present conditions there is no immediate necessity to incur expenditure' on reinstatement. There was never to be such a 'necessity', and the line has remained single ever since.

A further example of the need for financial stringency is seen from proposals considered by another LNER Committee. The Suburban & Road Transport Committee considered a proposal in 1929 to replace passenger trains on a number of lines in the North East, including Scarborough to Whitby. In the event the plan was not adopted, but one line in the region also on the list, Malton to Gilling, did lose its passenger service in 1930. Closer to home, intermediate stations between York and Scarborough, including Rillington, were closed from 20 September 1930.

More positively, the LNER introduced some innovations designed to reduce cost and capitalise on North Yorkshire's scenic attractions. The NER 'auto-car' trains had reappeared after the war on routes around Whitby, including to Goathland. By the time of the Grouping the elderly 'BTP' ('Bogie Tank Passenger') tanks used on these trains were approaching 50 years of age and were becoming life-expired. They were withdrawn

Top: **Early in the LNER period, on 4 August 1925, Class G5 0-4-4T No 1319 crosses the River Esk bridge at Ruswarp with the 10.54 Middlesbrough to Whitby service.**
K. L. Taylor, North Eastern Railway Association

Above: **'G5' 0-4-4T No 1886, with a Whitby to Malton train, passes Kingthorpe on the Levisham to New Bridge section of line singled during the First World War.**
Ken Hoole Study Centre

Left: **Station staff at Rillington pose for the photographer, possibly around the time the station was closed by the LNER in 1930.** *Alf Williamson Collection*

Below left: **Two-cylinder Sentinel steam railcar No 22 stands at Whitby during a test run from York on 6 April 1927. The car is in the teak livery adopted by the LNER for such railcars until replaced by green and cream. No 22 was later named *Brilliant*.** *H. G. W. Household, Ken Hoole Study Centre*

Bottom left: **A six-cylinder Sentinel steam railcar (either No 246 or 248) ascends the 1 in 49 gradient at Darnholm with a Whitby to Pickering service in the summer of 1935.** *C. M. Doncaster, Pendragon Collection*

within a few years, and with them went the 'auto-car' working. In an attempt to recreate the same flexibility the LNER started to invest in a fleet of steam railcars. The majority came from Sentinel Waggon of Shrewsbury; a firm better known for its range of steam road vehicles. Its sales stand at the 1924 British Empire Exhibition had clearly impressed the LNER, and in late 1924 a prototype vehicle was given a test run from York via the Malton to Whitby route, returning via Scarborough. This gave a varied route of steep gradients on the moors and coastal sections contrasting with the faster, relatively level Scarborough to York line, ideal for testing the new railcar's capabilities. In the event this became a regular test circuit from 1927 for Sentinel and a few Clayton steam railcars. An Armstrong-Whitworth diesel-electric railcar, *Lady Hamilton*, was also trialled in January 1932. Despite the test route, it was not until the 1930s that the largest and latest of the Sentinel cars were introduced on local services working from Whitby and Malton locomotive sheds.

On 23 July 1930 a dramatic summer storm deposited vast quantities of rain on the high ground that feeds the River Esk. The resultant torrent led to extensive flooding in the Esk Valley and demolished bridge 82, one of three stone bridges carrying the railway over the Esk between Grosmont and Glaisdale. Most of the stonework disappeared, leaving the track suspended over the gap. Further east there was damage to two other railway bridges between Grosmont and Sleights. At the latter village the bridge carrying the main A169 road from Pickering to Whitby was also washed away. The current road bridge at Sleights was constructed as a replacement, and spans both the river and the railway. The damaged bridges between Grosmont and Sleights were repaired sufficiently to allow the reopening of the Whitby to Pickering route a week later for the August Bank Holiday (then held at the beginning of the month), traffic being worked under single-line working conditions. Bridge 82 inevitably took much longer, during which time trains from the west terminated at Glaisdale, and a Sentinel railcar shuttled between Whitby and Egton. The new single-span steel girder bridge was commissioned in May 1931, but the weather had not yet done with bridge 82. Less then four months later, on 4 September 1931, it was brought down again in a further bout of flooding. It appeared that the flooding had caused the river to alter course, demolishing the east abutment and depositing the new girder span on the river bed. This time the replacement was a double-span girder, including re-use of the fallen span, with a new centre pier and new east abutment. The bridge was completed and the line re-opened in December 1932.

A significant innovation by the LNER in this period was the development of Camping Coaches, providing holiday accommodation for hire in withdrawn coaches specially adapted for the purpose. The first Camping Coaches were introduced in 1933 when the LNER converted a number of redundant former Great Northern Railway six-wheelers. Four were deployed on each of the lines radiating from Whitby, with the facility for users to request that the coach be located at a choice of stations along each line. This facility appears to have been withdrawn in 1935, but the number of static coaches had expanded, with more than 60 sites across the LNER. Some stations had more than one coach, with Sandsend having five on two sites less than half a mile, but two viaducts, apart. Over the years the initially quite rudimentary accommodation was improved. By 1938 the sites within the scope of this book included Levisham, Goathland, Kildale, Castleton Moor, Danby, Lealholm, Glaisdale and the Whitby area (East Row and Sandsend). It was also possible to book a week's 'Touring Camping Holiday'. Starting at York, the coach (an NER-built ex-East Coast Joint Stock vehicle) was moved to a different site by ordinary passenger train, with Glaisdale part of an itinerary that included the Yorkshire Dales.

The 1930s were also to see some of the busiest days ever experienced for passenger traffic on the prime holiday routes to Whitby from both Malton and Scarborough. Regular excursion trains to Whitby and along the Yorkshire Coast were a development fostered strongly by the LNER, particularly from the towns and cities of the West Riding, but also including for a brief period the prestigious 'Northern Belle' land cruise trains. Cheap half- or full-day excursion fares on ordinary trains were a further way to exploit the potential of the leisure traveller. More details of these operations are given in Chapter 6.

Unfortunately, however, this business was highly seasonal, and passenger numbers were significantly lower outside the relatively short summer peak. By the early 1930s the Depression and economic downturn were taking their toll. With much of heavy industry in recession, demand for the area's traditional raw materials was also down, reducing freight forwarding. At the same time, growth in road competition was beginning to bite, affecting passenger and freight traffic alike. Faced by these twin threats, the future for the region's railway routes was no longer certain. One minor economy made in 1930 was conversion to a ground frame of Deviation Junction signal box at Grosmont, which controlled the Beck Hole branch. The LNER estimated an annual saving of £133, with the conversion work costing £550. At around the same time similar action was taken with Foundry Siding signal box on the approach to Whitby, while Newton Dale signal box was taken out of use as a block post (the signals remained until 1952, and there is evidence that the siding was operated by a ground frame very occasionally for engineering work).

The onset of the Second World War inevitably brought more immediate change. Effectively the war brought the years of economic decline to an end and, as it developed, the demands of the war effort brought a dramatic, if brief, increase in traffic. Organisationally, steps were taken in 1940 against the risk of invasion, including the LNER's Evacuation Scheme, which involved moving locomotives inland from vulnerable coastal locations. The stated aim was to avoid leaving any engine overnight on the coast, although in practice this was impossible. In Whitby's case, at least four engines seem to have been moved to Malton out of a pre-war allocation of 14.

Top: **Bridge 82, near Glaisdale, was totally washed away on 23 July 1930 following flash floods caused by heavy storms.** *J. F. Addyman Collection*

Centre: **Washed out again, the girder for bridge 82 rests on the bed of the River Esk after the second flooding on 4 September 1931.** *J. F. Addyman Collection*

Above: **Bridge 82, rebuilt with a longer span, is being crossed by 'G5' No 67343 with an Esk Valley line train in 1953.** *J. W. Armstrong Trust*

Left: **In Newton Dale in the early 1930s a down train is headed by an ex-Hull & Barnsley Railway 0-6-0, by then LNER Class J23.** *Sidney Smith, Beck Isle Museum*

Below left: **A mainstay of local services in the 1930s, 'G5' 0-4-4T No 394 departs from Goathland with a Whitby to Malton train in August 1938. Note the camping coach in the right background.** *J. W. Armstrong Trust*

Above right: **Another locomotive type that saw regular use on the Whitby to Malton line throughout LNER days was the former Class W Pacific tank, which became LNER Class A6. No 686 departs from Whitby with a Malton train.** *NYMR archive*

On the night of 16 September 1940 Whitby came under aerial attack, and significant damage was caused on the approach to Whitby Town station*. As in the First World War the goods warehouse was damaged, but this time rather more severely with the southern portion effectively destroyed; the building was to remain truncated until closure and demolition. The running lines were cratered adjacent to the engine shed where the north end offices were destroyed; evidence of this can still be seen today with a new brick wall across the northern end of the shortened building. Clearance of rubble and track repairs was completed to allow the line to reopen within a few hours. Enemy action also affected a few other locations on the region's lines. Among the more significant was a bomb at Grosmont that made a hole in the roof of the Station House, causing the station master and his family to move out until repairs were completed. Near Pickering an early morning train from York was strafed by a German fighter, killing a passenger. The same plane also attacked the coal yard in

---

* the term 'Town' does not appear in timetables until after Nationalisation, however, it was clearly in use locally much earlier and for ease of reference is used in this book irrespective of date

Left: **In the summer of 1935 a heavily loaded scenic excursion accelerates away from Levisham after the token exchange off the single line from New Bridge. The train engine, Class D49 4-4-0 No 336 *The Quorn* from York shed is assisted by Class A8 4-6-2T No 1330.** *C. M. Doncaster, National Railway Museum*

Above: A busy scene outside Whitby shed on 1 June 1936, as 'G5' 0-4-4T No 1319 heads a lengthy train away from the station. A well-cleaned 'A8' rests on shed while a 'J23' 0-6-0 is stabled alongside the goods shed. *T. E. Rounthwaite, NYMR Collection*

Left: The clouds of war gather on 31 August 1939 as Class A6 4-6-2 No 686 accelerates away from Grosmont with a Leeds train, probably the 12.10 from Whitby. Note the banking engine providing assistance up the 1 in 49 gradient to Goathland. *J. W. Armstrong*

Below: Bomb damage at Whitby on 16 September 1940. *Pendragon Collection*

Bottom: The same scene following the clear-up, with both the engine shed to the left and the goods shed to the right now somewhat shorter. *Ken Hoole Study Centre*

Southgate, Pickering, leading staff to fear emptying the wagons in case there were shells inside.

Britain's railway system emerged from the war tired and worn out. The war had strained the system to its limit, but the revenue-sharing arrangement, effectively imposed by government, meant that in the last three years of war the railway companies received less than half the revenue due for the traffic carried. Yet the increased costs of conveying the huge increases in goods and passengers still had to be borne. The result of this financial settlement was hardly a recipe to address the massive backlog in maintenance, or help post-war recovery. Predictably, as the weakest of the 'Big Four', the LNER emerged in the poorest financial shape, having the lowest net revenue per route mile in 1946. With the Labour Party's victory in the 1945 General Election, nationalisation now became a certainty. But if financial stringency had been a factor throughout LNER days, there was little that would make the position any easier once owned by the state. In the two years following the war, the LNER lost 25% of its passenger volume (albeit from an artificially high wartime level), and the pressure to make economies was only set to accelerate, with decline punctuated by closures set to mark the next two decades for the North York Moors rail network.

Nationalisation took place on 1 January 1948, with responsibility for the 'Big Four' railways transferring to the new British Transport Commission (BTC) and its Railway Executive, more popularly known as British Railways (BR). Lines in North Yorkshire were now part of BR's North Eastern Region. Change was

Above: **Whitby Town, as it had now become, in 1948, the first year of nationalisation. Staple motive power in the immediate post-war years is displayed, with an 'A8' 4-6-2T on a Scarborough train and 'G5' 0-4-4T No 67288 on an Esk Valley line service. The overall roof would be removed in 1952.** *Ken Hoole Study Centre*

Left: **The first rationalisation came with the withdrawal of Forge Valley line services from Pickering to Scarborough on 3 January 1950. In May 1949 a 'G5' 0-4-4T enters Pickering with a push-pull set ready to form a Forge Valley train.** *Peter Ward*

Above: **A disused bridge on the Beck Hole branch, probably photographed around 1935.** *C. M. Doncaster, Whitby Museum*

not long in coming, with the loss of one of Pickering's passenger services in 1950. The Forge Valley line had never been the most heavily used of branch lines and, with many stations remote from the villages they served, it suffered from the development of competing bus services. Nevertheless, the branch had provided a useful link east to Scarborough, and the LNER had attempted to make economies by introducing Sentinel railcars to the branch in the 1930s. By the time the war was over the line had reverted to locomotive operation, albeit working push-pull trains. A respectable service frequency of up to six trains a day each way in the 1939 summer timetable had been reduced to three in each direction by 1948. Perhaps closure was inevitable, but it came early for the Forge Valley with the last train running on 3 June 1950. A short section of the branch remained open between Mill Lane Junction, Pickering, and Thornton Dale Quarry to handle stone until 25 January 1963.

A more open-and-shut case existed with the Grosmont branch to Beck Hole. Following the First World War the active length of the branch had gradually been cut back as traffic at the various sidings served died out, and one of the 1847 bridges over the Murk Esk, a short distance north of Beck Hole, was washed away in the 1931 floods. By the 1940s the line's only purpose was as a supply line to the roadless hamlet of Esk Valley, where an occasional freight train brought groceries and other essentials to the few residents. The arrangement made little sense and, citing a need for expensive track renewals – some of the rails were 70 years old – BR issued an ultimatum. In April 1951 it advised the local authority, Whitby Urban District Council, that the line was to close. North Riding County Council was prevailed upon to build a road down to the hamlet, and this opened on 2 October 1951. According to a newspaper report quoted by the late Ken Hoole, the last supply train should have run on that day, but no wagon was available. Thus the actual last train on the branch had already run on 18 September 1951.

Next to go was Pickering's remaining branch service, west to Gilling and York. The route's geography meant that journey times were never impressive, coupled with a service frequency that had declined from four trains each way to two by the early 1950s, plus a Saturday extra and a Helmsley to Pickering school train. BR withdrew the service completely on 31 January 1953, a day more generally remembered for the storms and floods that devastated much of the East Coast. Although the branch remained open between Gilling and Kirbymoorside for freight, and occasional summer ramblers' excursions, until 7 August 1964, so far as Pickering was concerned, that was that, with closure being total east of Kirbymoorside.

The focus of attention now moved north, with withdrawal of the Whitby to Stockton, via Picton, passenger service on 14 June 1954. More correctly, this was a re-routing, with an increase in the number of trains from Whitby to Middlesbrough via Battersby. This involved complete closure of the old NY&C route between Picton and Stokesley, with a freight service continuing between Battersby and Stokesley until 2 August 1965.

A period of relative stability followed for a few years before a significant closure affected Whitby directly. Although the old WR&MU route along the coast had continued to enjoy quite a frequent service, particularly in the summer, patronage outside the holiday period was declining, and the line had never been easy to work. From 5 May 1958 trains were withdrawn between Whitby and Loftus, the high cost of maintaining the five viaducts on this section being a key factor in BR's decision. A truncated service from Middlesbrough served Loftus for a short period. The northern end of the line continues in use today as far as Boulby mine, about two miles from Staithes, to handle a considerable tonnage of potash requiring several freight trains a day. South of the Boulby site, closure was total, with track recovered and the steel viaducts at Staithes and Sandsend dismantled over the next two years. More positively, the closure coincided with the introduction of DMU operation to the area. Initially they were introduced onto Scarborough-Whitby-Middlesbrough services, in connection with re-routing to run inland from Whitby to Middlesbrough via Battersby, together with a few Whitby to Goathland workings.

It was not all doom and gloom, however. More extensive use of DMUs followed in 1959 (see Chapter 6), undoubtedly helping to popularise the rail service in the eyes of the general public. In 1952 BR had reintroduced Camping Coaches, and by 1955 they were as extensive as ever. Near Whitby there were now six coaches at the two sites at Sandsend, and one was back at Goathland. With closure of the line, however, the Sandsend coaches had gone by 1961, but Grosmont and Ruswarp were new loca-

Above: **Class D49 4-4-0 No 62735 *Westmorland* crosses to the Gilling line at Mill Lane Junction, Pickering, with a York train on 31 January 1953, the day passenger services on this route were withdrawn.** *NYMR Collection*

Left: **On 13 June 1954, the last day of passenger services on the line from Battersby to Picton, Stockton shed has provided 'B1' 4-6-0 No 61034 *Chiru* in place of the more usual 'G5' for what appears to be the last train, the 17.40 Whitby to Stockton, even though the load is only three coaches. The driver picks up the single-line token from the Grosmont signalman for the section to Glaisdale.** *J. W. Armstrong Trust*

tions. Former Great Eastern Railway non-corridor vehicles seem to have been the predominant vehicles deployed at this time. A condition of hire was to travel to the Camping Coaches by train. Campers would also have used the local trains during their stay, no doubt taking advantage of one of the 'runabout' tickets extensively promoted by BR's North Eastern Region. All North Eastern Region Camping Coaches were withdrawn at the end of the 1964 season, but in recent years they have been re-introduced by NYMR at Levisham and Goathland.

West Cliff station in Whitby was now a dead end, with DMU services reversing en route between Scarborough and Whitby Town. Away from the main town centre and not heavily used, BR gained approval to close the station from 12 June 1961, and thereafter the Scarborough trains reversed at Prospect Hill Junction – yet another closure, but worse was to come, for 1961 also saw Dr Richard Beeching take charge of BR upon his appointment as BTC Chairman. With a successful track record in ICI, Beeching's remit from the Conservative Government was clear: to stem the mounting tide of BR's financial losses. The impact

Above: **More modern motive power made an appearance from the mid-1950s, including Standard Class 3 2-6-0 No 77012, seen here passing Darnholm on 5 September 1958 with the 08.55 Whitby to Malton train.** *C. Ord, NYMR Collection*

Right: **The Whitby to Malton pick-up goods makes a spirited departure from Goathland behind Malton shed's Class J25 0-6-0 No 65671 in August 1953.** *Kenneth Field, Rail Archive Stephenson*

Left: A Whitby to Malton train climbs the 1 in 49 of the deviation route above Beck Hole at Easter 1954 headed by 'A8' 4-6-2T No 69861 of Whitby shed. The stock is a typical three-coach formation of the period comprising an NER 'Toplight' brake and, from LNER days, a Thompson Composite Lavatory and Gresley Brake Third. *Jim Jarvis, Colour-Rail*

Right: At Whitby Town on 14 April 1958 'A8' 4-6-2T No 69861 is waiting to depart with the 18.50 service to Malton. *Mike Feather*

Below: An up summer express begins the descent into Newton Dale at Ellerbeck on 10 August 1961 behind 'B1' 4-6-0 No 61053, piloted by Ivatt Class 2 2-6-2T No 41265 probably as far as Malton, where this engine was based. *Neville Stead*

on the railways through the North York Moors and to Whitby would be profound.

Already dubbed 'The Beeching Report' after being heavily trailed for some months, *The Re-Shaping of British Railways* was published in March 1963 by the British Railways Board, as the BTC had by then become. It proposed widespread passenger service withdrawals, and closure of 1,924 stations. Freight services were also tackled, and a move away from the traditional wayside goods yards towards more block train movements was advocated. Specifically, Whitby's three remaining passenger services, from Malton, Scarborough and Middlesbrough, were all proposed for withdrawal. A limited freight service would survive along the Esk Valley line, mainly for coal to Whitby, but with a short section of the Scarborough line retained against the possibility of potash traffic from a potential mine at Hawsker Bottoms. The track via Prospect Hill over Larpool Viaduct to Hawsker was

Below: On 19 July 1957 'A8' 4-6-2T No 69891 enters Glaisdale with the 17.35 Whitby to Middlesbrough Esk Valley line train. This was the last summer before most passenger services on this route were handed over to DMUs. *Michael Mensing*

Top: The new order: a Metro-Cammell DMU departs from Whitby for Malton. *T. H. Mason, Ian Allan Library*

Above: The signalman collects the tablet as 'B1' 4-6-0 No 61276, a regular on the Malton to Whitby route, comes off the single line at New Bridge just north of Pickering with the summer 17.28 Whitby to York train. Note the Austin A35 Countryman (digitally enhanced). *Brian Rutherford*

Below: On 13 April 1964 preserved LNER 'K4' 2-6-0 No 3442 *The Great Marquess* was used for a BBC filming assignment from Leeds to Whitby. Here the train approaches Pickering, passing 'B1' No 61021 *Reitbok* shunting the Pickering goods yard. Note the Y&NM retort house behind the 'B1', which used to supply gas for both the railway and the town in the 19th century. *D. J. Mitchell*

in fact retained for some years after the Scarborough branch shut in anticipation of this development. The 'Re-Shaping' report caused a huge political storm, and ensured that the name 'Beeching' would for ever be associated with closure. But it was clear that he had the support of government, and the closure programme would go ahead. As we have seen, in reality such a policy had already been under way for some time; many earlier line closures by BR have often wrongly been attributed to Beeching, whereas he merely accelerated the process.

The closure proposals for the Whitby routes were duly published in February 1964. True to the report, all passenger services were to go. BR's case rested on published losses on all three routes. Despite, or perhaps because of, being the 'main line', the route of the old W&PR to Malton had the biggest net loss of £49,200, with an operating ratio (traffic expenses to revenue) of 245%. In other words, £1 of receipts cost £2.45. The Scarborough line was next, with a net loss of £30,700, but an even worse operating ratio of 254%. Only the Middlesbrough Esk Valley service came close to respectability in that revenue did at least exceed half the costs. Here the loss was £23,000 and the operating ratio 150%. Of course there were many who questioned the figures, but they were not open for debate.

Opposition to the closures was strong and vocal, with North Riding County Council coordinating matters for all the local authorities. Not surprisingly, Whitby Urban District Council was vehemently opposed, and organised a campaign for individuals to make written objections during the statutory public consultation period, eagerly supported by the local newspaper, *The Whitby Gazette*. Provided there was an objection – there were a record 2,260 – closure could not take place until the proposals had been considered by the regional Transport Users' Consultative Committee (TUCC), with a public hearing required to receive evidence of hardship.

Hearings for the Whitby closures were held in the town by the Yorkshire Area TUCC on 8 and 9 July 1964. Opposition was led by the local MP, Sir Alex Spearman, even though he was a member of the governing Conservative Party. The problems of winter weather in the moors were highlighted, when roads and bus services could often fail to function. Much evidence was given of hardship for daily travellers, including children who used the trains from Goathland and the remote Esk Valley villages to get to school in Whitby. The other big area of concern was the threatened impact on tourism. Although there was much anxiety expressed by Whitby hoteliers, proving actual hardship to rail users on this point was difficult. BR acknowledged the issue in relation to schoolchildren, but directed the problem at the education authorities (a not dissimilar situation arose over seating

Right: **The BBC filming special of 13 April 1964 waits to leave Whitby on its return journey to Leeds with No 3442 *The Great Marquess*.** *Gavin Morrison*

Below: **The 1964 Closure Notice for the routes to Whitby.** *Author*

BRITISH RAILWAYS BOARD

PUBLIC NOTICE – TRANSPORT ACT 1962

Withdrawal of Railway Passenger Services

The North Eastern Region of British Railways hereby give notice in accordance with Section 56 (7) of the Transport Act, 1962, that they propose to discontinue all railway passenger services between Malton and Whitby (and from the following stations):–

MARISHES ROAD	GROSMONT
PICKERING	SLEIGHTS
LEVISHAM	RUSWARP
GOATHLAND	WHITBY (TOWN)

It appears to the Board that the following alternative services will be available :–

ROAD

Operator	No.	Service
United Automobile Services Ltd. jointly with West Yorkshire Road Car Co.	91	Leeds–York–Malton–Whitby
United Automobile Services Ltd.	92	Whitby–Ruswarp–Sleights

Any users of the rail service which it is proposed to discontinue and any body representing such users may lodge an objection in writing within six weeks of Friday, 21st February, 1964, i.e., not later than Saturday, 4th April, 1964, addressing the objection to :–

The Secretary,
Transport Users Consultative Committee for the
North Eastern Area,
Toft Green Chambers,
Toft Green,
YORK.

if the objection relates to the withdrawal of services from stations in the North Riding of Yorkshire, or to:–

The Secretary,
Transport Users Consultative Committee for the
Yorkshire Area,
Toft Green Chambers,
Toft Green,
YORK.

if the objection relates to the withdrawal of services from stations in the East Riding of Yorkshire.

If any such objection is lodged the service cannot be discontinued until the Transport Users Consultative Committee has considered the objections and reported to the Minister of Transport and the Minister has given his consent to the closure under Section 56 (8) of the Transport Act, 1962.

The Committee may hold a meeting to hear objections. Such a meeting will be held in public and any persons who have lodged an objection in writing may also make oral representations to the Committee, if they so wish.

If no objections are lodged to the proposal the service will be discontinued on Monday 5th October, 1964.

capacity on the Esk Valley Line for schoolchildren 40 years later). For the winter roads threat there was no obvious answer.

1964 was the final year of a Conservative Government that was generally thought to have run out of steam. Rail closures were a potential election issue, and Transport Minister Ernest Marples had already made clear that railways to holiday resorts would be protected for the summer. This was cold comfort for Whitby, however, where it was 1965 and beyond that mattered. But hopes ran high when the TUCC published its findings, stating that closure of the Esk Valley line would cause grave hardship, and the Malton line severe hardship. Surely in an election year the government would back off, or at least defer a decision until after the election? The answer was a partial 'yes', for on 11 September 1964, during the dying days of the outgoing government, Marples announced his decision. Two of the lines would close, including the route to Pickering and Malton south of Grosmont. In the case of the Esk Valley, the Minister accepted the claims of hardship, and refused consent. Justifying his decision, Marples said that he 'took into account the importance of Whitby itself', and 'of retaining a rail service to connect it with the nearest large centre of population, the importance of the tourist trade to the town and to the area as a whole, and the extreme difficulty of operating buses over the Esk Valley roads, especially in winter.'

So was this a victory? Marples's reputation on closures had hardly been encouraging, with only a handful declined out of the dozens put to him over the previous year. On the same day as the Whitby decisions were announced, another 36 closures were approved (and two more reprieved). Against this unpromising background, to have salvaged something was an achievement. There had been some expectation that if any route was to be reprieved it would have been Whitby to Malton, given its links to York and the south. But the Middlesbrough service had the most traffic, and would be remaining open for freight. The problem of school travel was also more acute, with several villages along the Esk Valley, rather than just Goathland on the Malton line. However, as a route in for holiday traffic from the main catchment areas – the towns and cities of the West Riding – an enforced journey via Middlesbrough was not ideal.

Meanwhile, the fight went on in the hope that a change of government would bring a change of heart. The General Election of 16 October 1964 did indeed bring Labour to power, and expectations were again raised. This was particularly so since the new Prime Minister, Harold Wilson, had stated in April 1963 that 'No decision, no major decision on closures shall be made until there has been a comparable and equally ruthless survey of transport as a whole....', and there were similar even more forceful assurances subsequently. Referring specifically to Whitby, *The Whitby Gazette* quoted a letter to the local constituency Labour Party, where Mr Wilson confirmed that 'an obviously major decision such as the proposed Scarborough-Malton-Whitby rail closure would be covered by the statement in the Labour Party manifesto...'

It was not to be, however, for the new Transport Minister, Tom Fraser, quickly made clear in a statement in the House of Commons on 4 November that, while he would withhold consent to major closures likely to conflict with proposed regional transport plans, he was advised that he 'had no power under the Transport Act 1962 to withdraw a consent already given'. Closures already approved would stand, but he could vary or add to the conditions attached to those consents. Sophistry indeed, but he did state that he was asking BR to retain the track on closed lines where there was as yet no commitment to dispose of it. In the event, this was an important action since it meant that the line from Grosmont to Pickering stayed intact long enough to be rescued. Internal briefing notes to the Transport Minister released to the National Archives also confirm that BR was asked to consider keeping the track between Goathland and Grosmont in working order in case the schoolchildren were cut off by winter snows. Signalling records show that an inspection trolley traversed the line regularly and, unlike further south, signalling at Goathland remained intact until the NYMR came on the scene.

There were some further attempts to force a last-minute reprieve, both at national and local level, including a protest train organised by Richard Rowntree, the local Liberal Parliamentary candidate and later NYMR chairman, but in truth these never had any chance of success. BR set Monday 8 March 1965 as the

Below: In February 1965, during the last few weeks before closure, a DMU enters Goathland on a down service. The weather demonstrates why there was so much concern about communities becoming isolated in winter without the railway. *Charles Allenby*

date for closure. It only remained for the Road Traffic Commissioners to approve new bus routes to Goathland and Robin Hood's Bay, which they did in February, although with some reluctance in the case of Goathland. With no Sunday service the last trains would run on Saturday 6 March. The final day was marked by snow showers and a grand finale through the running of 'The Whitby Moors' railtour from Manchester by the Stephenson and Manchester Locomotive Societies. Double-headed by preserved 'K4' 2-6-0 No 3442 *The Great Marquess* and fellow Mogul 'K1' No 62005, this train traversed both the Scarborough to Whitby and Whitby to Malton lines. The final southbound train was the 18.54 Whitby to Malton, worked by English Electric Type 4 No D259, while the last northbound train, the 17.55 York to Whitby, was formed by a Metro-Cammell DMU.

This was not quite the end of the passenger service south from Grosmont. On Monday 29 November 1965 heavy snow fell over the North York Moors. The snow prevented the school bus bringing children home from reaching Goathland. With the bus and children returned to Whitby, BR was prevailed upon to run an emergency train, in line with the earlier ministerial request. Formed by a DMU, the train ran again on the Tuesday from

Right: Snow is still on the ground at Goathland as the 08.55 Whitby to Malton service calls on 6 March 1965. The lady on the platform will need to find another form of transport in future, as this was the day on which all services were withdrawn between Grosmont and Pickering. *Maurice Burns*

Below: Saturday 6 March 1965 was the final day of services over both the Scarborough and Malton routes from Whitby. Having arrived via the coastal route from Scarborough, the empty stock of 'The Whitby Moors' railtour is shunted in Bog Hall sidings prior to heading south over the route to Malton behind preserved 'K4' 2-6-0 No 3442 *The Great Marquess* and 'K1' 2-6-0 No 62005. English Electric Type 4 No D259 waits with stock for the last up passenger train on the route, the 18.54 Whitby to Malton. *Gavin Morrison*

Left: After arrival at Pickering on the evening of 6 March 1965, passengers alight for the last time from the 18.54 Whitby to Malton. Although it would take another ten years, passengers would one day be able to arrive by train at Pickering after the station was reopened by the North Yorkshire Moors Railway in 1975. *Maurice Burns*

Below: The last hurrah! Class V2 2-6-2 No 60886 runs into Pickering on 3 June 1965 with the empty stock of the Royal Train after it had been stabled overnight at Marishes Road. *Frank Dean, courtesy of Nigel Trotter*

Goathland, returning in the evening. With improved weather the school bus was back by Wednesday, and BR made it clear to the education authority that in future they would only consider putting on a train if children actually needed rescuing. This scenario never recurred, and thus the school train from Whitby on the afternoon of Tuesday 30 November 1965 was the last BR passenger service to Goathland.

At the southern end of the route, however, a freight service had been retained from Rillington to serve New Bridge Quarry and the coal yard at Pickering. This section of line was also destined to see one final passenger working following withdrawal of normal services. On the night of 2 June 1965, the Royal Train was stabled at Marishes Road, from whence on Thursday 3 June the Duke of Edinburgh made a visit to Fylingdales Early Warning Station. It is said that after his departure local residents were invited to view the train's interior and take coffee. Under the direction of York District Inspector Alfred Maud, the empty train then ran forward to Pickering for the engine to run round the stock. Arriving at a deserted station, word soon spread and the crowds descended for this last spectacle. York shed had turned out Gresley 'V2' 2-6-2 No 60886, possibly the largest ever locomotive to visit the route prior to preservation, while the Duke of Edinburgh appears to have been the last passenger to use Marishes Road station. A brief moment of glory perhaps, but the truncated line only lasted another year, with the last trip freight to Malton running on 1 July 1966, worked by BR diesel shunter No D2066, driven by driver Len Blades.

The impact of closure was significant for the men and women who worked on the railway. Passenger services were now based on DMUs working out and back from Middles-

Top: Driver Len Blades of Malton leans out of BR 204hp diesel shunter No D2066 shunting Pickering coal drops for the last time with the final trip to Malton on 1 July 1966, the day freight services were withdrawn and the line from Rillington to Pickering and New Bridge Quarry was closed. *Frank Dean*

Above: With signs of rationalisation well in evidence, a Middlesbrough-bound DMU leaves Whitby on 27 May 1980. *Brian Morrison*

Left: Completion of the 'basic railway': BR Class 47 No 47309 stands with an engineers' train at Sleights on 30 September 1984 during work to single the final section of double line into Whitby. *Ian S. Carr*

brough, with freight handled by trip workings from Tees Yard, and the need for staff at Whitby dropped rapidly. The infrastructure on the surviving Esk Valley line and at Whitby remained little altered for several years, but rationalisation was inevitable eventually, and started with singling of the line between Grosmont and Sleights in 1972. Thereafter the march towards the basic railway continued, albeit at quite a slow pace (see also Chapters 6 and 8).

Above: **A lifeline to the community, a Class 101 DMU calls at Commondale on a wintry 4 January 1985 with an Esk Valley line service.** *Ian Allan Library*

Below: **On Easter Monday, 29 April 2007, Whitby sees the usual single Class 156 diesel unit (No 156497) strengthened with Class 142 No 142017 to form the Esk Valley train back to Middlesbrough.** *Author*

4

Grosmont to Pickering Resurrection (1966-2008)

The widespread concern in the community about the loss of the rail lines did not die down following closure. Much of this concern centred on Goathland, where the plight of the schoolchildren highlighted the village's transport problems. *The Whitby Gazette* had kept the debate going, and matters were sufficiently high profile for Transport Minister Barbara Castle to send a junior minister to Goathland on a fact-finding mission early in 1966. But it was also made clear that the line would not reopen. Matters turned to the possibility of reopening under private hands.

An embargo had been placed on BR preventing track recovery for two years, but by early 1967 there were rumours that removal was now imminent. Enquiries to BR by the local Liberal Association confirmed this to be the case; in fact, a works order authorising the recovery had already been issued to the Chief Civil Engineer. On 22 June BR wrote to the Clerk of Whitby Rural District Council advising that, since it was clear that there was no real likelihood of local authority financial support, track removal on both the Scarborough and Malton lines from Whitby would be progressed during the summer of 1967.

However, matters were in fact already moving, as a meeting had been held at the home of Tom Salmon in Ruswarp on 3 June. Six people attended with four apologies. There was debate about which route to focus on – should it be through the moors towards Pickering, or the coastal Whitby to Scarborough line? The latter was complicated by the possibility of potash traffic from Hawsker, and the moors route was by general consensus felt to be the better option. Although the needs of Goathland were a primary consideration, the ultimate objective would be to progress reopening of the line in stages from Grosmont through to Pickering. It is interesting to note that the driving force at this early stage was as much community need as preservation. An immediate expression of interest was sent to BR, and this seems to have put a halt on track removal, as a memo from Derek Barrie, the Eastern Region General Manager (by this time the Eastern & North Eastern Regions had merged), dated 29 June 1967 advises BR Headquarters:

'I am afraid this does not leave us free at the moment, however, to lift the track on the Whitby/Malton line because an approach has been made by a firm of solicitors on behalf of the society who are seeking to lease part of the line between Grosmont and Pickering. As you know such approaches have to be reported to the Ministry (by the BRB) after preliminary enquiries have been made... In the meanwhile this is presumably an inhibition to lifting the track.'

Top: **Early days in the preservation era: in 1969 volunteers are at work near Beck Hole before British Rail recovered the second track.** *NYMR Collection*

Above left: **The fledgling NYMR's first motive power, AC Cars railbus No W79978, has arrived at Grosmont on 9 August 1968, having travelled under its own power from Grangemouth in Scotland. The gentleman third from the right with the white shirt and tie is Fred Stuart, the NYMR's first chairman.** *John Boyes, Murray Brown Collection*

Left: **Another epic day: the NYMR's first steam engine, *Mirvale*, a Hudswell Clarke 0-4-0ST, is prepared at Pickering for the journey to Grosmont on 2 February 1969.** *John Boyes, NYMR Collection*

Above: **On 30 March 1969 two more steam locomotives followed the example of *Mirvale* and made the journey from Pickering to Grosmont under their own steam, with the limited water capacity leading to a little improvisation near milepost 14! The locomotives are Borrows No 3, an 0-4-0WT, and *Salmon*, an Andrew Barclay 0-4-0ST.** *John Boyes, J. W. Armstrong Trust*

Right: **AC Cars railbus No W79978 stands at High Mill, Pickering, on 21 October 1968 having arrived from Goathland on a fact-finding journey for the North Riding County Planning Officer – in effect the NYMR's first 'passenger train'.** *John Boyes, J. W. Armstrong Trust*

Below right: **High-tech coaling arrangements at Grosmont in 1970! The locomotive is the 'Q6' in LNER livery as No 3395.** *John Hunt Collection*

Later that year the North Yorkshire Moors Railway Preservation Society (NYMRPS) was formed, holding its first public meeting at Goathland Village Hall on 18 November 1967. By then membership had already reached 450. Discussions now commenced in earnest with BR to stave off track removal. BR quoted £120,000 for purchase of the route and track from Grosmont to Pickering, a huge sum that was way beyond the fledgling NYMRPS's resources. The Society was given six months until 1 April 1968 to come up with a viable proposition during which time the track would be left intact. This was the start of what has always remained a very positive relationship for NYMR with BR and its successor organisations, Railtrack and Network Rail.

A great deal of activity and fundraising followed and, by the time of the Society's first anniversary in 1968, membership had passed the 1,000 mark. It was also possible to announce that agreement in principle had been reached with BR to purchase the land from Grosmont to Pickering, together with a single line of rails as far south as Ellerbeck (near Goathland Summit signal box) for £42,500. BR would recover the rest of the track. By this stage it was recognised that the railway's success would depend primarily on attracting tourists, drawn by the preservation aspects of the railway and the scenery of the National Park. The immediate objective would be to operate over the 5½ miles from Grosmont to Ellerbeck, where a terminus and run-round loop

Above left: **On 23 July 1971 a special train was run from Grosmont to Pickering for the benefit of the Chairman and Councillors of North Riding County Council. Worked by ex-Lambton Colliery and NCB Robert Stephenson 0-6-2T No 5, the train is seen with civic dignitaries after arrival at Pickering. Richard Rowntree the NYMRPS chairman is second right and the railway's long time President Lord Downe far left.** *Chris Cubitt Collection*

Above: **Work is under way in 1973 on the building of the first phase of Grosmont Motive Power Depot.** *John Hunt*

Above: **On the advertised first day of NYMR public services, Easter Sunday, 22 April 1973, a DMU waits at the temporary High Mill station at Pickering prior to returning to Goathland.** *John Hunt*

Below: **The Duchess of Kent talks to driver Chris Cubitt at Grosmont prior to joining the special train to Pickering, run to mark the official opening of the NYMR on 1 May 1973.** *John Hunt*

would be constructed. The first item of rolling stock was acquired in 1968, when, on 9 August, BR AC Cars four-wheel railbus No W79978 made the long journey from Grangemouth in Scotland to Grosmont under its own power. It was envisaged that this would be used for a local community service between Goathland and Grosmont, an idea that never materialised.

From 10 November 1968 BR allowed Society working parties access to the line with maintenance trolleys. This paved the way for the arrival at Pickering on 25 January 1969 of the NYMR's first steam locomotive, *Mirvale*, a 1955-built Hudswell Clarke 0-4-0ST on loan from Mr R. E. Dixon. A week later, on 2 February, the locomotive made a historic first journey from Pickering to Grosmont under its own steam. Two more locomotives, Andrew Barclay 0-6-0ST *Salmon* and Borrows 0-4-0WT No 3 of 1898, similarly worked north on 28 March 1969. A further milestone came on 19 May 1969 when the NYMRPS was able to hand over the 10% deposit agreed with BR – renovation of the line could now start. Then the North Riding County Council (NRCC) and the North York Moors National Park (NYMNP) Committee stepped into the debate. On 21 October 1969 the railbus was allowed to run from Goathland to Pickering for a visit by the County Planning Officer. No W79978 was driven by the Society's first chairman, Fred Stuart, himself a County Councillor and former Whitby engine driver. As a result of this trip the Planning Officer agreed to seek support from the NYMNP in persuading BR to delay removal of the whole of the track through to Pickering. While generally supportive of the proposed re-opening, both authorities had grave doubts about the idea of a terminus in the middle of the moors, with all the attendant road access and car parking issues this would create. It would be far better, surely, for the line to continue on to Pick-

Left: **The NYMR opening special was given dispensation to run into Pickering station, even though a dispute over future land use of the station site was to prevent its regular use for another two years. Ex-Lambton Colliery and NCB Kitson 0-6-2T No 29 and NER 'P3' 0-6-0 No 2392 shunt the special train, run as a Royal Train.** *John Hunt*

ering, and provide a regular transport link through the Park. The NYMR was now encouraged to pursue this goal at a much earlier stage than previously envisaged. In return NRCC would give the railway direct financial help by purchasing from BR the track through to Pickering.

Given the NRCC offer, the Society had some hard thinking to do. Should the NYMR stick to its plan, being confident that as a volunteer project Grosmont to Ellerbeck was achievable, while forgoing the chance to secure the track to Pickering? A drive to Pickering could hopefully follow in stages, if and when money and resources allowed, although, with the track lifted south of Ellerbeck, it might never happen. Alternatively, was not the chance to achieve a rapid re-opening of the whole line too good an opportunity to miss? But this was 18 route miles of railway, far longer than any preserved railway had taken on before, and to make sense trains would have to run daily in season. The scale and nature of the operation made it more than just a volunteer project – some element of paid support would be inevitable. The decision was not easy, but the membership voted to go to Pickering. A steam service would run between Grosmont and Goathland, with railcar operation thence to Pickering. The 1 in 49 gradient of the deviation route to Goathland could provide plenty of interest for steam operations, while the greater levels of visibility available from DMUs would be well-suited to the scenic attractions of the more open southern section through Newton Dale.

Meanwhile, with retention of one line of rails now secure throughout from Grosmont to Pickering, BR undertook recovery of the remaining track during 1969, working southwards through Pickering towards Rillington Junction. The last scrap train, worked by English Electric Type 4 No D399, retreated back to Malton and York on 2 November. With it seemed to go any realistic prospect of a revived southern rail link; not that this was seriously in anyone's mind at the time, given the busy level crossings that would have had to be re-opened in Pickering town centre.

Before the railway could commence advertised passenger services, negotiations had to be completed with BR and a Light Railway Order (LRO) granted by the Secretary of State to allow train operations by the NYMR. This process involved BR applying for the LRO, which would then be conferred on the NYMR by a second Light Railway Transfer Order. Before then it was possible, however, to run trains for Society and Trust members, and a scheme was devised that allowed travel by

Above: **By 15 August 1976 trains were running regularly from Pickering's original station. A well-filled Metro-Cammell DMU on hire from British Rail waits to depart for Goathland.** *John Hunt*

purchase of membership tickets on the day. From Easter 1970 onwards such events at weekends and bank holidays became increasingly frequent, opening up the railway to a wider audience. Apart from gaining new members, the income raised paid the operating costs, and generated funds towards the re-opening. On 23 July 1971 another milestone was achieved with the running of a steam train over the whole line to Pickering station for the chairman and members of NRCC.

Preparing 18 miles of moribund railway for public operation was a huge undertaking for a dedicated, but still volunteer, workforce (the first paid employee was not engaged until 1972). Much of the track had to be re-fettled, weeds needed clearing, ditches required emptying, stations had to be painted, and a host of other tasks carried out. Obviously important was the securing of appropriate locomotives and rolling stock. The North Eastern Locomotive Preservation Group (NELPG), formed in 1966 to save BR locomotives in the North East, set up home on the NYMR; the beginning of a relationship that has continued ever since. For coaching stock, a number of former LNER and earlier coaches were secured.

On 31 December 1971 the North York Moors Historical Railway Trust (NYMHRT) was incorporated as successor to the

NYMRPS. Registered as a charity on 14 February 1972, the NYMHRT had the unique distinction of being the country's first passenger railway to achieve charitable status. The Trust's Objects are worth quoting from:

'To advance the education of the public in the history and development of railway locomotion by the maintenance in working order of the historic and scenic railway line situated between the towns of Grosmont and Pickering in the County of York...'

At the end of 1972 the second NYMHRT chairman, Richard Rowntree, was able to issue a call to arms in the railway's house magazine *Moorsline*. The railway would commence operations at Easter, and although a number of paid staff had now been appointed, more volunteers were sought. His closing words were:

'1973 is a year of destiny for the NYMR just because its future will depend on what we are all going to be able to contribute in its vital opening year. There is a big job to be done. Of course we will make some mistakes and hope to learn from them. But it will be fun, it will be worthwhile and it will certainly be challenging. Provided we all pull together we can make a great success of our railway. I believe we will.'

A public timetable was issued early in 1973. The plan was still for a steam shuttle between Grosmont and Goathland, with DMUs operating services from Grosmont to Pickering. In fact, it was not possible at this stage to terminate in Pickering station due to a dispute with Pickering Urban District Council, who wanted the site for a car park, and were pursuing compulsory purchase. The matter would have to go to Inquiry, but in the meantime a temporary platform was constructed north of High Mill level crossing. An Extraordinary General Meeting was held at Pickering on 17 February 1973 to give approval for the Trust to apply for a Light Railway Transfer Order, an essential final step to enable the LRO to be transferred from BR to the NYMR. Certain works needed attention to satisfy HM Railway Inspecting Officer, Major Peter Olver, but the way was clear for public services to commence. This they did between Grosmont and Pickering on Sunday 22 April, although charter trains had run from Grosmont to Goathland the previous day carrying passengers from a special train to Scarborough (interestingly hauled by A4 Pacific *Sir Nigel Gresley*, an early link between the NYMR and this locomotive, based today on the railway). While the NYMR had sufficient steam locomotives and rolling stock to operate shuttle trains between Grosmont and Goathland, a three-car Metro-Cammell DMU was hired from BR for the Grosmont to Pickering service. Steam trains over the opening weekend were worked by NELPG's 'J27' (re-painted in NER livery as 'P3' No 2392) and former Lambton Railway Kitson 0-6-2T No 29.

On Tuesday 1 May 1973 HRH the Duchess of Kent officially re-opened the line as the North Yorkshire Moors Railway, an appropriate choice given that the Duchess's family home was in

Above: **Steam trains cross at Levisham on 30 May 1976, for the first time since 1962.** *John Hunt*

Left: **The NELPG's 'K1' 2-6-0, masquerading as LNER No 2005, passes the derelict Newton Dale signal box with a northbound train in the early 1980s.** *John Hunt*

the Howardian Hills, only a few miles from Pickering. In echoes of the first opening of the W&PR in 1836, the day dawned sunny and bright with Union flags and bunting adorning the stations. Arriving first at Whitby, the Duchess unveiled a commemorative plaque on the Angel Inn and, after a celebratory luncheon at the Royal Hotel, was driven to Grosmont for the opening ceremony. Ironically, it had been agreed with BR for the opening train to run through from Whitby, but a May Day rail strike prevented this. After the unveiling of another plaque to mark the opening, arrangements had been made to enable the Duchess to clear the departure signal before boarding the special train for its journey to Pickering. Double-headed by No 2392 (driver Chris Cubitt) and No 29 (driver Norman Ash), accompanied by Inspector Jim Brodie, the train was worked as a Royal Train carrying 300 invited guests.

At the NYMHRT AGM in August it was reported that 48,370 passengers had been carried. Ticket receipts were £16,284, with £9,000 of catering and other sales. Interestingly, 66.1% of passengers had booked at Grosmont, quite a contrast to the pattern established in later years, where Pickering has become very much the predominant starting station. By the end of the first year 75,037 tickets had been sold, with total traffic receipts of £23,636. At the 1974 AGM the chairman reported on a satisfactory first year with a surplus of £845 posted; however, this was after a £5,000 grant from North Yorkshire County Council (NYCC) in relation to the cost of the track through to Pickering purchased from BR. The railway had needed to spend £21,000 on track renewals rather than the anticipated £6,000 at the time of purchase, largely because anticipated used rails were no longer available. Although a good second season was in progress, the long-term future of the Pickering operation was stated as not yet secure, even if the concept of a National Park transport service was right. These remarks seem to have been clearly aimed at an external audience; the NYMR needed financial support if it was to perform a social function. This was to have positive results over the next two years, for in 1975 the NYMNP Committee made a £20,000 loan to the railway in recognition of the valuable role the railway was playing in transporting visitors into the Park. Then in 1976 the trackbed between Moorgates and Pickering was sold for £15,250 to NYCC, which leased it back to the railway on a long-term basis for a nominal rent. Several years later the NYMR's finances had advanced sufficiently for the line to be returned to NYMHRT ownership.

The year 1974 saw a 51% increase in traffic receipts to £35,834. By the end of that year a favourable decision had also been received from the Pickering station Inquiry. The site would not be redeveloped, and all that was required was a further Light Railway Transfer Order for trains to start running. In the event this took slightly longer than expected, and the station came into use for the Spring Bank Holiday weekend on Saturday 24 May 1975.

With services now running over the complete route, more attention could be given to the NYMR's long-term development. One key issue was traction policy. Up until now steam operation on the southern route section to Pickering had been limited to occasional specials. Partly this had been out of necessity due to the limited availability of steam locomotives with haulage and water capacity needed to work the longer route section, and the problems of locomotive run-round at Pickering. There was also a belief that regular operation of coal-fired locomotives would be

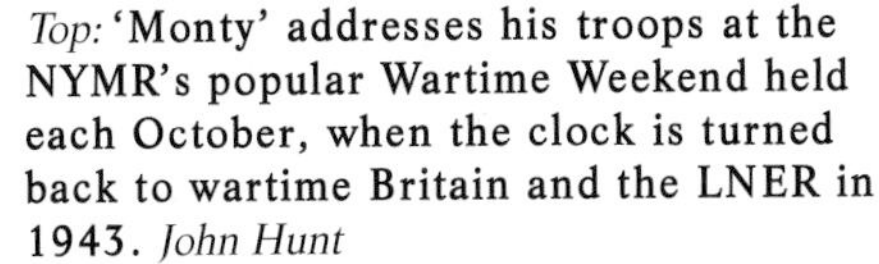
Top: 'Monty' addresses his troops at the NYMR's popular Wartime Weekend held each October, when the clock is turned back to wartime Britain and the LNER in 1943. *John Hunt*

Above: Freight is not generally associated with the modern NYMR. but in 2001 the line was used for the movement of scrap from Pickering. Loaded at New Bridge, the traffic was moved out by English, Welsh & Scottish Railways, whose Class 66 No 66024 is seen departing Levisham. *John Hunt*

Left: The modern railway is depicted in another form during a visit by a Virgin 'Voyager' Class 220 on 28 April 2002, seen here at Goathland. *John Hunt*

unacceptable to the Forestry Commission and Duchy of Lancaster, through whose land much of this section of line ran. Insurance was seen as another inhibiting factor. In *Moorsline* in 1973, Richard Rowntree had argued that conversion of some locos to oil-firing would probably be the only option. Nevertheless, by 1975 coal-fired locomotives were working regularly to Levisham, and timetabled steam services to Pickering started in 1976. The NYMR remained heavily dependent on diesel traction for many years, but as more steam locomotives became available this became the dominant form of traction.

The basic pattern of train operations was now established, and would remain similar for the next 30 years, although timetable frequency increased as passenger demand grew, and on 23 April 1981 Newton Dale Halt was opened to cater for walkers and hikers. Space will not permit a detailed account here of the many other and varied developments on the NYMR over the years that followed, but there are a number of milestones to mention.

Grosmont was established as the main operational base, with the motive power depot developed south of the tunnel, initially on the site of the former Grosmont turntable siding, but eventually expanding to cover a much greater area. Work began in 1971, with the first locomotive shed coming into use in 1973. From basic facilities in those early days, the depot has grown to handle both running maintenance and heavy overhaul of locomotives. Immediately north of Pickering station a Carriage & Wagon maintenance depot was established. At first all activities had to be carried out in the open air, but a shed was brought into use in 1984, with further facilities added over the next few years. The site of a siding to one of the old stone quarries at New Bridge became the location for the railway's permanent way depot. The only signalling left by BR was at Goathland, and new equipment was needed throughout the line. In due course colour light signals and track circuiting were installed in the Pickering area, controlled remotely from New Bridge signal box, and a totally new NER-design signal box was commissioned at Grosmont in 1996 (see Chapter 8).

As passenger numbers grew the limitations of the NYMR's stations became apparent. More passengers now meant trains of up to eight or more coaches. While even longer trains had occasionally run on the route in LNER and BR days, these were predominantly excursions bound for the coast and either 'drew up' or missed the smaller intermediate stations. Now it was possible to have several hundred passengers wanting to join and alight from the NYMR's busiest trains, yet station platforms could only accommodate three, or at most four, coaches. Nothing much could be done about Goathland or Levisham without destroying the character of the stations, but an extension to the up platform at Pickering came into use in 1990. Work at Grosmont, including a third platform face, completed in 2004, also greatly eased operation of the NYMR's highly successful Pullman dining service, a train that regularly loads to eight coaches.

Today the NYMR is the busiest heritage railway in Britain, carrying more than 320,000 passengers a year. The railway is also probably the country's longest registered museum.

Above: **Founders' Day, 3 June 2007, celebrating 40 years of the North Yorkshire Moors Railway: Tom Salmon (in whose home the first meeting was held to discuss a possible rescue bid for the line), Charlie Hart, Michael Pitts and Tom's wife Erica pose on the platform at Grosmont.** *Margaret Pitts*

Right: **Restored by the NYMR from Barry Scrapyard condition, Standard Class 4 2-6-4T No 80135 is a firm favourite among the railway's members and staff. The engine is painted in BR green at the request and in memory of its long-time Dutch owner, the late Jos de Crau, who saved the locomotive for use on the NYMR. The engine is heading a Pickering-bound train approaching Darnholm on 10 April 1994.** *John Hunt*

Above: A 'B1' back on the Whitby to Malton line: the Thompson B1 Locomotive Trust's No 61264 departs from Grosmont on 28 September 2005 with the 09.50 to Pickering. *Author*

Below: Owned by the Sir Nigel Gresley Locomotive Preservation Trust, Class A4 4-6-2 No 60007 ***Sir Nigel Gresley*** heads away from Goathland with the NYMR's popular Sunday lunch Pullman diner 'The Moorlander' on 4 November 2007. *Author*

5

A Photographic Journey along the Line

Left: Malton was where most trains over the Rillington to Whitby line started their journey. Class A8 4-6-2T No 69861 is on just such a working on 21 July 1958, heading the 16.00 service to Whitby. *Michael Mensing*

Below: Around 1955, almost brand-new Standard Class 4 2-6-4T No 80118 passes through the remains of Rillington station with a Malton to Whitby service. The original NER signal box controls the Whitby line junction. *J. W. Armstrong Trust*

Below: In September 1904 an up train approaches Kirby old station headed by Worsdell Class G1 4-4-0 No 557. The train has just passed over Black Bull crossing. *G. W. J. Potter, John Minnis Collection*

Below right: Near Haygate Lane, south of Pickering, our old friend 'A8' No 69861 heads a down Malton to Whitby train in September 1957. *C. G. Pearson, Ian Allan Library*

Left: Class D49 4-4-0 No 62726 ***The Meynell*** stands in Pickering station in 1951 with a York via Gilling train. The overall roof was removed in 1952. *W. A. Camwell, Peter Ward Collection*

Below left: At the north end of Pickering station on 19 April 1951 'G5' 0-4-4T No 67330 is taking water before heading through the moors with a Malton to Whitby service. *Peter Ward*

Below: A 'B1' heads north near Kingthorpe on the single-line section between New Bridge and Levisham on a snowy 20 February 1964. *Doug Hardy*

Bottom: Looking north from Pickering, a North Eastern Railway Whitby-bound train heads towards Kingthorpe in the early years of the 20th century before this section of line was singled. *Sidney Smith, Beck Isle Museum*

Right: Levisham in 1937, with 'G5' No 1886 of Malton shed departing with a down train. *NYMR Collection*

Below left: Standard Class 3 2-6-2T No 82029 makes a spirited departure from Levisham with the 15.50 Malton to Whitby train in 1962, a working that retained loco-hauled stock as it formed the up evening mail train back from Whitby. *Brian Rutherford*

Belowright: Heading through the wooded lower section of Newton Dale, a down express for Whitby has a 'B1' 4-6-0 as train engine with No 41251, one of Malton's two Ivatt Class 2 2-6-2Ts, as pilot for the climb through the North York Moors and over Goathland Summit. *P. Wilson, NYMR Collection*

Left: A Standard Class 3 2-6-2T heads through Northdale with an afternoon Malton to Whitby service in the summer of 1962 or 1963. The first two coaches are through from London King's Cross, having worked north from London on the 'Scarborough Spa Express'. *M. Dunnett, NYMR Collection*

Left: During the line's last summer before closure by British Rail, a three-car Metro-Cammell DMU approaches Goathland Summit with the 10.23 York to Whitby service, in the shadow of the newly built Fylingdales Early Warning Station. *John Clarke*

Below: 'G5' No 67315 heads an up train from Whitby Town to Malton in the early 1950s near Moorgates. The trackbed of the old Whitby & Pickering Railway route joining the 1865 deviation route is just discernible as the slightly raised ground to the left of the engine. *Ken Hoole Study Centre*

Right: Worsdell Class J24 0-6-0 No 65671, a Whitby engine, shunts Goathland goods yard with the Whitby to Malton pick-up goods in August 1953. The two former NER wooden-bodied coal hoppers are of note. *Kenneth Field, Rail Archive Stephenson*

Left: 'A8' No 69861 waits for the 'right away' at Goathland on 15 April 1958 with a Malton to Whitby Town local. *Mike Feather*

Below left: In 1935 a typical Whitby to Malton train of the time climbs past Darnholm headed by a 'G5' 0-4-4T. *C. M. Doncaster, Ian Allan Library*

Bottom: 'B1' 4-6-0 No 61337 climbs past Water Ark with the afternoon SO Whitby to Leeds express in 1964. *David Sutcliffe*

Above right: Shortly after the Second World War in 1946, 'D49' 4-4-0 No 2759 *The Craven* climbs under the road overbridge above Beck Hole village with a Whitby to York train. *Dr C. Cobb, Ken Hoole Study Centre*

Right: In the late 1950s 'B1' 4-6-0 No 61218 is piloted by Ivatt Class 2 2-6-2T No 41251 in the early stages of the 1 in 49 climb to Goathland Summit at Greenend, about a mile south of Grosmont, with the summer 14.10 (SO) Whitby to Leeds express. *Cecil Ord, Rail Archive Stephenson*

Bottom left: At Grosmont, looking north in 1954, the ubiquitous 'A8' No 69861 approaches the station with a late-afternoon Whitby to Malton train. The chimney in the background was part of the brickworks that adjoined the line at this point. Remnants of the brick kilns can still be seen alongside today's NYMR carriage sidings.
J. W. Armstrong Trust

Below: Thompson Class L1 2-6-4T No 67766 takes the Esk Valley line and platform at Grosmont as the fireman prepares to collect the single-line tablet from the signalman for the section to Glaisdale on 16 April 1958.
Mike Feather

Left: In the late 1930s, 'G5' 0-4-4T No 1886 nears Grosmont with a Whitby to Malton train. *Ian Allan Library*

Below: 'G5' No 67343 departs from Sleights in March 1954 with a Whitby to Malton train. *Jim Jarvis, Colour-Rail*

Bottom left: A new bridge was built at Sleights to carry the Pickering to Whitby A169 road over the railway and the River Esk after the old river bridge was severed in the 1930 floods, replacing a level crossing in the process. 'A8' No 69889 departs under the bridge with the 16.05 Whitby to Middlesbrough service in August 1955. *Peter Cookson*

Bottom right: In August 1957 'B1' 4-6-0 No 61038 ***Blacktail*** enters Sleights with the 14.10 SO Whitby to Leeds express. The goods yard is still doing plenty of business. *Tony Ross*

Left: On 31 August 1978 a Metro-Cammell Class 101 DMU enters Ruswarp with the 11.40 Middlesbrough to Whitby service. *N. Mitchell, Ian Allan Library*

Below: An 'A8' passes under Larpool Viaduct and along the bank of the River Esk on 8 May 1958 with a Whitby to Malton train. *C. Hogg, Colour-Rail*

Above: Thompson Class B1 4-6-0 No 61071 propels the stock for the Summer-only 18.10 express from Whitby to York past Bog Hall signal box on 21 July 1958. *Michael Mensing*

Left: At Whitby Town at Easter 1954, after the train-shed roof had been removed, Malton's 'G5' No 67332 prepares for a smoky departure with an up train back to its home town. *Jim Jarvis, Nigel Trotter Collection*

Above: A photograph of Whitby Town taken in the early-1950s before the train-shed roof was removed. The locomotive is a 'D49' 4-4-0. *Lens of Sutton, Nigel Trotter Collection*

Above: At Whitby West Cliff station on 23 June 1957, the 'Yorkshire Coast' enthusiasts' special organised by the Railway Travel & Correspondence Society is ready to depart after reversal for the short run via the chord line down to Whitby Town. The locomotives are 'A8' 4-6-2T No 69881 and 'D49' 4-4-0 No 62731 ***Selkirkshire.*** *Gavin Morrison*

Left: A8' No 69867 from Scarborough shed climbs slowly away from Larpool Viaduct and heads for home with a train from Middlesbrough in July 1957. *Michael Mensing*

Below: On 19 July 1957 Gresley Class V1 2-6-2T No 67646 heads a Whitby to Middlesbrough Esk Valley line train near Glaisdale. *Michael Mensing*

Left: An 'A8' heads for Whitby at Kilkdale in 1953, three years before the loop at this station was abolished.
J. W. Armstrong Trust

Below: Also in 1953, 'A8' No 69886 takes water at Battersby with an Esk Valley line train. *J. W. Armstrong Trust*

Bottom: 'L1' No 67754 crosses East Row Viaduct at Sandsend in 1954 with a Middlesbrough to Whitby Town train.
Colour Rail

6

Train Services and Railway Operations

Horse-drawn days

When the first W&PR horse trains started running between Whitby and Grosmont, the railway appears to have had only the First Class coach *Premier* available. The directors' minutes show that initially a morning and an afternoon return trip had been planned between Whitby and Tunnel Inn, Grosmont, including Sundays. By the time services actually began, however, this had been modified to a single trip leaving Whitby at 14.00 returning at 19.00 or 20.00 in the evening. A number of shareholders had expressed disquiet at the idea of a Sunday operation, and at a Special General Meeting it was decided not to provide one at that stage. A second service was run on Saturdays to cater for 'market people', the times from Whitby being 07.45 and 17.00, returning at 09.00 and 19.00 from Tunnel. From July 1835 a Second Class coach was available to share the operation, and it was also now possible to reach Beck Hole by arrangement. By October times had been changed to 10.00 from Whitby, coming back from Tunnel at 15.00.

With the opening of the railway throughout between Whitby and Pickering, the Sunday issue seems to have been resolved. The timetable published on 1 June 1836 advertised two return trips daily leaving Whitby at 06.30 and 17.00. From Pickering the morning coach departed at 10.30 (Sundays 07.00) and the evening one at 17.00, or upon arrival of the stagecoach from York. A coach to Beck Hole and Tunnel was also advertised at 13.30, returning from Tunnel at 19.00. William Turnbull, who was one of the first guards on the railway coaches, used to transfer to the connecting stagecoach at Pickering, then acted as guard on the road journey through to York. Times of the horse trains changed over the years, with the advertised journey times also varying between 2½ and 3 hours. In 1838 the *Lady Hilda* was shown as leaving Whitby at 08.00 and arriving in Pickering at 10.45, then returning at 14.00 to arrive at Whitby 'around' 16.30. In 1843 Bradshaw's railway timetable gave the time as 08.30, giving a York arrival of 14.30, while in the other direction departure from York was at 12.00, having connected with a number of trains, with a Whitby arrival at 18.00. Bradshaw also referred to a luggage train at a lower fare taking 4 hours. Interestingly, this apparently deliberately slow service predated by a year the Act requiring one daily train on every line at a fare no greater than 1 penny a mile. By 1844 the morning coach was leaving Whitby at 07.00, giving a 12.30 arrival at York.

In his 1906 book Potter relates an account given by William Wardell, who was a postillion-rider, of the operational arrangements. It appears that the NER had put Potter in touch with Wardell in 1899. He had become a platelayer when horse operation finished and, according to the NER, was still working as a

Above: 1838 Whitby & Pickering Railway poster showing the Spring and Summer timetable. *NYMR*

NORTH MIDLAND RAILWAY.
OPENING of the ENTIRE LINE.

THE PUBLIC is respectfully informed that this RAILWAY WILL BE OPENED THROUGHOUT FROM DERBY TO LEEDS, for the Conveyance of Passengers and Parcels, on WEDNESDAY, the First Day of July next.

Passengers may be booked through to Leeds and York, at the London and Birmingham Railway Station, Euston-square.

Further Particulars as to the Times of Departure of the Trains will be duly announced.

By Order,
H. PATTESON, Secretary.
13, George-Street, Mansion-House, London,
May 9, 1840.

WHITBY AND PICKERING RAILWAY.

THE PREMIER COACH leaves WHITBY every Morning (except Sundays) at SIX o'Clock, arriving in YORK at a Quarter before TWELVE, in time for the Trains on the YORK and NORTH MIDLAND RAILWAY, by which Passengers may, after the 30th instant, proceed without delay to Hull, Leeds, Liverpool, Sheffield, Birmingham, and London, and other places in the South.

The same Coach returns from York at TWO, and reaches Whitby at EIGHT o'Clock in the Evening.

The TRANSIT COACH leaves PICKERING for WHITBY every Morning at Half-past EIGHT, and starts from WHITBY for PICKERING in returning at Half-past FOUR o'Clock in the Afternoon, on the arrival of the Coach from Stockton and the North, so that Passengers from thence may proceed immediately to Pickering.

Coaches for a party of not less than Eight, and Trucks for the conveyance of Carriages may be had at any time, either at Whitby or Pickering, and even a Single Person will find the engaging of a Railway Carriage to himself less expensive than a Post Chaise.

Railway Office, Whitby, June 20, 1840.

Left: An 1840 Whitby & Pickering Railway press advertisement showing connections to York from Whitby via stagecoach from Pickering. The other advertisement, presumably placed by the York & North Midland Railway, announces the introduction of through trains between Derby and Leeds with through tickets now available via the London & Birmingham Railway to reach York, and thus no doubt Whitby. *Graham Reussner Collection*

Top right: William Wardell, who had worked as a postillion in the earliest horse-drawn days of the railway, was still at work in 1905 as crossing-keeper at Mill Lane, Pickering. (He appears to have moved from nearby Hungate, where he was reported as working in 1899.) *G. W. J. Potter, John Minnis Collection*

crossing-keeper at Hungate, Pickering, at the age of 72. A single horse and driver would work a coach from Pickering as far as Raindale (near Levisham), where it was replaced by two horses working in tandem, with the help of the postillion, for the climb to the summit near Fen Bog. The postillion then brought the second horse back to Raindale while the remaining animal worked through to the incline top at Goathland. According to Wardell, the coach would be allowed to freewheel from the bottom of the incline at Beck Hole, usually getting close to Grosmont from where another horse would work on to Whitby. A similar arrangement applied in the southbound direction, although, with gentler gradients, only one horse was required over each section.

In the Whitby & Pickering's early days, it was apparently possible for individuals to bring their own vehicle on to the railway upon payment of a toll. These were quoted as varying between 2d and 6d per mile per ton, with passengers charged at 2d per mile. A supplement of 1s a ton applied up the incline. Just how much use was made of this facility is unclear, but it was also possible to travel in your own road carriage loaded upon a rail truck. An account is given of a journey by Mr Chapman, the uncle of the local MP Aaron Chapman, who in his 86th year travelled up the line this way in the family carriage. He was 'exceedingly delighted with so novel a mode of travelling, as well as with the beautiful scenery through which he was conveyed.'

Information about goods operations during the horse-drawn days is limited. But Joseph Watson, aged 84 in 1899, recalled driving the horse-drawn wagons between Pickering and Raindale, which was evidently a stabling and exchange point, as he used to return with wagons that had come through from further north. It appears that initially operations were contracted out to local farmers, but were taken 'in-house' within about a year. Each truck was capable of carrying 2 tons, this being an approximate load for a single horse. Mr Watson also confirmed that dandy carts for horses 'were not used for passenger trains, but that they had a kind of a horse box in which horses, which had assisted goods wagons up the bank, rode down from Fen Bog to Levisham.'

York & North Midland services

Conversion to steam operation brought about a dramatic improvement in the pattern of services. The first passenger train from Whitby to the foot of the incline at Beck Hole was worked by driver Edward Laws, who recollected that it had three vehicles. The fireman was William Pickering. Locomotive haulage resulted in a rapid upturn in stone being forwarded from the Esk Valley. Driver Laws recalled that a second locomotive, *Firefly*, had to be introduced on the Whitby section to clear loaded wagons from Grosmont to Whitby Harbour. At this early stage capacity was around 3½ tons per wagon, at least an improvement on the horse-drawn days.

In 1848, when Bradshaw started publishing full details of the service, the August timetable was showing three trains between York and Whitby in each direction supplemented by additional Pickering services from and to York and Rillington. The 07.00 from York and the 15.15 from Whitby ran as mail trains, starting a practice that lasted until the line's closure. Journey times generally varied between 2 hours down from Malton, and 2¼ hours in the up direction, although the 15.15 mail train from Whitby was advertised to reach Malton in 1 hour 55 minutes (see Table 6.1). Winter saw a reduced service of two trains each way between Whitby and Pickering, while on Sundays just the mail train ran in each direction.

Table 6.1: York & North Midland (principal stations only), August 1848

YORK & NORTH MIDLAND – August 1848							
Down		Mail					
Class	1,2,3	1,2	1,2,3	1,2,Gov	1,2,3	1,2,3	1,2,3
York		07.00		09.15	12.00	16.00	17.30
Malton		08.00		10.15	13.00	16.45	18.30
Rillington	08.00		10.03		13.20	17.10	18.55
Pickering	08.20	08.30	10.23	10.50	13.40	17.30	19.10
Goathland		09.15			14.25		19.55
Grosmont		09.40			14.50		20.15
Whitby		10.00			15.05		20.35
Up						Mail	
Class	1,2,Gov	1,2,3		1,2,3		1,2	1,2,3
Whitby		07.45		11.15		15.15	
Grosmont		08.05		11.40		15.40	
Goathland		08.20		12.00		16.00	
Pickering	07.20	09.15		12.45		16.45	16.55
Rillington	07.48	09.48		13.18		17.00	17.15
Malton	08.00	10.00		13.30		17.10	
York	09.05	11.00		14.30		18.10	

Table 6.2

		NORTH EASTERN RAILWAY - January 1861												
Down		Goods	Mail Pass	Goods	Pass	Coal	Goods	Goods	Exp Pass	Goods	Goods	Pass	SUNDAY Mail Pass	Pass
Malton	d		07.00	09.05	10.45	10.20	13.30	15.20	15.50			19.33	07.00	
Rillington	a		07.09		10.49				16.00			19.44	07.09	
	d		07.25	09.20	10.55	11.35		15.40	16.05		17.45	19.53	07.18	19.15
Marishes Rd			07.30	09.30	11.00				16.10			20.00	07.25	19.25
Kirby														
Pickering	a		07.40	09.50	11.12	12.00	14.20	16.00	16.20	↴	18.20	20.10	07.33	19.35
	d		07.42	10.10	11.15	12.30		↳	16.22	16.40		20.12	07.35	
Levisham			07.57	10.40	11.38	12.53			16.37	17.10		20.27	07.50	
Goathland			08.20	11.20	11.57	13.30			17.00	18.00		20.50	08.13	
Beck Holes		09.00	08.28	13.30	12.03				17.08	19.00		20.58	08.28	18.05
Grosmont		09.15	08.34	13.45	12.12				17.14	19.10		21.04	08.34	18.15
Sleights		09.45	08.44	14.05	12.22				17.24	19.20		21.14	08.44	18.25
Ruswarp		09.50	08.54	14.20	12.28				17.30	19.30		21.19	08.54	18.30
Whitby	a	10.00	09.00	14.30	12.38				17.40	19.45		21.30	09.00	18.35
Up		Pass	Goods	Goods	Pass	Goods	Goods	Exp Pass	Coal	Goods	Mail Pass	Goods	Pass	Mail Pass
Whitby	d			06.30	08.10		10.00	12.40		15.09	17.25	18.00	07.30	17.25
Ruswarp				06.45	08.15		10.15	12.45			17.30	18.10	07.35	17.30
Sleights				07.00	08.20		10.30	12.50			17.35	18.20	07.40	17.35
Grosmont				07.15	08.30		10.45	13.00		15.30	17.45	18.35	07.50	17.45
Beck Holes				07.30			11.00			15.50		18.45	08.05	
Goathland					08.50	10.05		13.20	14.00	16.10	18.05	19.30		18.05
Levisham					09.15	10.55		13.42	14.30		18.30	20.05		18.30
Pickering	a				09.28	11.15		13.55	14.50		18.43	20.30		18.43
	d	06.45	07.45		09.30	12.15		13.57	15.15	16.55	18.45	20.45	06.45	18.45
Kirby						12.25						20.55		
Marishes Rd		06.55			09.40	12.35					18.55	21.05	06.55	18.55
Rillington	a	07.05			09.50	12.45		14.16		17.20	19.05		07.05	19.05
	d				09.55			14.25	15.35	17.30	19.10	21.15		19.10
Malton	a		08.45		10.10	13.00		14.35	16.00	18.00	19.20	21.45		19.20

The North Eastern in the 19th century

The January 1861 working timetable listed four passenger trains down to Whitby, one being the mail train and another described as an express, but only three in the up direction. Pickering, however, had an early morning connection to Rillington, with a return working possibly combined with the down mail vehicles from York, detached from the Scarborough service. Similar balancing is apparent between Whitby and Beck Hole for the Sunday mail train (Beck Hole otherwise had no up passenger service). Two down and up goods services worked the full length of the line, with the afternoon return from Whitby running fast, almost certainly for perishable fish traffic. Trip working is evident between Grosmont and Whitby, with other local coal trips at the Pickering end of the line (see Table 6.2).

Not surprisingly, opening of the Goathland deviation line in 1865 led to a radical recast of the timetable. The fastest passenger time in both directions between Malton and Whitby was now 1 hour 35 minutes, an improvement of 10 minutes resulting from elimination of the rope incline. Frequency remained unbalanced with five down services, plus an early-morning fast mail train, but only four up services. For the brief period of services to Scarborough via Rillington two return trains ran from Whitby calling only at Pickering, giving a journey time of just 1½ hours. Potter tells us that William Pickering, whom we have already met, was the regular driver of these trains. Driver Pickering was one of the staff members referred to in the 1899 NER briefing paper, having retired from the NER in 1893. The most striking aspect of the working timetable, however, is the increase in provision for freight trains, including many clearly being scheduled to service the ironworks at Grosmont. Whether all these trains ran regularly must be debatable; indeed, some of the timings all but conflict (See Table 6.3).

Opening of the NY&C branch from Picton to Grosmont in 1865 brought another four trains a day in each direction along the Esk Valley, virtually doubling Whitby's passenger service. Stockton was the starting point for these trains rather than Middlesbrough, with the link line from Battersby to Middlesbrough not opening for passengers until 1868. Initially trains left Stockton at 07.45, 10.40, 15.30 and 20.40 for the journey of just over 2 hours. Return times from Whitby were at 07.15, 10.30, 15.15 and 18.15. The service had expanded to five by 1900, with an additional train leaving Whitby around lunchtime.

Goods traffic on the NY&C was dominated by the ironstone traffic from the Rosedale branch to the blast furnaces of Teesside, and does not concern us here. Nevertheless, the mineral traffic from the Esk Valley area around Grosmont and Glaisdale also needed moving west, and in the opposite direction there was a daily coke train to feed the blast furnaces at Grosmont. By 1898, however, with the Esk Valley blast furnaces by then shut down, a single 'Stockton Mineral' train was timetabled from Whitby in the morning, returning in the afternoon.

The arrival of the other two routes into Whitby obviously increased the number of trains serving the town. With the

Right: **Table 6.3** (Principle Stations only)

Notes:
L – Two additional return goods trains scheduled to Levisham (depart 08.50/11.00) and return (depart 09.50/12.00) to convey coke and limestone
Q – Runs as required

NORTH EASTERN RAILWAY - Weekdays August 1865

Down		Mail	Coke	Pass (Mail)	Fish Q	Coal	Goods	Min	Goods	Pass	Pass	Goods	Min	Goods	Exp Pass	Pass	Exp Pass	Pass
Malton	d	04.33	06.00	07.05	07.30	08.00	08.30		09.00		10.55			14.30	15.50	19.30		20.10
Scarborough	d									09.50							18.40	
Pickering	a		06.40	07.40	08.05	08.40	09.05		09.40		11.20	↱		15.10	16.13	19.52		20.35
	d		06.50	07.42	08.15	09.00	↳	09.05	10.00	10.30	11.22	12.00	13.30	16.20	16.15	19.53	19.20	20.37
Goathland Mill				08.18		10.00			11.10		11.58	13.20		17.30		20.26		20.52
Grosmont (L)	a		08.05	08.28		10.15		10.30	11/30		12.08	13.45	15.00	17.40	17.00	20.35		21.13
Whitby	a	05.35		08.50	10.15				12.15	11.20	12.30	14.30		18.20	17.25	20.51	20.10	21.45

Up		Pass	Goods	Exp	Pass	Coal Empties	Goods & Empties	Goods	Pass	Goods & Empties	Goods	Fish Q	Goods	Goods	Pass	Pass (Mail)	Goods
Whitby	d	05.20	06.30	08.00	08.25			10.00	13.00		15.00	15.15		16.00	16.45	18.05	18.10
Grosmont (L)	d	05.39	07.10		08.44	10.45	11.10	11.15	13.20	13.25	15.25		15.35	16.40		18.25	18.35
Goathland Mill		05.48	07.20		08.53	11.00		11.25	13.30	13.40	15.40		15.50	17.10		18.33	18.50
Pickering	a	06.20	08.20		09.28	11.50	12.10	12.30	14.08	14.30	16.30	16.50	16.50	18.10		19.08	19.50
	d	06.22		08.50	09.30	12.05		12.50	14.10	14.40	16.40	17.00	17.10	18.40	17.35	19.10	20.00
Scarborough	d			09.30											18.15		
Malton	a	06.50			10.00	12.40		13.35	14.40	15.30	17.10	17.35	17.45	19.20		19.40	20.35

Table 6.4 (Principle Stations only)

NORTH EASTERN RAILWAY - October 1898-April 1899														
Down		**Exp Pass (Mail)**	Thro' Goods Y	**Slow Pass**	Goods	**Slow Pass**	**Pass**	Cattle (Alt TuO)	Goods Q	**Pass**	**Pass**	Goods	**Exp Pass**	ECS (SO)
Malton	d	**05.11**	05.35	**07.19**	09.10	**10.00**	**10.45**	11.00		**14.20**	**16.43**	16.50	**19.30**	
Pickering	a	**05.28**		**07.41**		**10.21**	**11.07**	11.30		**14.41**	**17.03**		**19.52**	
	d	**05.31**	06.05	**07.42**	A		**11.08**		12.00	**14.43**	**17.04**	A	**19.53**	
Goathland	d	**B**	07.00	**08.15**	A		**11.41**		A	**15.14**	**17.36**		**20.26**	
Grosmont	d	**06.04**	07.15	**08.24**	12.05		**11.50**		13.40	**15.25**	**17.45**	A	**20.35**	21.25
Whitby	a	**06.20**	07.50	**08.43**	12.35		**12.09**		14.30	**15.44**	**18.04**	19.25	**20.51**	21.45
Up		Pilot Engine	Goods Q	**Exp Pass**	**Slow Pass**	**Pass**	Goods	Pass	Thro' Goods Y C	**Exp Pass**	**Slow**	Exp Fish	**Slow Pass (Mail)**	**Pass (SO)**
Whitby	d	06ll43	07.05	**07.30**	**08.25**	**09.23**	09.35		11.10	**12.18**	**15.05**	15.50	**18.10**	**21.00**
Grosmont	d	06ll57	A	**07.45**	**08.43**	**09.40**	A		A	**12.36**	**15.23**	A	**18.28**	**21.18**
Goathland	d		A	**07.55**	**08.53**	**09.50**	A		A	**12.47**	**15.34**	A	**18.39**	
Pickering	a		09.15	**08.24**	**09.23**	**10.19**	11.15			**13.18**	**16.04**	A	**19.09**	
	d			**08.26**	**09.24**	**10.21**	13.50	**10.45**	A	**13.19**	**16.05**		**19.10**	
Malton	a			**08.47**	**09.42**	**10.40**	14.20	**11.07**	13.25	**13.40**	**16.27**	17.20	**19.32**	

Additional summer services

Down	Pass W	Exp Pass Y	Pass	Exp Pass Z	Pass
York		**14.30**	***15.05***	**16.05**	***20.00***
Malton	**10.00**	**15.03**	**15.45**	**16.38**	**21.00**
Whitby	**11.25**	**16.18**	**1708**	**17.53**	**22.24**
Up	Exp Pass Y	Pass	Pass Z	Pass	Pass
Whitby	**10.40**	**11.25**	**12.18**	**13.50**	**19.10**
Malton	**11.50**	**12.42**	**13.38**	**15.00**	**20.25**
York	**12.23**		**14.12**	***16.10***	

Notes:

A – Stops as required

B – Stops to leave mailbags at Goathland and Sleights

C – Stops as required at Ruswarp and Sleights for perishable traffic to be transhipped for York, Levisham for livestock and perishable traffic for Malton and beyond

Q – Runs as required

W – 10.00 Malton-Pickering extended

Y – From/to York

Z – Winter equivalent runs between Malton and Whitby only

Above: **Marishes Road around 1900, with passengers having alighted from an up train formed of NER 45-foot bogie stock, a new innovation for the Malton to Whitby line at this time.** *NYMR Collection*

Above right: **An up goods north of High Mill, seen from Pickering Castle around 1900, with lime kilns and quarrying activity evidence. The locomotive appears to be a Fletcher Class 93 0-6-0.** *W. J. Potter, Whitby Museum*

route from Loftus opening first in 1883, Whitby gained a second station at West Cliff, but the trains from Saltburn still continued down the hill to terminate at Town station. The opening of the Scarborough line in 1885 allowed the possibility of through working between Saltburn and Scarborough via West Cliff, with a connecting shuttle service between West Cliff and Town. This would eventually expand to as many as 14 trains a day.

This was a time of expansion, both for the country and for railways. By the final year of the 19th century there were six trains each way between Malton and Whitby even in winter, plus a return working from Malton to Pickering. Good connections for York were provided at Malton, and the best journey time between York and Whitby was now 2 hours. In the summer two trains each way ran through between Whitby and York. It was now possible to reach the capital in 6 hours from Whitby, about the same time as it took to York when the railway first opened, and through coaches had been running between Whitby and London King's Cross for some years. The winter Sunday service was back to just the mail train each way, although additional trains ran in summer. Finally there was a 21.00 short working from Whitby to Grosmont after Saturday market.

Freight services, however, did not continue at the optimistic levels provided for immediately after the deviation route opened, particularly as the local iron-making declined. The 1898 Working Timetable shows an early morning through goods from York to Whitby and return, with a note indicating that the up train would stop at Levisham to attach livestock for Malton and beyond. From Whitby a morning goods ran through to Malton, with a lay-over of 2 hours 35 minutes at Pickering, returning in the late afternoon. Malton also had a goods to Whitby with the locomotive working back on the afternoon fish train. An 'as required' early-morning pick-up goods was timetabled from Whitby to Pickering, serving the branch stations. The Malton route was never an easy one to work, and Whitby shed provided a banking locomotive to assist trains up the 1 in 49 gradient from Grosmont to Goathland Summit. (Table 6.4 gives a summary of train times between Malton and Whitby in the 1898/9 NER Working Timetable – the principal stations only are shown.)

Above: **Just prior to the Grouping a McDonnell '59' class 0-6-0 climbs into Goathland with a lengthy goods train, banked in the rear.** *Nigel Trotter Collection*

The North Eastern in the 20th century

The growth in tourism in the Edwardian years saw 'auto-car' services begin from Whitby in 1905. At first these concentrated on the coastal beauty spots such as Robin Hood's Bay, but from 1 July 1908 services commenced on the Beck Hole branch. The summer of 1912 saw five return trains scheduled, with 'auto-cars' also augmenting service frequencies from Whitby to Goathland (12) and Glaisdale (11). A special handbill was issued to promote the service.

General excursion traffic was also growing fast, presenting some challenges for the limited track and siding capacity at Whitby. Stock from incoming specials often had to be stabled at

The small station at Beck Hole was built for summer tourist services in 1908. An NER 'auto-car' train waits at the platform with the Fletcher 'BTP' locomotive sandwiched between two push-pull coaches. *Ken Hoole Study Centre*

NORTH EASTERN RAILWAY – July 1922 SUMMER THROUGH SERVICES				
Down		Through Train	K	L
London King's Cross	d			13.55
Leeds	d	13.05	16.05	
Malton	a	14.28	17.31	18.48
	d	14.35	17.42	19.10
Whitby	a	15.55	18.59	20.20
Up		Through Train	K	L
Whitby	d	07.52	10.40	12.10
Malton	a	09.05	11.47	13.28
	d	09.10	12.02	13.57
Leeds	a	10.40		15.24
London King's Cross	d		17.00	

Table 6.5

Notes:

K – Detach/attach to Leeds-Scarborough train and vice versa at Malton

L – Detach/attach to King's Cross-Scarborough train and vice versa at Malton

outlying stations. The following working notice for the Whitsuntide Holiday in 1911 is a good example of the arrangements made:

'GENERAL ARRANGEMENTS AT WHITBY TOWN STATION, WHIT MONDAY & TUESDAY

Loco Foreman, Whitby, to arrange for engines to assist Excursions and Ordinary trains between Pickering and Grosmont morning and evening as required, and provide an engine to shunt at Whitby.

The Empty Excursion trains to stand at Whitby, Ruswarp, Sleights, Eskdale Mines, Grosmont, &c, and Station Masters concerned must see the trains are returned to Whitby in sufficient time to admit of the Return Excursion being started punctually.

Guards being sent to work Return Excursions to enquire at Grosmont whether their train is standing there.'

The route from Malton on that particular holiday saw four excursions on Whit Monday, and six on Whit Tuesday, the latter comprising trains from Leeds (two), Bradford (two), Colne and Sheffield.

Freight traffic could best be described as steady, but in June 1907 the District Superintendent reported the opening of a new siding at Eskdale ironstone mines at Grosmont. Traffic expectations were high, with 12 wagons a day already being forwarded to Middlesbrough blast furnaces. Unfortunately, just a year later the sidings were reported out of use due to a drop in demand.

The First World War produced some cutbacks, of which the most obvious was the immediate suspension of the summer 'auto-car' services, only ever aimed at the now vanishing tourist market. The war really marked the end of rail's golden age, at its zenith in the first decade of the 20th century. Nevertheless, the NER's last summer of 1922 saw a weekdays-only service of seven trains in each direction between Malton and Whitby, with through daily coaches or trains linking Whitby with Leeds and London King's Cross (see Table 6.5). There were now no Sunday trains, however, even in summer, and it would be another decade before these reappeared.

Grosmont had its own morning commuter train to Whitby (worked out from Whitby as empty stock), but there was also a summer-only 'auto-car' service between Whitby and Goathland (three trains) and Grosmont (one train). The Esk Valley summer service consisted of five trains in each direction (split between Stockton and Middlesbrough), plus a Whitby to Castleton and return short working.

The last NER Working Timetable in October 1922 saw a passenger service of five trains in each direction on the Malton line, plus the Grosmont morning commuter service. The 12.10 from Whitby, and the 15.42 from Malton, conveyed through Leeds coaches. There were now just two goods services in each direction. A morning 'Class D' pick-up from Malton served Pickering, Levisham, Goathland, Grosmont, and Sleights and Ruswarp as required, a pattern that would remain largely unaltered until closure. The train returned as a 'Class B' fast goods from Whitby, calling only at Grosmont and Pickering. An up 'Class D' pick-up left Whitby, also in the morning, taking most of the day to shunt intermediate stations south of Grosmont, working back from Malton with traffic calls only at Pickering and Grosmont. On Mondays this train stopped at the remote railway cottages to enable platelayers' wives living between Newton Dale and Farworth to do their shopping in Pickering. A similar facility

At Whitby around 1900 a Class A 2-4-2T is in Platform 3 on a train of what appear to be six-wheel coaches, possibly forming a Stockton service. *Ken Hoole Study Centre*

NORTH EASTERN RAILWAY - 02 October 1922										
Down		**Pass (Mail)**	**Pass**	**Slow**	Goods (E)	**Pass**	Light	**Pass (L)**	Goods (G)	**Pass**
Malton	d	**05.38**		**07.44**	08.15	**10.42**		**15.25**	16.30	**17.55**
Pickering	a	**05.54**		**08.07**	08.42	**10.56**		**15.46**	16.57	**18.16**
	d	**05.58**		**08.08**	09.24	**11.03**		**15.48**	17.20	**18.18**
Goathland	a	**B**		**08.36**	10.22	**11.31**		**16.16**	G	**18.46**
Grosmont	a	**06.34**	**08.10**	**08.43**	10.51	**11.38**	15ll 00	**16.23**	18.40	**18.53**
Whitby	a	**06.50**	**08.30**	**09.03**	12.10	**11.57**	15ll 20	**16.42**	18.58	**19.12**
Up		**Pass**	ECS	**Pass**	Goods (H)	Light Engine	**Pass (L)**	Goods (J)	**Pass (Mail)**	**Pass**
Whitby	d	**07.10**	07.25	**08.00**	10.00	11ll 55	**12.10**	13.30	**16.10**	**19.00**
Grosmont	d	**07.25**	07.40	**08.18**	12.40	12ll 10	**12.28**	14.00	**16.29**	**19.18**
Goathland	d	**07.35**		**08.28**	14.05		**12.38**		**16.39**	**19.28**
Pickering	a	**08.04**		**08.57**	14.20		**13.06**	14.50	**17.07**	**19.56**
	d	**08.08**		**08.57**	14.40		**13.08**	15.18	**17.10**	**19.58**
Malton	a	**08.27**		**09.13**	15.22		**13.28**	15.45	**17.29**	**20.18**

Table 6.6 (Principal Stations only)

Notes:

B – Stops at Goathland to leave mailbags

E – Class B (Class D Pickering to Whitby), SO 5 minutes extra allowed at Levisham to Goathland to take up platelayers' wives

G – Class B (Class C Pickering to Grosmont), stops at Goathland to pin down brakes

L – Through coaches to/from Leeds

H – Class D, calls at Black Bull as required

J – Class B, SO stops between Goathland and Levisham to set down platelayers' wives.

was provided by the morning trip from Malton and the afternoon goods from Whitby for the Saturday market in Whitby. The ladies had to be fast shoppers, however, since only 1 hour 20 minutes was available before the train back, later reduced by the LNER to 35 minutes. (See Table 6.6)

Frequency on the Esk Valley was four trains a day in the winter timetable. The first morning train from Whitby ran to Middlesbrough with the remaining three still routed to Stockton. In the return direction, however, Stockton and Middlesbrough had two trains apiece to Whitby. Timings were arranged to ensure good connections for either Stockton or Middlesbrough at Battersby. The Working Timetable shows the single Esk Valley goods from Whitby now running to Battersby at 07.35 (apart from alternate Mondays, when it left at 05.55 to serve Stokesley).

Pickering's train service was augmented by the Gilling and Forge Valley services. For much of its life the Gilling line had four trains a day, but this was cut back to three by the LNER with a Saturday extra. Most trains ran through between Pickering and York, although a journey time of 1 hour 40 minutes was hardly competitive with the route via Malton. Before and after the First World War one train from Pickering ran via the north curve at Sunbeck Junction to terminate at either Pilmoor or Thirsk on the East Coast Main Line (ECML). A Thursday market-day service also ran between Pickering and Helmsley for a time. Goods services were a single daily pick-up in each direction. The service to Scarborough along the Forge Valley line varied between three and four trains a day, with a Thursday extra, presumably to serve Pickering market.

'Whitby Willie' Class W 4-6-2T No 695, rebuilt from a 4-6-0T, heads a well-loaded freight east through Sleights shortly after the First World War. *Pendragon Collection*

LNER developments

The pattern of operations remained much the same during early LNER years. Whilst the winter passenger service between Malton and Whitby was still a basic pattern of five trains each way, a much expanded service operated in the summer. Despite the country's economic problems, the LNER was keen to promote the tourism potential of the area. The daily service increased by two trains each way, with up to a further four on Saturdays; usually two of these ran through between Whitby and either York or Leeds. Saturdays in the height of summer saw through coaches from and to London King's Cross, attached to the summer 'Scarborough Flyer' south of Malton or York.

The summer 'auto-car' trains from Whitby re-started after the First World War apart from those to Beck Hole, however, the withdrawal of the life-expired push-pull-fitted 'BTP' locomotives in the mid 1920s meant reversion to conventional loco-hauled operation. In 1932, Sentinel steam railcars were introduced to the service with up to six round trips a day between Whitby and Goathland. The railcars were also ideal for the Town to West Cliff shuttle, with the LNER Sectional Appendix giving special

Right: In LNER days, around 1935, 'G5' No 381 coasts downhill past Water Ark with a Malton to Whitby train. *C. M. Doncaster, Whitby Museum*

Below: Although passenger trains to Beck Hole finished for good with the outbreak of the First World War, the 'BTP'-worked 'auto-car' trains resumed operations on other routes around Whitby, continuing into early LNER days. Such a combination is seen at Goathland on 3 August 1925. *K. L. Taylor, North Eastern Railway Association*

Bottom: The first Sentinel steam railcars introduced into the area by the LNER for revenue-earning service were the two-cylinder cars used on the Pickering to Scarborough Forge Valley line. Car No 2236 ***British Queen*** departs from Scarborough in the mid-1930s with a Pickering train strengthened with a four-wheel trailer car. *Lens of Sutton, Martin Bairstow Collection*

authority for two railcars to work together provided both were fully manned and facing the same way. Multiple unit operation was definitely not possible. Railcars also worked the coastal route on Middlesbrough to Scarborough services, and a number of local summer excursions, including a Scarborough-Pickering-Whitby-Scarborough circular tour, were actually intended for diesel railcar operation. The Forge Valley had already become a candidate for Sentinel steam railcar operation. In 1928 a railcar was based at Pickering, but from November 1931 the working transferred to Malton, leading to a balancing 06.40 service between Malton and Pickering (and 22.00 return empty railcar).

In the early years there had been restrictions on both locomotive types and coaches allowed over the routes to Whitby (more details are given in Chapter 7). Gradually these had been relaxed and by 1924 all normal rolling stock could be worked. One unusual restriction that appears to have been introduced rather later, possibly during the Second World War, allowed the placement of coaching stock in only one of Whitby Town's Platforms 3 or 4 at the same time. The range of motive power that could operate over the routes had also expanded, with restrictions on six-coupled locomotives removed early in the LNER period. This opened the way for much greater operating flexibility.

Summer excursion traffic had been developing strongly before the First World War, and the inter-war period saw this expand significantly. A pattern of scenic excursions was established based on a circular route. Trains started from various stations, usually in the West Riding, travelling out via York and Malton to Whitby. The return was via the coastal route to Scarborough and the main line back to York. The most exotic excursion was the 'Northern Belle', a lavish sleeping-car-based operation that covered the more scenic parts of the LNER network in England and Scotland over the course of a week. Starting at London King's Cross, both day and night portions were included in the train formation, often split to meet the needs of the tour programme. The train first ran in June 1933, and included Malton to Whitby in its itinerary, reached from the ECML via Pilmoor and Gilling. At Town station the train reversed up the hill to West Cliff for another reversal prior to heading south to Scarborough and thence to York. The schedule omitted the Yorkshire coast in subsequent years, but a similar, less prestigious operation was later provided for the Boy Scout movement. As an example, such a 'Scout Cruise' train, with separate day and night portions, visited Whitby on 14 and 15 April 1939. Arrival was from Middlesbrough via Battersby, with the day portion recorded as departing south via Pickering and Malton behind 'D49' class locomotive No 273 *The Holderness.*

Sunday services did not reappear after the First World War until 1933, when a summer service of five return trains was introduced between Whitby and Goathland/Grosmont, worked by a Sentinel railcar. The following year a 10.00 Leeds to Whitby Sunday service was provided, returning at 19.50 from Whitby. There was a gradual expansion of summer Sunday services up to 1939, by which time a second Leeds train was running, and there were also three return summer Sunday services on the Esk Valley line. A Sunday winter service was still not provided on any of the lines to Whitby.

A new bay platform was built at Whitby West Cliff in 1934 to accommodate the Town to West Cliff shuttle service. This followed an increase in traffic on the coastal route after the northern terminus was changed from Saltburn to Middlesbrough. The number of passenger trains on the single-line coastal route expanded hugely, and as a consequence the two local pick-up goods could only run at night: from Whitby to Carlin How near

Skinningrove, and from Gallows Close, Scarborough, to Whitby. Late-night services, often worked by steam railcar, were a regular feature in the summer, providing a night out for revellers and theatre-goers in Scarborough. At weekends the last passenger train did not arrive back at Whitby until 00.50 Sunday morning.

The late 1930s became the busiest period for rail traffic at Whitby, with around 50 departures from Town station on summer Saturdays, and a similar number from West Cliff. As many as 12 trains a day were scheduled on the Malton route on peak summer Saturdays, in addition to six Whitby-Goathland return shuttles. These included two services from London, one of which was a full restaurant car train at 11.25 from King's Cross, reaching Whitby at 16.39. The return left Whitby at 09.40, suggesting some rather poor stock utilisation during the intervening week, although through coaches to and from King's Cross, rather than a complete train, ran on other weekdays. Sunday afternoon saw through coaches returning to King's Cross at 13.55, balancing the second of the Saturday northbound workings.

Draconian service reductions introduced across Britain upon the outbreak of the Second World War saw all this come to a sudden end. After a national outcry at the savage cuts, a more considered 'Emergency Timetable' was issued on 2 October 1939. Nevertheless, between Malton and Whitby services were cut back to four a day, with similar reductions on the Esk Valley. The coastal route was down to only three services in each direction, one of which, from both Middlesbrough and Scarborough respectively, started and terminated at Whitby Town, leaving just two through trains. This reduced the need for the shuttle between Town and West Cliff to just one round trip. Like most of Britain's railways, demand on the routes around Whitby increased during the war, although perhaps not quite as much as some other parts of the country. The lines were not trunk routes and local geography meant that there were less military installations than in some other parts of Eastern England.

After the war it took some years for the timetable to regain pre-war levels. In 1947, the LNER's last summer, there were still

Top: **One of the six-cylinder Sentinel cars, No 2219 *Telegraph*, is seen out of use, and possibly stored, at Whitby in 1942. These cars, more powerful than their two-cylinder counterparts, were felt necessary for the hilly routes out of Whitby.** *R. C. Riley, The Transport Treasury*

Above left: **Class D49 4-4-0 No 235 *The Bedale* enters the single-line section to New Bridge at Levisham in the summer of 1935 with a Whitby to York train, passing an ex-Hull & Barnsley Railway 'J23' 0-6-0, possibly on an engineers' train.** *National Railway Museum*

Above: **A 1930s goods train behind Class J24 0-6-0 No 1892 heads for Whitby past the out-of-use Eskdale Mines signal box, north of Grosmont.** *E. R. Wethersett, Ian Allan Library*

Left: **A down train in the 1930s sees one of the last 'J23' 0-6-0s, No 2460 of Malton shed, pressed into passenger service near Raindale siding, north of Levisham.** *C. M. Doncaster, David Joy Collection*

Right: **'D49' No 231 *The Badsworth* shunts a train of Gresley's 1930s green and white excursion stock into the sidings at Bog Hall, Whitby, in the years before the Second World War. In all probability this was during the Whitby call of one of the popular circular scenic excursions.**
T. G. Hepburn, Rail Archive Stephenson

only four trains each way between Malton and Whitby, with a Saturday-only extra. Apart from two trains through from York on Mondays and Saturdays, all trains started and terminated at Malton. On the Esk Valley there were just three Monday to Friday trains, with two Saturday extras. Middlesbrough was the destination for two trains, leaving a mere one via Picton to Stockton. Eastbound, one train started at Middlesbrough with the other two running from Stockton and West Hartlepool. On the coastal route Whitby saw four trains in each direction on Mondays to Fridays, of which two from both the Middlesbrough and Scarborough ends started and terminated at Whitby Town. The Town to West Cliff shuttle was three in each direction.

Nationalisation

Initially matters began to look up under BR, particularly during the early/mid-1950s. Service levels on the lines remaining open crept back towards those of the 1930s. A service frequency of five trains was established between Malton and Whitby, with morning and lunchtime return workings between Whitby and Goathland. Summer Saturdays saw additional services timetabled on all the routes into Whitby. On the Malton line, frequency only went up by one, but most trains started or terminated at York or Leeds, and the through coaches between London King's Cross and Whitby were re-introduced. Summer excursions to Whitby also returned, with trains originating not just from the industrial centres of Yorkshire and

Above centre: **A classic 1950s scene as 'G5' No 67335 departs from Levisham with a Malton to Whitby train made up of a parcels van and three former NER coaches. Four vehicles was the limit for a 'G5' over the steeply graded route between Pickering and Grosmont.**
Cecil Ord, Neville Stead Collection

Above: **'G5' No 67273 takes water at Pickering on 1 May 1949 after arrival with the 14.50 push-pull train from Scarborough.** *John Edgington*

Left: **On 19 September 1950 'A8' No 69861 (of course!) enters Pickering with the 15.20 Whitby to Malton service.**
Peter Ward

Lancashire, but also from the Midlands. The circular scenic excursion tours pioneered by the LNER were also re-introduced, running as before out via Malton to Whitby, returning down the coast through Scarborough.

Esk Valley line frequency was five trains a day, with Middlesbrough now very much the predominant destination, even before the route between Battersby and Picton closed in 1954. The most frequent service was provided on the coastal route, with up to 12 trains running both north and south of Whitby. As many as 13 trains a day used the chord line between Whitby Town and West Cliff, and authorisation was given in 1955 for trains of no more than two coaches to be propelled over the line in the uphill direction only. In effect this could apply to all trains in the quieter winter months, but only to the shuttle service in summer. Any through train serving Whitby Town either had to run-round at

Top: **Proving that more than one 'A8' operated on the Malton line, No 69886 approaches Bog Hall Junction with the 08.15 Goathland to Whitby commuter service on 24 July 1958.** *Michael Mensing*

Above left: **On 22 August 1958 'A8' No 69861 enters Whitby Town with the early-evening train from Malton. The first two coaches are through from London King's Cross, having travelled north on the 'Scarborough Flyer'.** *Peter Cookson*

Above: **The evening train from Whitby was extended to York in high summer, and is seen here departing past Bog Hall signal box on 22 July 1958 behind 'B1' 4-6-0 No 61071. Note the second and third vehicles, former LNER streamline-era articulated coaches.** *Michael Mensing*

Centre left: **A high day for 'G5' No 67342 piloting a 'B1' 4-6-0 on a southbound express at Ellerbeck in 1953.** *Cecil Ord, NYMR Collection*

Left: **In August 1953, the year before withdrawal of these services, 'G5' No 67262 calls at Glaisdale with a Whitby Town to Stockton train. Note the signal box.** *J. W. Armstrong Trust*

Left: Rush hour at Battersby: Class V3 2-6-2T No 67646 runs round the 12.45 Middlesbrough to Whitby service, while in the distance 'L1' No 67754, having just run round, prepares to draw forward onto the 12.05 Whitby to Middlesbrough train on 1 July 1957. This was the last year before DMUs were introduced on most Esk Valley line services. *Michael Mensing*

Below left: Although there were fewer of them than on the other lines, the Esk Valley line saw some summer excursions. In 1955 'L1' No 67754 heads such a train from Darlington to Whitby near Egton. *Cecil Ord, NYMR Collection*

Below: At Whitby West Cliff on 25 June 1951 'A8' No 69880 prepares to leave for Scarborough, having reversed with the 11.15 train from Whitby Town. Fellow class member No 69858 prepares to depart down the hill to Town station with the 09.23 service from Middlesbrough via Loftus. *John Edgington*

Bottom: On 19 July 1957 a Standard Class 4 2-6-4T propels a Whitby Town to West Cliff train up the bank from Bog Hall Junction round Airy Hill and under Larpool Viaduct towards Prospect Hill Junction. *Michael Mensing*

Above: **Super power' for a Sheffield to Whitby excursion: a combination of two 'B1' 4-6-0s, headed by No 61053, negotiates the 1 in 60 climb past Yorfalls in Newton Dale.** *Cecil Ord, NYMR Collection*

Top: **Reversal at Whitby 1: having reversed at Town station on 15 June 1958, Fairburn Class 4 2-6-4T No 42083 ascends from Bog Hall Junction approaching Prospect Hill Junction with a Scarborough-bound scenic excursion. 'B1' No 61084 is at the rear of the train ready to head forward towards Scarborough following the second reversal at West Cliff.** *Ken Hoole, NYMR Collection*

Above: **Reversal at Whitby 2: on this occasion in 1955 no fewer than three engines are involved in the reversal at West Cliff. 'A8' No 69860 heads a 'B1' about to depart for Scarborough, while exhaust from the third engine that has headed the train up from Town station can be seen in the distance.** *J. W. Armstrong Trust*

Below: **Reversal at Whitby 3: the West Cliff reversal behind it, a scenic excursion from Wakefield heads for Scarborough past Prospect Hill Junction, double-headed by 'A8' No 69882 and 'B1' No 61085. The train will have arrived at Whitby Town via the Malton line, reaching West Cliff via the line in the foreground from Bog Hall and Town station.** *J. W. Armstrong Trust*

both West Cliff and Town stations, or have another engine attached on the north end of the train to avoid propelling. For the frequently double-headed heavy scenic excursions this could mean the use of three locomotives.

Rationalisation

Closure of the Loftus route on 5 May 1958 led to a complete re-cast of the timetable between Whitby and Scarborough. From the date of closure, these were converted to DMU operation and re-routed via the Esk Valley to Middlesbrough, in the process giving this line a dramatically increased service level of up to 11 trains a day. Train reversal was clearly easier with DMUs, and the Scarborough to Middlesbrough service did so four times: at Scarborough, to access the Whitby line at Falsgrave; Whitby West Cliff (or Prospect Hill Junction after West Cliff station closed in 1961), for the run down to Town station); Whitby Town; and Battersby.

The short workings between Whitby and Goathland also saw some DMU operation in 1958, with a more widespread takeover by DMUs on the Malton to Whitby line in April 1959. Thereafter only the morning and evening trains conveying mail and parcels, together with their balancing workings, remained loco-hauled. The overall service frequency on the route was still five trains in each direction, with an additional train in the summer, a pattern that would remain little changed until closure. The two Whitby to Goathland shuttles were also still a standard feature, and in most timetables at least two services were extended from and to York. Summer Saturdays saw the majority of trains start back at York or beyond. The 1963 summer Saturday service of six trains included four starting and terminating at York, and a through Leeds service. Through coaches from London King's Cross were detached from the 'Scarborough Flyer' at York, going forward to Whitby at 15.35, more than 40 minutes after the main train had left for Scarborough. The return King's Cross coaches departed from Whitby at 09.30, with arrival in London at 15.25, again attached to the 'Scarborough Flyer' at York. A through train from Leeds arrived at 12.11, returning at 14.12. Echoing the LNER of the late 1930s there were two through Sunday services to Whitby, one from Leeds and the other from Selby.

Following the Malton and Scarborough line closures, Whitby's remaining DMU-worked Esk Valley service initially had a frequency of seven trains a day, working out and back from Middlesbrough. In 1990 the frequency was reduced to four trains a day, based on the service that could be operated by just one unit and two sets of train crew. This remains the basic service level commitment laid down by the Department for Transport, to be provided by the franchise-holding TOC, currently Northern

Rail. However, a summer Sunday service of five trains operates between May and September, with two of these running through from Newcastle and Bishop Auckland.

Freight operations in the post-war period played a gradually diminishing role. With many of the traditional extractive industries in decline, the service reduced to little more than one pick-up goods on each line by 1965. Although forwarding of stone from Thornton Dale Quarry had finished in 1963, quarrying activity was still producing some stone traffic from New Bridge. A Malton-based 'trip' engine serviced this traffic, and Pickering coal yard, until this too came to an end on 1 July 1966. But goods services along the Esk Valley were to linger on until April 1983 when the freight facility at Whitby was closed. The potash development at Hawsker, anticipated in 1965, never did materialise.

Top: In 1958 Whitby Abbey looks down on the ubiquitous No 69861 piloting a 'B1' 4-6-0 as they draw the stock of a returning summer express out of Bog Hall sidings, prior to reversing into Whitby Town station. *Colour-Rail*

Above: On 1 August 1958 Class L1 2-6-4T No 67766 heads the 11.47 Middlesbrough to Whitby Town train away from Grosmont, a rare steam turn on the Esk Valley following the May 1958 dieselisation. *Michael Mensing*

Left: A busy scene at Whitby Town on 23 July 1958, during the transition period from steam to diesel. 'L1' No 67754 heads one of the few remaining Esk Valley steam turns, the 18.00 to Middlesbrough, while 'B1' No 61071 has charge of the 18.10 to York. The DMU, on a Scarborough service, is arriving from Middlesbrough. *Michael Mensing*

Left: In 1958 DMUs had yet to make major inroads on the Malton route from Whitby, but on 1 August two three-car Metro-Cammell sets were deployed on the lunchtime Whitby to Goathland shuttle service. It can be assumed that there was no shortage of space on this six-vehicle formation seen here arriving at Grosmont with the returning 13.20 from Goathland. *Michael Mensing*

Top: In the summer of 1964 'B1' No 61319 traverses Northdale with the 16.08 Malton to Whitby train. The through coaches from King's Cross, by now BR Standard Mark 1s, are the first two vehicles. *David Sutcliffe*

Above Left: By 1961 steam was beginning to give way to diesels on some of the remaining longer locomotive-hauled workings. On 10 September two Brush Type 2s (later designated Class 31), Nos D5809 and D5693, pass through Pickering with an excursion from Heeley (Sheffield) to Whitby. *D. P. Leckonby*

Above: Withdrawal of the Malton to Whitby service is only a couple of weeks away as a Metro-Cammell two-car DMU calls at Grosmont with a Whitby-bound train in February 1965. *NYMR Collection*

Left: Modern-day Esk Valley line services are generally handled by two-car Class 156 'Sprinter' units. No 156471 calls at Sleights with the 10.30 Middlesbrough to Whitby service on 8 January 2001. *John Hunt*

Left: **Class J24 0-6-0 No 65656 passes Pickering engine shed with the up Whitby to Malton pick-up goods in June 1951.** *Alec Ford*

Below left: **By 1958 motive power on the pick-up goods had been upgraded to the later NER Class J27. On 16 April Malton shed's No 65848 makes a strong showing away from Grosmont with the up train.** *Mike Feather*

The preservation era

Following re-opening, a standard pattern developed relatively quickly for NYMR services, once trains were able to run over the full length of the preserved line from Grosmont through to Pickering station. At peak periods an hourly service of up to nine trains a day is operated over the 17¾ mile route, with journey times of 1 hour 5 minutes (down) and 1 hour 10 minutes (up), together with an evening dining train several times each week. Under the terms of the LRO, the line speed on the NYMR line is limited to 25mph. The number of trains run to Whitby is governed by available 'train paths' beyond Grosmont, where the track is also used by the Northern Rail service. On the majority of operating days in 2008 three NYMR trains ran through between Pickering and Whitby, completing the journey in 1 hour 35 minutes.

Staffing the railway

Finally in this chapter some reference is appropriate to the people who operated the railway. Long service has always been a trait of railway employees, or 'servants' as they were known until quite recently. Nevertheless, it seems remarkable to find that men employed when the W&PR opened were either still working, or only recently retired, when the NER was gathering information about the railway's origins some sixty years later. Despite the 19th-century industrial activity of the Esk Valley, this part of North Yorkshire was and has increasingly become a largely rural area. The railway offered secure and comparatively well-paid employment, becoming a major employer in the local community. As early as 1849 the Y&NM had 49 staff on its payroll between Rillington and Whitby, at an annual cost of £2,061.

The range of jobs was considerable. Engine sheds at Malton, Pickering and Whitby provided employment for drivers, firemen, cleaners, fitters and shed labourers. Every station had a station master, with a number of porters, signalmen, crossing-keepers, and one or more clerks (at all but the smallest). Malton, Pickering and Whitby had train guards, and separate goods departments requiring shunters, rulleymen (in charge of delivery horses), more porters and clerks. Track maintenance required large numbers of lengthmen, gangers and labourers, often living in remote cottages by the lineside. By the time the NER was established and all the lines built, the total number of staff working for the company between Malton and Whitby would have been several hundred.

Above: **With the closure of Malton shed in 1963, responsibility for working the Whitby freight passed to York, with the service working out of York Dringhouses Yard via Malton. 'B1' No 4-6-0 No 61319 approaches Sleights with the Whitby-bound train on 25 May 1964.** *John Boyes*

Right: **An Esk Valley line 'trip' goods also served Whitby, becoming the only freight link in March 1965. Operating latterly out of the 1950s-built Tees Yard, the service continued until 1984. Traffic was not exactly heavy on 14 May 1964 as Thornaby-based English Electric Type 3 (later Class 37) No D6766 heads away from Whitby near Bog Hall.** *John Boyes, J. W. Armstrong Trust*

The Depression, the General Strike and the LNER's efforts to cut costs generally led to some staff economies between the two wars. For example, in this period the following station masters' posts were amalgamated:

- Rillington and Marishes Road
- Levisham and Goathland
- Sleights and Ruswarp
- Whitby Town and Whitby West Cliff

As already mentioned, several signal boxes were either downgraded to ground frames or permanently switched out of use, but these were mostly already regularly unstaffed. In the main, however, numbers would not reduce significantly until the closures of the 1950s and 1960s. The most dramatic impact came with the two line closures of March 1965. At Whitby alone a staff of 43 dropped overnight to 18. Eleven drivers' jobs disappeared, as did three out of four guards, and both carriage-cleaners. Four out of five porters left the railway, as did two out of six signalmen. The other stations faired even worse, with several station masters, for example, either retiring or taking jobs as booking clerks. This was the human side of railway closure. Some local railwaymen, such as signalling inspector Charlie Hart, permanent way inspector Joe Brown, and Tom Robertson, Whitby's last station master, became active in the nascent NYMR, while Ron Cana, the station master responsible for Grosmont and Goathland, was destined to do the same job again in preservation – as a volunteer. But all this was still some years off.

The gradual run-down in staff continued on the surviving Esk Valley line. Stations were de-manned completely, and signal boxes closed. Today the only railway staff at Whitby are employed by the NYMR running the rail travel office. The NYMR, incidentally, is also now a major employer in the area. The first paid employee was engaged in 1972, and in 2007 there were around 85 permanent and 50 seasonal staff, together with several hundred active volunteers. How can so many people be required? To quote the NYMR's archivist, Graham Reussner, the company had to 'establish its own maintenance and administrative infrastructure; it could no longer rely on a head office at York and heavy engineering works at York, Darlington, Doncaster and elsewhere.'

Above: **The all-male staff of Whitby Goods Office pose for the camera in 1888.** *Ken Hoole Study Centre*

Left: **The station master stands proudly on the platform of Levisham station around 1900. Levisham lost its station master in the economies of the 1930s when responsibility was transferred to Goathland.** *John Addyman Collection*

Below left: **Staff and, most probably, family members pose at Beck Hole station between 1908 and 1914, against the backdrop of a 'BTP'-worked 'auto-car' service to Whitby. The neighbouring hamlet of Esk Valley had railwaymen among its residents, as it does NYMR staff and volunteers today.** *Tammy Naylor Collection*

Below: **Snow is being cleared from the Esk Valley platform by the station porter at Grosmont in 1931; he is no doubt welcoming the break for the photograph.**
Ken Hoole Collection, Chris Cubitt Collection

7

Locomotives and Rolling Stock

Whitby & Pickering days

The first horse-drawn passenger coaches were effectively stage-coaches on rails following the fashion of the time for such vehicles. The first coach was ordered in September 1834 from Beeston & Melling, a coach-building firm in Manchester, at a tendered price of £170, although the final bill was £190. The 3-foot-diameter wheel-sets were ordered separately from Messrs Tayleur & Co of Newton. Designed to be drawn by a single horse, the coach was four-wheeled and, in true stagecoach style, the driver sat up front on a 'dickey seat' with a footboard and hand-brake lever. The coach was for First Class travellers and weighed 2 ¾ tons; it carried six inside passengers, four in front outside and four behind outside, with more able to ride on top. On 24 January 1835 the directors decided to name this initial coach *Premier*, and also ordered a second coach. Described at the time as a 'market coach', this and subsequent similar vehicles appear to have been very much cheaper, and were probably uncovered. Having seen the plan, the directors left it to the Engineer, Mr Swanwick, to order the coach 'as he may consider best and cheapest'. At least some of these market coaches were built by a different contractor, George Vassey, for a price of £42. In readiness for the full opening of the railway, a further First Class coach was also ordered later in 1835, probably *Lady Hilda*. A third and final First Class coach was named *Transit*. *Premier* and *Lady Hilda* appear to have been painted yellow (an early painting supports this), with *Transit* painted green.

The first goods wagons were ordered from yet another company, Messrs Hawkes & Co of Newcastle. Each had a floor of sheet iron and sides of 1⅛ inch wood, fitted with removable ends for loading/unloading. The body was 8ft 5in long, tapering to 7ft 9in at the bottom, and 6ft 2in wide with a height above sole-bar of 2ft 6in. The sole-bar had a depth of 10 inches, projecting 13 inches at each end to form buffers. The vehicle was sprung, with 3-foot-diameter wheel-sets, and a net weight of 34¼cwt. Reference is also made to a smaller design of 'truck' at 2 ¾ cwt. As was common practice, the ironwork was painted in black and the wooden bodies with lead paint.

A sketch of a W&PR horse train at Whitby, drawn by George Weatherill, who became Whitby station booking clerk. *Whitby Museum, courtesy of Tammy Naylor*

Locomotives

The Y&NM built an engine shed at Whitby in 1847 for the start of steam operations, with a shed at Malton following in 1853. Together with the small sub-shed at Pickering, these housed the area's motive power until the advent of diesel traction. Turntables were provided at Malton, Whitby and Pickering, and until 1948 also at Deviation Junction, Grosmont. The Y&NM used a number of 2-2-0 locomotives, described as having solid driving wheels, for the first steam trains, and it was one of these that worked the first train into Whitby in 1847, although its exact identity appears to have gone unrecorded. Other locomotives of similar design known to have worked at Whitby around this time include *Firefly* and *Greyhound*. The origin of these locomotives is uncertain, since the Y&NM does not appear to have had any of its own 2-2-0s. In 1840, however, it had acquired the locomotive stock of the Leeds & Selby Railway (later taking over this company), including 11 2-2-0s supplied between 1834 and 1839. The latest five were supplied by Kirtley & Co in 1839, and it may be that the Whitby locos came from this batch. Reference can also be found to an 0-6-0 goods engine called *Achilles*, this too having solid driving wheels.

The sharp curvature of the route, and restrictions arising from the Goathland incline limited the line initially to four-coupled or short-wheelbase six-coupled locomotives. Between 1854 and 1861 a small number of 0-4-0 tender locomotives, with 5-foot-diameter wheels and 15in x 20in cylinders, emerged from the NER's York Works, designed by the first NER Locomotive Superintendent, Edward Fletcher, specifically for the Whitby line. Although virtually new engines, they were all rebuilds of locomotives built in the 1840s. In his book, Potter quotes no less a source than the NER's then Locomotive Superintendent, Wilson Worsdell, in giving the following details of these engines:

Loco No.	Original builder	Date	Original Wheel Arrangement	Date Rebuilt	Scrapped
263	R Stephenson	1841	2-2-2T	1859	1889
264	R Stephenson	1841	0-4-0	1854	1878
272	Kitson	1845	2-2-2T	1861	1888
278	Murray & Jackson	1846	0-4-0	1854	1887

Initially the rebuilt locomotives had a curious arrangement of 'raised springs', possibly out of concern for the sharp changes of gradient when being manoeuvred on and off the 1 in 15 Goathland incline (something that only happened when they needed a visit to York Works), but the arrangement was not perpetuated.

Another new design of locomotive was introduced in 1864 specifically for passenger working on the Whitby branch. Designed by Edward Fletcher, and built by Robert Stephenson & Co, the ten '492' class 4-4-0 locomotives had 5-foot driving

Right: One of Edward Fletcher's NER rebuilds to produce a 0-4-0 specifically to cater for the sharp curvature of the Malton to Whitby line, No 272 emerged from York Works in 1860, having started life from Kitson & Co in 1845. It is seen at High Mill, Pickering, around 1870. *Beck Isle Museum*

Right: Another Fletcher design for the Whitby road was the Class 492, built specifically with through train working in mind when the Goathland deviation route opened in 1865. No 500 is seen at Malton in near original condition apart from the single equalising spring replacing the separate springs on the front bogie. This engine was replaced by a new No 500 and scrapped in February 1885.
Ken Hoole Study Centre

Left: A later view of a Class 492 at Whitby in 1893: the former No 496 has acquired a still rather rudimentary cab during rebuilding, and the new number 1809. Driver O. Hart is wearing the bowler, with foreman G. R. Laws on the ground.
B. Mashiter, Pendragon Collection

Below: Fletcher Class 93 0-6-0 No 512 is seen at Malton on 2 May 1908. Malton was the class's last outpost with the last survivor, being withdrawn from there in 1909.
Ken Hoole Study Centre

wheels, 16in x 22in cylinders, and were unusual at the time in having a four-wheel bogie. Referred to as 'Whitby bogies', various improvements were made over the years, including replacement of the basic weatherboard with a marginally more protective cab. They operated over both the Malton and Stockton routes to Whitby. Originally numbered 492-501, some were renumbered between 1887 and 1889, although withdrawals had already started in 1883. The last of the class was withdrawn in 1893.

Freight traffic in the later half of the 19th century was handled by a variety of 0-6-0s of both NER and Stockton & Darlington Railway (S&D) origin, after the latter amalgamated with the NER in 1863. These included the '93' class of outside-framed 0-6-0s introduced by Fletcher in 1866, the last of which (No 1766) was taken out of service from Malton shed in 1909. Four of these locos were rebuilt in 1871 as 0-6-0 saddle tanks for banking work, including between Grosmont and Goathland. Fletcher's Class 398 0-6-0s of 1875 also worked in the area. The S&D influence came from the '1001' class of 0-6-0, also seeing long service in the area. The design, by William Bouch, went back to the 1850s, its key features being inside frames, a short wheelbase but a long boiler. After the two railways amalgamated, Bouch worked in parallel with Fletcher for some years, and his '1001' class continued to be built until 1875. The short wheelbase was ideal on the Malton to Whitby road and the last

Right: **Class 577 No 2262 stands at Whitby around the turn of the 20th century. The locomotive was rebuilt from a Class 93, and was used for banking up to Goathland. Note the bank coupling release cord looped from the cab roof, re-appearing at the front of the engine.** *Whitby Museum*

Right: **A slightly later design, the Fletcher Class 398s first emerged in 1873. This is No 1333 shunting at Bog Hall around 1900. Note the ancient short-wheelbase stock.** *Ken Hoole Study Centre*

Below: **A view of Whitby shed, thought to have been taken around 1890, with 'BTP' 0-4-4T No 958 and Bouch Class 1001 0-6-0 No 1667 on shed. Behind them can be seen a McDonnell Class 38. Even goods engines were kept clean.** *Pendragon Collection*

Left: **The Class 1001 0-6-0s were designed by William Bouch for the Stockton & Darlington Railway, but also worked well on the Whitby line. No 1275 was the last in service when withdrawn from Malton in 1923; it is seen here at Darlington in sparkling condition, probably ready for its part in the 1925 S&D Centenary celebrations. The engine survives in the care of the National Railway Museum.** *Ken Hoole Study Centre*

Right: **In LNER days, on 29 July 1925, one of the surviving Edward Fletcher 'BTP' 0-4-4Ts, No 63 (by then LNER Class G6), stands on Whitby shed alongside a McDonnell Class 59 0-6-0 (LNER Class J22), No 1485. Class A (LNER 'F8') No 1583 stands in the background, and a further 'BTP' and Class J22 are also evident. Note the ancient four-wheel stock, possibly in departmental use.** *J. Hayes, K. L. Taylor Collection*

Below: **One of the less than popular McDonnell Class 38 4-4-0s, No 158, stands on Whitby shed around 1919. McDonnell's influence is complete in this scene, with a Class 59 in the background.** *Ken Hoole Study Centre*

locomotive (No 1275) was not withdrawn from Malton until 1923; it is now part of the National Collection.

The final significant development from this period was Fletcher's 'Bogie Tank Passenger' ('BTP') design. First introduced in 1874, these worked from Whitby for many years, becoming the basis of the NER's steam 'auto-car' workings in the Edwardian period. The last was not withdrawn until 1929 as LNER Class G6, with Whitby losing its final 'BTP' (No 1020) on 4 August 1925.

In 1882 Alexander McDonnell took over as NER Locomotive Superintendent. During his tenure, he built two classes that saw extensive use on lines to Whitby. Both were a decided break with the previous Fletcher tradition and with new features, such as left-hand drive, they were not well liked by footplate crews. In fact, McDonnell's tenure with the NER was to be a mere two years, with the changes he sought to bring being too controversial after the long and revered Fletcher regime. Nevertheless, the '38' class of passenger 4-4-0 came to dominate longer-distance passenger workings on the Malton to Whitby line in the 1890s, while the '59' class 0-6-0 freight locomotives, introduced in 1882, would continue into LNER days (becoming LNER Class J22). Until 1917, however, the '59s' were not allowed south of Grosmont.

By the turn of the 20th century a number of more modern locomotives were appearing. The Class A (LNER Class F8) 2-4-2T, introduced by T. W. Worsdell in 1886, was deployed from both Malton and Whitby sheds on local passenger work. Then, in 1894, after Wilson Worsdell succeeded his brother as NER Locomotive Superintendent, came the Class O 0-4-4T (LNER Class G5). These popular and versatile passenger tanks were to have a more than 60-year association with the area. In 1904

Left: On 4 August 1925 LNER Class J22 (former NER Class 59) 0-6-0 No 506D stands at Sleights with a goods train. *Ken Hoole Study Centre*

Below left: T. W. Worsdell NER Class A 2-4-2T No 674 stands on Whitby old turntable around 1900. *Whitby Museum*

Bottom left: In LNER days former Class A (now LNER 'F8') 2-4-2T No 1581 waits with a local train at Whitby. *A. Williamson Collection*

Above right: An excellent 1949 study of typical former NER train, with Wilson Worsdell Class G5 (NER Class O) 0-4-4T No 67273 takes water at Pickering in 1949 on a push-pull-fitted Forge Valley train. *W A Camwell, Beck Isle Museum*

Right: Class G1 No 217 stands at Malton in 1904. These lightweight 4-4-0s were introduced by T. W. Worsdell in 1887 for secondary lines. Built initially as 2-4-0s, front bogies were fitted between 1900 and 1904. *G. W. J. Potter, Ken Hoole Study Centre*

Below right: An LNER and BR Class J24 (NER Class P) 0-6-0, introduced by Wilson Worsdell in 1894, stands on the turntable at Bog Hall. Despite the date of 19 June 1951, the engine still carries its LNER number 5644 prefixed by 'E' for Eastern Region, as a 'quick fix' following nationalisation. *Alec Ford*

T. W. Worsdell's Class G1 4-4-0s (LNER Class D23), recently rebuilt from 2-4-0s, were introduced onto the longer-distance summer passenger workings, gradually replacing the McDonnell Class 38s. This followed the introduction of heavier bogie stock and installation of a new 50-foot turntable at Bog Hall in place of the smaller 42-foot one in Whitby shed yard. The 'G1s' were allowed to work 125 tons up the bank to Goathland without assistance; equivalent to five 45-foot bogie coaches plus either two four-wheel or one six-wheel van (one more coach was allowed if not stopping at Grosmont). Other examples of the later and larger NER 4-4-0s also visited the area from time to time, but only 'G1s' were the allocated to the local sheds.

A new range of goods 0-6-0s were built during the Worsdell era, starting with T. W. Worsdell's Class C (LNER 'J21') introduced in 1886. Wilson Worsdell developed increasingly more powerful designs, progressing from Class P in 1894 (LNER 'J24') through 'P1' (LNER 'J25'), 'P2' (LNER 'J26') to culminate in 1906 with the 'P3' (LNER 'J27'). All appear to have worked regularly on the Whitby lines at some stage, although it was not until LNER days that they were permitted between Grosmont and Pickering.

In 1907 Wilson Worsdell introduced a new locomotive specifically aimed at the rugged Scarborough to Whitby line, with its steep gradients around Ravenscar, and the equally challenging Whitby to Malton route. Initially, however, operation of the ten Class W 4-6-0Ts was limited by bridge restrictions, and only one was allocated to Whitby shed. After coal capacity was found to be inadequate, Worsdell's successor, Vincent Raven, rebuilt them as 4-6-2Ts with extended bunkers and an additional well tank to increase coal and water capacity (the LNER classification was 'A6'). Following the renewed growth in holiday traffic after the First World War, more of the engines came to be allocated to Whitby, justifying their 'Whitby Willie' soubriquet.

Another large tank engine design that would become closely associated with the routes around Whitby was the Class D (LNER 'H1'), introduced in 1913 by Vincent Raven. These locomotives were built as 4-4-4Ts, in which configuration they had a tendency to slip in conditions of poor rail adhesion. After one engine was converted by the LNER to a 4-6-2T in 1931, the remaining locomotives were all modified over the next five years and re-classified 'A8'. The 1930s' increase in passenger traffic on the coastal route found the 'A6' tanks struggling to cope. Gradually more 'A8s' were allocated, after a relaxation to allow use of 'J39' 0-6-0s ended in 1937 when one derailed at Prospect Hill. By the late 1930s, 15 'A8s' were avail-

Left: **Class J25 (NER Class P1) 0-6-0 No 65685 is on shed at Whitby on 30 July 1955. In the background is visiting Gresley 'V3' 2-6-2T No 67638 from Middlesbrough.** *L. Brown*

Below left: **The most modern of the NER 0-6-0s was the 'P3' class. Later classified 'J27' by the LNER, they took over from the earlier 0-6-0 designs on Malton to Whitby goods workings in the mid-1950s. No 65827 approaches Mill Lane Junction, Pickering, in July 1957 with the down Whitby goods.** *C. G. Pearson, Ian Allan Library*

Below: **In around 1922 Wilson Worsdell Class W No 688 is seen at Whitby following conversion from 4-6-0T to 4-6-2T to give increased coal capacity.** *W. Leslie Good, Peter Ward Collection*

Bottom: **The LNER classified the 'W' 4-6-2Ts as Class A6. No 686 is seen at Whitby on 3 June 1935. Note the coal-loading crane adjacent to the 'G5' locomotive, introduced in 1910, – compare with the photograph on page 24.** *H. C. Casserley*

able between the three sheds working the route: Scarborough (three), Whitby (three) and Middlesbrough (nine). Thereafter they were increasingly deployed in the area, with allocations eventually extending to Malton in 1953.

LNER days saw some changes to motive power policy affecting shed allocations at both Malton and Whitby. A number of former Hull & Barnsley Railway 0-6-0s, designed by Matthew Stirling (LNER Class J23), had become surplus in their home area. In 1927/8 Malton acquired four, while another four arrived at Whitby in 1930/1. Not hugely popular with footplate crews, they seem to have been used as a last resort, but were allocated not only to freight duties but also summer passenger services. The last two (Nos 2460 and 2476) were withdrawn from Whitby on 5 November 1938. Earlier still, the last two 'F8' 2-4-2Ts (Nos 1580 and 262) disappeared from Malton shed in 1933 and 1934, with a compensating increase in the number of 'G5s' allocated. The inter-war years also saw Nigel Gresley's Class D49 'Hunt' 4-4-0s appear on the Malton to Whitby line. Although none were allocated to either Malton or Whitby, the class worked in regularly from York. In July 1939 Whitby received a Wilson Worsdell 'D20' 4-4-0, No 2012, but this was rapidly despatched back to York on 11 September, barely a week after the outbreak of war.

A sub-shed of Malton, Pickering was allocated a variety of different classes to work its local goods, Gilling and Forge Valley turns. These included 'BTP' tanks, with 'G5s' and various 0-6-0s ('J21', 'J22' and 'J23') based at Pickering in LNER days. Worsdell-era 'N8' and 'N9' 0-6-2Ts were also drafted in after footplate

Above left: Vincent Raven introduced the Class D in 1913 as 4-4-4Ts. In this configuration they were always light on their feet, and Gresley rebuilt them as 4-6-2Ts, classified as Class A8. No 1531 stands on shed at Whitby around 1938. *C. A. Davies, Pendragon Collection*

Left: A number of ex-Hull & Barnsley Railway Class J23 0-6-0s were drafted in to Malton and Whitby sheds by the LNER. No 2453 is in charge of a lengthy down goods at Levisham in 1935. (The train is standing on the single line from New Bridge, and, with the points set from the up line and the Home signal at danger, shunting may be taking place.) *National Railway Museum*

Below: A splendid portrait of a Class D20 (former NER Class R) 4-4-0. No 1207 is at High Mill, Pickering, shortly before the Second World War. The engine may have just been turned prior to working a Gilling line train back to York. *Nigel Trotter collection*

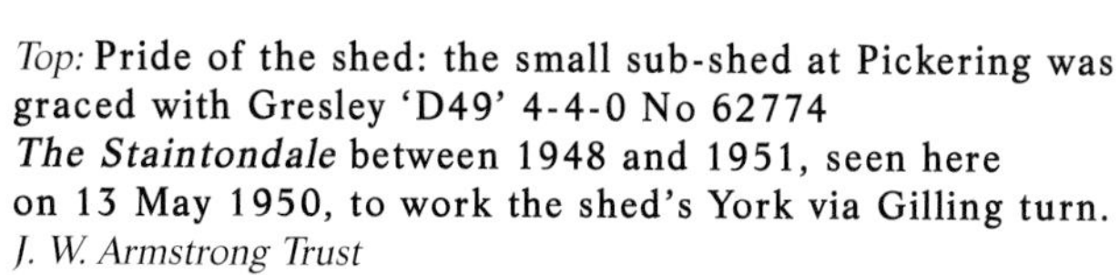

Top: Pride of the shed: the small sub-shed at Pickering was graced with Gresley 'D49' 4-4-0 No 62774 ***The Staintondale*** between 1948 and 1951, seen here on 13 May 1950, to work the shed's York via Gilling turn. *J. W. Armstrong Trust*

Above: Pickering shed's Sentinel Class Y3 No 81 is serviced by the shed crane some time in the 1930s. *Beck Isle Museum*

Above right: Perhaps the most remarkable visitor to the small shed at Pickering was former Great Northern Railway Ivatt 4-4-2 Class C1 No 3277. Details of the working and the date are unknown, but the locomotive probably worked in from York on a Gilling line train. *R. C. Riley, Ian Allan Library*

Right: Sentinel 'Y3' No 81 heads a loco shunting movement near Pickering coal yard in the 1930s. Mill Lane Junction signal box can be seen in the background and Pickering gasworks is to the right. *NYMR Collection*

crew complaints about tender-first running on the 0-6-0s. For a short period during the Second World War an NER 'D20' 4-4-0 (No 1232) was sent from York, but Pickering's big moment came in 1948 when 'D49' No 62774 *The Staintondale* was allocated to work the Gilling line. This turn alternated with a York engine, covering the 07.10 to York, 10.35 York to Pickering and 17.32 back to York. The loco also saw some local goods work, including a Mondays-only turn to Goathland. Another 'D20' (No 62343) replaced 'D49' No 62774 in 1951, working the Gilling line turn until closure in 1953. A Sentinel 0-4-0 shunting locomotive (LNER Class Y3) was based at Pickering in LNER and early BR days to shunt the goods yard and sidings in the immediate area. No 81 was allocated from 1928 to 1942, when No 192 (later No 68157) took over until withdrawn in 1952. The 'Y3' was also intended as a standby for the Forge Valley Sentinel railcar, with No 81 being vacuum-fitted, although there is no evidence that it was ever used for that purpose.

The scenic excursion trains that became such a feature in the 1930s were generally formed of modern Gresley stock, and could load up to eight vehicles. For such heavy trains an assisting engine, often an 'A8', was regularly provided for the run to Whitby and along the coast to Scarborough. At Whitby Town, where the train reversed, the assisting loco was attached to the opposite end of the train to head up the hill to West Cliff for the second reversal. There it ran round again to become the leading loco, double-heading forward to Scarborough.

The first appearance of Sentinel steam railcars appears to have been in October 1924 on the trial circuit from York via Malton, Whitby and Scarborough. The route became established as a regular test route on 6 April 1927 when the two-cylinder car No 22 again ran this way. The two-cylinder car No 237 *Rodney* was allocated to Pickering from new in 1928 for use on the Forge Valley line, being joined in November 1928, and later replaced, by six-cylinder No 2136 *Hope*. Further north, however, timetabled operation with Sentinel railcars did not begin between Whitby and Goathland until 1932, using the larger six-cylinder vehicles deemed necessary for reliable operation over such steep routes. The Sentinels could be temperamental machines, capable of raising steam quickly, but equally able to rapidly lose it on the hills. Nevertheless, in certain circumstances they were permitted to haul a four-wheel passenger trailer or goods van.

Hope again features as the first railcar allocated to Whitby, and by the mid-1930s three railcars were regularly based there. As an example, in 1934 the allocation was No 2219 *New Fly*, and two twin six-cylinder cars, Nos 246 *Royal Sovereign* and 248 *Tantivy*. One of the experimental Armstrong-Whitworth diesel railcars, *Tyneside Venturer* (and possibly sister railcar *Lady Hamilton*), regularly operated the Scarborough-Pickering-Whitby circular excursions until withdrawn in early 1939, with the last summer season before the war being covered by the Scarborough-allocated steam railcar No 220 *Defence*. Railcar operation reduced significantly with the onset of the Second World War, although various vehicles remained on Whitby's allocation until October 1944. Malton shed, by now working the Forge Valley line, also had an allocation until 15 June 1946 when No 2219 *New Fly* was condemned. With the withdrawal of railcar working, loco-haulage took over, usually by 'G5' 0-4-4Ts. On the Forge Valley line push-pull-fitted 'G5s' were deployed working with newly converted NER driving trailers, although this was a different vacuum based system compared to the mechanical/Westinghouse air-braked system used on the earlier NER 'auto-cars'.

Following the LNER relaxations to allow the Worsdell 0-6-0s to work over the Grosmont to Rillington line, two 'J24s' were allocated to Whitby in 1926 and one to Malton in 1927. Increasingly 'J24s' took over goods services from the old McDonnell 'J22' and Stirling 'J23' classes. In turn, these gave way in the 1950s first to 'J25s' and finally to the more powerful 'J27s', which started to appear at Malton in 1955. For a period Malton shed also had an allocation of four of the more modern Gresley-built 'J39' 0-6-0s, although they were used on the Gilling and Driffield branches rather than to Whitby. In the final years of steam Raven 'Q6' 0-8-0s appeared on the Esk Valley line, working out of the newly built shed at Thornaby.

Other LNER classes introduced to the area in later years included Gresley's 'V1'/'V3' 2-6-2Ts, Edward Thompson's 1945-designed 'L1' 2-6-4Ts, and a few Robinson Great Central

Top: **Sentinel six-cylinder steam railcar No 220 *Defence* at Whitby on a test run in 1932.** *Ken Hoole Study Centre*

Above: **Sentinel six-cylinder steam railcar No 248 *Tantivy* waits at Goathland to return to Whitby in the summer of 1936. Note the Camping Coach behind the waiting shelter.** *NYMR Collection*

Left: One of the experimental Armstrong-Whitworth diesel-electric railcars passes Raindale in 1935, probably working one of the Scarborough-based summer excursions to Whitby via Pickering and return via the coast. The photograph states this to be the railcar ***Lady Hamilton***, although the regular car was ***Tyneside Venturer***. *C. M. Doncaster, Whitby Museum*

Below: A busy post-war scene at Whitby in August 1953 with no fewer than eight locomotives in view. Identifiable are 'A8s' Nos 69890 and 69888, 'V3' No 67656, 'J25' No 65691 and 'B1' No 61030 ***Nyala***. *Kenneth Field, Rail Archive Stephenson*

Top: Around 1960 Thornaby-based former NER 'Q6' No 63393 crosses the River Esk at Ruswarp with the return freight 'trip' from Whitby to Tees Yard. The 'Q6' 0-8-0s were only latterly used on the Esk Valley route, and did not venture south of Grosmont until NYMR days (in the form of preserved No 63395). *Ken Hoole Study Centre*

Above: At Whitby Town on 26 July 1958, Whitby-allocated Standard Class 3 No 77012 stands ready to shunt the stock of the 16.08 from Malton, while Thompson 'L1' 2-6-4T No 67754 is in charge of the 18.00 to Middlesbrough. *Michael Mensing*

Left: Staple motive power in the final years of steam to Whitby were the Thompson Class B1 4-6-0s. No 61276 from York shed, but a regular on the Whitby line, is turned on the table at Bog Hall on 14 May 1964 prior to working the evening 'mail' passenger from Whitby to Malton. *J. M. Boyes, J. W. Armstrong Trust*

Right: The LMS influence: Fairburn Class 4 2-6-4T No 42085, one of three allocated to Whitby, departs from Levisham on the way home with a train from Malton. This locomotive survives today on the Lakeside & Haverthwaite Railway. *Cecil Ord, NYMR Collection*

Left: **Whitby shed received five brand-new Standard Class 4 2-6-4Ts in 1955. On 15 April 1958 No 80117 propels out of Whitby Town with a shuttle train to West Cliff.** *Mike Feather*

Below: **Malton shed gained an allocation of Standard Class 3 2-6-2Ts. No 82026 departs from Pickering with the 08.47 Whitby to Malton train in 1962.** *Brian Rutherford*

Bottom: **A 1958 memo referring to the replacement of 'G5' locos by 2MTs.** *Chris Cubitt collection*

B.R. 3/2

BRITISH TRANSPORT COMMISSION
BRITISH RAILWAYS
N.E. REGION

YOUR REF.
DATED

OUR REF. F.T.L.B.
DATED 12.12.58.

TO Shunter C.L.Thompson,
Signalman, New Bridge.
Pickering. (Centre No.)

FROM STATION MASTER'S
PICKERING, N.E. REGION (Centre No.)
Extn.

Pickering : Pilot P.1.Working.

The G.5 type locomotive at present in use will shortly be replaced with a No.2 M.T. (tender) loco. The latter engine is graded Route Availability No.2 with a minimum working radius of 4 chains. As a G.5. has a minumum working radius of 5 chains, the Class 2 MT, having a lesser radius will, as far as radii are concerned, be able to work New Bridge Sidings.

As far as loadings are concerned, the 2 MT is placed in F.T.L.B. Group 2.F. The loadings from Thornton Dale to Pickering for a Group 2 F loco are 25 heavies.(25 heavies are eqqal to 16 large hoppers loaded).

Station Master.

Railway-designed Class A5 4-6-2Ts, built by the LNER at Darlington. These classes were prohibited south of Grosmont to Pickering, but allocations at Middlesbrough and Saltburn brought them to Whitby via either the Loftus or Esk Valley routes. In January 1957 two 'L1s' (Nos 67763/65) were allocated to Whitby shed, but moved away after a mere two months. The final LNER design to become regularly established in the area was Thompson's 1942-designed 'B1' 4-6-0. These locos became increasingly common during the 1950s on all routes, with York-allocated examples destined to see out regular steam working to Whitby in 1964.

Before then the 1950s period was something of an Indian summer for the remarkable variety of steam locomotives working over the routes to Whitby. In total more than twenty classes could be seen at some stage during the BR period, even though some only just made it. Most of the 'A6' 'Whitby Willies' had been moved inland from Whitby in 1940 under the wartime 'Evacuation Scheme', and the last (No 9799) left in October 1948. Three Fairburn LMS-design 2-6-4Ts were transferred to Whitby shed in the 1950s (Nos 42083/84/85), being joined by five new 1955-built Standard Class 4 2-6-4Ts (Nos 80116-20). Whitby also received two Standard Class 3 2-6-0s (Nos 77003/14), while a number of Standard Class 3 2-6-2Ts and Ivatt LMS-design Class 2 2-6-0s and 2-6-2Ts were allocated to Malton shed. These helped to displace the last 'G5s' (Nos 67248, 67315 and 67342), which were withdrawn from Malton in December 1958. Ivatt Class 4 2-6-0s, and

Above: **The LMS influence at Malton shed came in the form of Ivatt Class 2s 2-6-2Ts. No 41251 heads a freight 'trip' working at Pickering station in 1962.** *Brian Rutherford*

Right: **Malton's Ivatt Class 2-6-0 No 46473 heads the down Whitby goods between Pickering and New Bridge around 1962.** *Brian Rutherford*

Below right: **On 15 April 1963 Ivatt Class 4MT No 43055 waits to leave Malton with the shed's last steam turn, the 16.00 passenger to Whitby.** *Ken Hoole Study Centre*

Standard Class 2 2-6-0s, also worked over the inland and coastal routes during the 1950s. The occasional Stanier Black 5 reached Whitby, usually on excursions.

The introduction of DMU working in 1958 led to a rapid reduction in steam operations. On 6 April 1959 Whitby shed was closed, with the three LMS 2-6-4Ts and Standard Class 3 2-6-0s transferred away. For the record, on the last working day, Saturday 4 April, No 42083 had worked the 07.02 and 15.15 Whitby-Malton services, returning at 11.00 and 17.50, while No 42084 worked the 11.37 Whitby-Malton and the 14.15 back from Malton. There were still a few steam turns from Malton worked by Standard Class 3 2-6-2Ts and LMS 2-6-0s and 2-6-2Ts, but the shed eventually closed on 15 April 1963. The last turn, on Saturday 13 April, covering the 16.00 Malton to Whitby and 18.54 return, was worked by Ivatt Class 4 2-6-0 No 43055, ironically not a Malton engine.

Steam working continued between Malton and Whitby on the weekday 06.45 York-Whitby pick-up goods, and the two remaining loco-hauled passenger/mail workings, using York-based 'B1s'. These turns were converted to scheduled diesel

Left: Metro-Cammell DMUs (later Class 101) became a common sight on the routes from Malton and Middlesbrough to Whitby. On 1 August 1958, shortly after their arrival in the area, a lengthy formation of two three-car units approaches Grosmont with the 12.35 short working from Whitby to Goathland. *Michael Mensing*

Below: Even after withdrawal of the Malton and Scarborough line services, Whitby could still have its busy moments. On 6 August 1987 Class 143 'Pacer' units are seen on the approaches to Whitby in the shadow of the new road bridge across the mouth of the Esk estuary opened in 1980. By now the running line had been singled, and unit No 143019 is stabled on the old up line. The other unit, No 143023, is in Tyne & Wear Metro colours. In the background Brush Class 47 No 47528 stands on the stock of a return excursion. *Ian S. Carr*

operation in 1964, with English Electric Type 4s or Sulzer Type 2s being the normal traction, although 'B1s' still appeared regularly, until closure. The remaining freight trip from Malton to Pickering and New Bridge was handled by BR-built 204hp Gardner diesel-mechanical shunters up to withdrawal in 1966.

The DMUs employed both in the period up to closure, and subsequently on the remaining Esk Valley service to Whitby, were largely Metro-Cammell two- and three-car units, although other designs also appeared. In 1987 'Pacer' units (Classes 142-144) were introduced, occasionally substituted by Class 156 'Sprinters'. In 2004 it proved possible to allocate the 'Sprinter' units, with their better ride quality, on a regular basis. The remaining freight operations to Whitby were diesel-worked, usually by a Thornaby-based English Electric Type 3 (Class 37), until the service was withdrawn in 1983.

Coaching and freight stock

There are few details about the first passenger carriages used for the start of locomotive operations in 1847. They would have been four-wheeled, and no doubt uncomfortable, since the Y&NM was reputed to provide the worst passenger rolling stock in the country. Y&NM First Class carriages normally had three compartments, while Second Class had four with open sides and a roof supported on iron stanchions. Carriages were painted dark green and carried the armorial bearings of the City of York. It can be assumed that coaches for 'parliamentary' class passengers, and probably Third Class, would still have been open at the time of the NER takeover in 1854.

The NER soon improved matters, with one early decision being the abolition of open coaches following a fatality; an order to this effect was issued by the NER Locomotive Committee on 13 February 1857. However, the geography of the Pickering to Whitby route, with its sharp curves and the Goathland incline, prevented the introduction of six-wheeled coaches that would have given a better ride quality. This restriction also extended to the Loftus and Scarborough lines. For the Whitby to Stockton service, however, a batch of six-wheeled coaches was introduced with a 21-foot wheelbase and additional play on the centre axle to help cope with the Esk Valley line's curves. Thirty vehicles, made up into five-coach sets, had this modification. The restrictions necessitating continued use of these vehicles was removed in 1909.

It appears that at some stage in the late 19th century the NER may have relaxed the ban on its own six-wheeled 32ft 6in vehicles, but retained restrictions for other companies' vehicles. Thus even after the introduction of through coaches between London King's Cross and Whitby, the Great Northern Railway (GNR), which provided the stock, had to retain a number of four-wheeled coaches especially for this service because of the restrictions between Pickering and Whitby. Their nickname of 'Whitby bathing machines' gives a clue as to how they were regarded by their long-suffering passengers. Two new four-wheeled coaches were built by the GNR as late as 1887, the NER having stopped building such vehicles even for local services in 1885. The GNR vehicles were 26 feet long on a 16ft 8in wheelbase, and contained a luggage compartment, a First Class saloon seating nine, a Third Class compartment and a shared lavatory.

Despite the opening of the deviation route bypassing Goathland incline, and developments in coach design, real improvement only came to the Malton to Whitby line at the very end of the 19th century when, in 1898/9, the four-wheeled coaches were replaced with bogie vehicles built to a reduced length of 45 feet rather than the normal 52 feet. Three types were built over these two years:

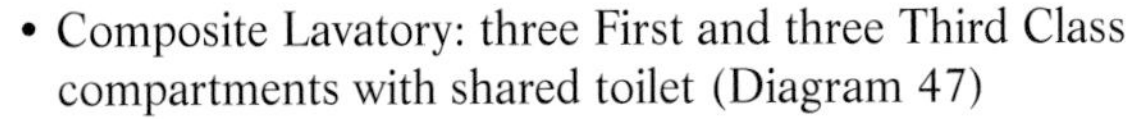

- Composite Lavatory: three First and three Third Class compartments with shared toilet (Diagram 47)
- Third: six compartments (Diagram 48)
- Brake Third: three compartments (Diagram 49)

Partly helped by a programme of track improvements, the NER realised that there was no practical reason to maintain restrictions on 52-foot stock, and they were removed on lines into Whitby in 1901. Some restrictions remained on other companies' six-wheeled and four-wheeled stock. Thereafter coaches from the standard NER fleet could increasingly be used, with East Coast Joint Stock allowed in 1909 and vehicles up to 65ft 6in by 1922. Finally, all restrictions on LNER coaches were lifted in 1924. The 1898 45-foot stock had clerestory roofs as was very much the NER pattern at the time. Elliptical roofs become standard for all non-gangway stock in 1906, and by 1909 some

Top left: **Four-wheel coaches are stabled near Bog Hall around 1900. Bogie coaches were only permitted into Whitby in 1898, and even then only of limited length and on the Malton route.** *Ken Hoole Study Centre*

Top: **One of the earlier clerestory build of NER 'porthole' 'auto-car' coaches converted from a conventional eight-compartment coach to Diagram 14 is seen at Whitby West Cliff. The conversion to Diagram 116 was introduced in 1905 to include a driving compartment for push-pull operation with 'BTP' engines.** *G. W. J. Potter, John Minnis Collection*

Above left: **A later build of 'auto-car' coaches appeared in 1908 with elliptical roofs to Diagram 162. For the push-pull operations introduced in later LNER/early BR days a number of new conversions were also made from conventional former NER Brake Third coaches. This is vehicle No E21020 at Forge Valley on the last train on this line, 3 June 1950.** *Ken Hoole Study Centre*

Above: **This view of Whitby Town on 27 July 1954 has a good selection of coaching stock on view, including both NER and LNER Gresley Brake Thirds, and a Thompson Composite Lavatory. The engine is an 'A8' 4-6-2T.** *H. C. Casserley*

Left: **The sole surviving Thompson Composite Lavatory, No 88339, forms part of a train at Goathland in 2008. Although this vehicle did not operate over the NYMR in BR days, identical coaches were part of the standard formation of local services on the routes to Whitby during the postwar period.** *Author*

remarkably spacious and modern gangwayed stock was being introduced for longer-distance services, including London to Whitby/Scarborough. The improvement in standards and comfort in just a decade was dramatic.

The steam 'auto-car' services employed specially modified or new-build driving trailers, with distinctive porthole windows. Rodding from the coach was linked to the locomotive, enabling the driver to control all essential functions from the leading vehicle, including regulator, reverser, brake and whistle. A number of six-compartment (one First and five Third) clerestory-roofed coaches were rebuilt in 1905 (from Diagram 14 to 116), with a second similar but elliptical-roofed batch built new in 1908 (Diagram 162). Both types operated on the services radiating from Whitby, while Pickering saw newly modified push-pull vehicles return in the Forge Valley line's final years.

On all routes both clerestory and elliptical-roofed non-gangway stock became standard for most local services. This was to remain the case throughout the LNER period, and on into the BR era. In terms of carriage working, on the Malton to Whitby service the stock was made up into three-coach sets (Brake Third, Composite Lavatory, Brake Third), with the route stencilled on the outer vehicle ends; although a Third might be added or substituted sometimes together with a Full Brake. Trains on the Whitby to Stockton and Middlesbrough route were similarly made up into three- or four-coach sets. In the 1950s some Thompson LNER and BR standard non-gangway suburban stock was allocated to the Malton and Esk Valley services. The scenic excursions of the 1930s saw both standard Gresley corridor stock and some of his green-and-cream articulated excursion sets. Through trains and coaches to more distant locations, such as Leeds and London, were diagrammed for standard LNER Gresley and Thompson corridor stock until Mark 1 vehicles were introduced around 1960.

There is little remarkable to note so far as freight rolling stock is concerned, once the Y&NM upgrade of the W&PR had taken place. Thereafter most railway wagons could inter-work generally without restriction. Open goods wagons (three- and five-plank) were common for local mineral traffic, with bolster wagons for handling timber becoming more prevalent in the 20th century. Vans were provided for perishable fish traffic from Whitby, with vacuum-brake-fitted vehicles becoming increasingly common following the Second World War. The usual range of coal and cattle wagons served the wayside stations. Raised coal drops, such a popular feature at NER stations, enabled bottom-discharge coal wagons to be handled at the larger stations. Both NER and former private-owner hopper wagons appear to have still been in use up to the 1950s, thereafter being replaced by BR steel 21-ton vehicles.

The NYMR era

Over the 35 years of operation, a wide range of steam and diesel traction has worked on the restored NYMR. In the early days the assumption was that steam operations would largely be limited to between Grosmont and Ellerbeck. The first steam locomotives were thus small industrial types such as Hudswell Clark 0-4-0ST *Mirvale* and Andrew Barclay 0-4-0ST *Salmon*. The AC railbus No W79978 was intended for local community services, with two 2-car Gloucester C&W DMUs procured for Pickering trains.

As the railway developed, it became clear that more and larger steam locomotives were needed, although the railway relied heavily on main-line diesels for some years. With the decision of the NELPG to make its base on the NYMR, larger locomotives became available. The first NELPG locomotive to arrive was 'Q6' 0-8-0 No 63395 on 25 June 1970, together with 1904 Kitson 0-6-2T No 29 from the Lambton Railway. Two months later another ex-Lambton locomotive came to the NYMR, Stephenson-built 0-6-2T No 5. Another NELPG loco, 'J27' 0-6-0 No 65894, arrived in October 1971. Standard Class 4 No 80135 came to the NYMR straight from Dai Woodham's Barry scrapyard in March 1973, and the following year saw the arrival of two more locomotives that were to become very much part of the railway. First, on 28 May, came NELPG's 'K1' No 2005, fresh from a two-year overhaul and painted somewhat controversially in LNER apple green, a livery it had never carried prior to preservation. As No 62005, this loco had of course been one of those that had worked over the line on the last-day special in 1965. The second loco was LMS Stanier Class 5 No 45428 *Eric Treacy*, owned at that time by Brian Hollingsworth and hitherto based at Tyseley.

Today the NYMR either owns, or is long-term custodian of, nine steam locomotives. Several more are on long-term 'home-based' hire agreements, including the NELPG locomotives and LNER 'A4' 4-6-2 No 60007 *Sir Nigel Gresley*, while others are on shorter-term agreements. The railway usually needs around ten operational steam locomotives in a season and, since at any one time a number are always under or awaiting overhaul, the annual hire commitment can be as high as eight. The NYMR also has in its care a number of diesel locomotives and vehicles.

Rolling stock consists largely of BR Mark 1 stock, together with a number of LNER Gresley/Thompson coaches, including several awaiting restoration. The NYMR's dining train includes 1929 and BR Metro-Cammell Pullman cars. A large range of goods wagons reside on the railway.

Top left: The North Eastern Locomotive Preservation Group's fifth birthday is celebrated in style in early-season snow on 20 November 1971 as 'Q6' 0-8-0 No 3395 climbs out of Grosmont near Esk Valley cottages. *John Hunt*

Left: A typical NYMR locomotive line-up at Grosmont in 1990. A southbound train emerges from the tunnel behind LMS Class 5 4-6-0 No 45428, named *Eric Treacy* following preservation. In the shed yard are Standard Class 4 2-6-4T No 80135, GWR '66xx' class 0-6-2T No 6619 and ex-Lambton Colliery Robert Stephenson 0-6-2T No 5. *John Hunt*

Above: Now very much part of the NYMR scene, the Sir Nigel Gresley Locomotive Preservation Trust's Class A4 4-6-2 No 60007 passes Moorgates on 21 October 2007 with the 15.50 Grosmont to Pickering train. *Author*

Below: The NYMR's 'Vintage Train' of restored LNER coaches on a special working at Needle Point in Newton Dale on 14 March 2008. The locomotive, Gresley 'V2' No 4771 *Green Arrow*, part of the National Collection, has since been retired and can currently be seen at 'Locomotion', Shildon. *Author*

8

Stations and Infrastructure

Stations and related buildings

Very few original W&PR buildings still exist. The most significant is the Weigh House at Whitby. Located alongside the track at a place called 'The Batts', a short distance from Bog Hall, it was built in 1834 by local stonemason John Bolton (Junior) to house machinery for weighing goods passing along the railway. Over the years the building has sadly fallen into ruin and only remnants survive today. The W&PR was developed in concept as almost a turnpike on rails, and as such the need for buildings would have been limited. What few there were seem to have been largely swept away during the Y&NM rebuilding. Nevertheless, it is known that sheds and stables were provided for the passenger coaches and horses at both Whitby and Pickering, while Raindale also appears to have had stabling for horses. The original Raindale Inn about half a mile north of Levisham, today known as The Grange', and the derelict 'Carter's House' in Northdale were both used by the railway as coaching inns for exchange of horses and refreshment purposes. Neither, however, are thought to be original W&P buildings, unlike 'Ash Tree Cottage' the only known survivor of a number of cottages and houses built for W&PR workers. Situated at the top of the old incline in Goathland, it may have been built for the resident overseer of the incline and remains as a private residence

The Y&NM's rebuilding programme was nothing if not thorough, with the York architect George Townsend Andrews engaged for building design. Andrews was the favoured architect for George Hudson's railways until they fell out when, in 1849, the year of his downfall, Hudson demanded a reduction in fees. Andrews left his mark throughout the North East, most noticeably with York old station and at Hull Paragon. His buildings had a distinctive design with low-pitched over-hanging roofs, and often incorporated arched chimneys. Most of the buildings on the Rillington to Whitby line were of his design, including stations, goods sheds, engine sheds and crossing-keepers' cottages. The stations at Malton, Rillington, Pickering and Whitby were particularly notable, with substantial facilities provided including G. T. Andrews's distinctive design of overall roof. Most numerous were the many lineside dwellings for railway workers. An NER census in 1862 recorded 52 cottages on the branch. The majority were to Andrews's design, and many survive today, albeit often modernised and in private ownership.

At Malton, development owed much to the existence of the Whitby line, with a range of sidings, yards and an engine shed growing up over the years on the banks of the River Derwent. An unusual feature of Malton station was a drawbridge enabling passengers to access the up main platform in the absence of a footbridge. Interlocked with the signalling, this was retracted beneath the platform whenever a train needed to enter the single down platform. At the east end of the station a bay platform and two sidings were provided primarily for Whitby trains, covered by a glazed roof designed by NER architect William Bell in 1883. When the train-shed was removed in the 1990s the glazing from the bay was used to create a new platform canopy. The two-road engine shed was constructed in 1853, and extended in 1867. Malton shed remained the principal supplier of motive power at the southern end of the Whitby line until closure in 1963.

At Rillington, 4½ miles from Malton, the Whitby line diverged from the main York to Scarborough line. Anticipating the importance of the station as a junction, a substantial building with an Andrews train-shed was constructed, including a bay platform for Whitby trains. Malton eventually assumed this function, after Rillington's layout was altered in 1865 to facilitate through train running between the Whitby branch and the Scarborough line, in readiness perhaps for the upgrading of services with the forthcoming opening of the Goathland deviation. The north-to-east curve at Rillington was removed in 1879. Although Rillington was included in the programme of station closures on 20 September 1930, surprisingly the train-shed with its overall roof lasted until the 1950s.

Above left: **The Whitby & Pickering Railway Weigh House on the outskirts of Whitby, when it was still largely intact in the early part of the 20th century.** *Ken Hoole Study Centre*

Left: **The remains of the Weigh House seen from a passing NYMR train in 2008.** *Author*

Left: Ash Tree Cottage, built by the Whitby & Pickering Railway adjoining Goathland incline, is thought to have been the incline overseer's house and possibly also a waiting room. It is seen here around 1905, but still survives today as a private residence.
G. W. J. Potter, Whitby Museum

Below: The interior of Malton station in 1956 showing the drawbridge used to provide access to the up island platform. *H. C. Casserley*

Bottom: The glazed roof at Malton station by William Bell was built in 1883 over the Whitby bay and sidings. Parts of the roof were used to provide a new platform canopy when the overall roof was removed in the 1990s.
H. C. Casserley

Above: **Malton shed viewed in the 1950s, with 'G5' 0-4-4T No 67248 and 'J27' 0-6-0 No 65827 'on shed'.** *P. Booth, Neville Stead Collection*

Left: **The overall roof of Rillington station is still intact in the 1950s, more than 20 years after the station had closed.** *Ken Hoole, Neville Stead Collection*

Below left: **Marishes Road station, level crossing and signal box on closure day, 6 March 1965.** *David Sutcliffe*

Some 3 miles from Rillington, Marishes Road station served the scattered community of High and Low Marishes. Always a remote country byway, station facilities were modest with a single-storey station building and cottage, down-side wooden platform shelter and small signal box. A siding on the up side provided basic goods facilities. Much of the station, including the platforms and platform shelter, remains today, and there are plans to install the signal cabin (in store at Goathland for many years) as an exhibit at Pickering station. Further north, the Malton to Pickering road was crossed near the short-lived station at Kirby, the crossing taking its name from the neighbouring Black Bull public house. The Andrews-designed Kirby station building is visible from the main road, in use as a private residence.

At Pickering, as befitted its status, a wide range of goods and passenger facilities were provided. A single-road engine shed was constructed, extended in 1875 to accommodate two engines. Although the shed closed in 1959, it still survives in industrial use. The Y&NM built a gasworks to provide light for the station complex, and the building that housed the retort and purifier is still in use (currently as a hair salon), although the adjoining gasometer has long gone. The facility not only supplied the station, but gas was also sold by the railway for street lighting and private use in Pickering town. Although the town eventually received its own independent gas supply, the station remained gas-lit until closure. In fact, Graham Reussner tells how, as a schoolboy looking round the disused station some time after closure, he idly pulled one of the gas lighting chains, only to find it flicker into life.

The Andrews station building at Pickering was a substantial affair with main buildings along the eastern wall of the train-shed, and an overall roof spanning the two platforms. It is thought that local stone was used for the building from Hildenley Quarry. The gabled roof, of standard Andrews design, was of slate, supported by a system of 'Euston truss' spans (named after the station where they were first used) and end bowstring girders, with a central glazed and vented clerestory. In order to reduce maintenance costs the overall roof was removed by BR in 1952, being replaced by the functional but inelegant canopies that remain today. A large goods shed, again to the standard G. T. Andrews gabled-roof design, was provided south of the passenger station, but did not survive the road scheme that now runs over the goods yard site. A 42-foot turntable was installed near the engine shed in 1870, but this was replaced in 1893 by a larger 50-foot table north of the station near High Mill, probably to facilitate turning of engines working the York-Gilling-Pickering service. This was removed in 1958, and the current 60-foot turntable from York was installed during the preservation era.

The picturesquely situated but misleadingly named station at Levisham was built 1½ miles and 300 feet below the village it purported to serve. Facilities were appropriately modest apart from a substantial station house, converted from a farmhouse. A pair of workmen's cottages was added in 1858, followed by a wooden passenger shelter in 1876, and a further brick waiting room in 1880. As part of its economy drive, in 1926 the LNER built a brick extension to the signal box to enable the signalman to sell tickets following withdrawal of the station master. A single siding and short loading platform sufficed for goods traffic, also used in LNER days for stabling the Camping Coach, but there was also a down refuge siding north of the station.

The next station north at Goathland was constructed as part of the 1865 deviation work, and thus did not follow the Andrews theme. The stone station buildings, including station house/ticket office and goods shed, were designed by the NER architect Thomas Prosser, presenting a Scottish look with distinctive 'crow-stepped' gables. As at Levisham, waiting accommodation was provided a few years later on the up platform, first with a combined waiting room and ladies' toilets, then a free standing waiting shelter. Rather more substantial goods facilities were

Top: **The former station at Kirby, near Black Bull crossing viewed around 1905, showing the distinctive style of the York & North Midland Railway architect G. T. Andrews.** *G. W. J. Potter, John Minnis Collection*

Above: **A scene full of interest is viewed from the coal drops at Pickering, looking north towards the station on 1 July 1966, the occasion of the last branch freight 'trip'. Hungate gate box is immediately behind the coal drops, controlling the level crossing over the A170 Thirsk to Scarborough road. Beyond is the goods shed, with Bridge Street signal box just visible ahead of the station. The engine shed is to just out of shot to the right.** *Frank Dean, Ken Hoole Study Centre*

Left: **The G. T. Andrews-designed Pickering engine shed is seen on 30 May 1954, with resident 'G5' 0-4-4T No 67308 at home.** *J. W. Armstrong Trust*

provided than at the other smaller stations, with separate sidings located on the down side to the goods shed and coal drop. On the up side four sidings served the stone-crusher and loading point. Here a water turbine was installed in 1936 of a type known as a 'Pelton Wheel' to provide power for the stone-crusher and for moving wagons around the site. Although out of use since the Sil Howe mine closed in 1951, NYMRPS members were able to restart it in 1969 to provide power within the station area, and its potential as a 'green' energy source is again being considered. A 1903 track plan also shows a further short up siding on the gradient north of the station, possibly for 'crippled wagons'. The date at which the station's name was changed from Goathland Mill is uncertain with timetables still showing this name in 1876.

A number of buildings were constructed in connection with the Goathland incline. These included a small engine shed, together with a turntable, at the top of the incline, where there was also a ticket office. Upon replacement of the initial 'water-balance truck', an engine house was built to house the stationary engine installed to drive the incline rope.

The work of G. T. Andrews is again in evidence at Grosmont station in the building incorporating the station master's house and passenger facilities (today much of the latter is taken up by the NYMR station shop). Here, as at Sleights and Ruswarp, a number of Tudor features were introduced to the design. Wooden waiting shelters were again provided on the platforms in NER days together with a range of outbuildings, one of which acted as the station master's office. The opening of the NY&C route along the Esk Valley resulted in a separate platform being constructed to serve this line with its own brick building containing waiting and ladies' rooms. Local goods facilities were located in the area between the Malton and Esk Valley platforms, with a loading dock road and three other sidings. Within the immediate vicinity of the station there were a number of other sidings serving the various industrial activities, including the old ironworks site and the brickworks.

The station buildings at Sleights and Ruswarp were similar, both being designed by Andrews as part of the Y&NM upgrading. Constructed of stone, these followed similar patterns

Above left: **The interior of Pickering station looking south around 1905. A train of stone wagons, no doubt from New Bridge Quarry, stands at the up platform. Note the station bookstall behind the left-most wagon.** *G. W. J. Potter, Whitby Museum*

Left: **The north end of Pickering station is seen around 1950 shortly before the overall roof was removed.** *Beck Isle Museum*

Below: **Pickering station viewed from the south end after replacement of the roof in 1952 with the functional platform canopies still in place today. Note the LMS-design BG van in the parcels dock, probably used for inwards newspapers.** *Beck Isle Museum*

Above: **Levisham station is seen in 1961, with the signal box, platform buildings and station house in a view that has changed little over the years.** *David Sutcliffe*

Left: **The main station building at Goathland, with the goods shed beyond, in 1957. Note the similarity of the building design to that at Lealholm, built at the same time around 1865 to the design of NER Architect Thomas Prosser. Standard Class 4 2-6-4T No 80118 is arriving with a down train.** *David Sutcliffe*

to Grosmont with a station house combined with passenger accommodation opening out on to one of the platforms. The second platform gained a wooden passenger shelter. Goods facilities consisted of two sidings and a small loading dock.

At Whitby the station was developed around a substantial double-span train-shed, and was located closer to the town centre than the original W&PR terminus. The contract for construction of the station was let on 20 August 1846 to Messrs Bellerby & Shaftoe at a price of £10,640. The train-shed was to the standard Andrews design but, in order to incorporate a central siding between the platform lines, two spans were required, supported on a row of columns. The shed was curved, necessitating some adjustments to accommodate two spans of unequal width. A cross platform behind the buffer stops linked the arrival and departure platforms (later Platforms 1 and 2). Station facilities were provided in buildings on the north and east sides of the train-shed. Unusually, although the main entrance was on the east elevation, entrance porticos were provided both there and on the north wall.

While two platforms were adequate to deal with the Pickering and Malton service, the opening of the Esk Valley line in July 1865 brought additional demands on the station. To meet these it appears that the two bay platforms, 3 and 4, located on the east side outside the train shed, were also constructed in 1865. A number of additional outbuildings developed over the years; however, as with Pickering, major change came in 1952 when BR replaced the train-shed roof with functional glazed awnings over the platform areas. Since the 1965 closures the station has seen considerable rationalisation, with only Platform 1 now in use, although a trackless portion of Platform 2 still remains. The south-east corner of the station site, where Platforms 3 and 4 used to be, is now a supermarket. Goods facilities at Whitby

Left: Looking south from Grosmont station towards the tunnel in 1900. The scene has changed remarkably little over the last century, despite the opening up of an additional platform and construction of a new signal box in recent years. *G. W. J. Potter, John Minnis Collection*

Below: Grosmont Junction around 1905, showing the extent of the Andrews-designed station building, the old signal cabin (replaced in 1907), and the Esk Valley platform shelter. *National Railway Museum/Pendragon Collection*

Bottom: The view west at Sleights station as it looked around 1905. Today the western end of the station is dominated by the A169 road bridge constructed after the 1930s floods. *G. W. J. Potter, John Minnis Collection*

Above: Ruswarp station and signal box looking towards Whitby just after the Second World War. *E. E. Whyman*

Left: The interior of Whitby station in 1952, before the removal of the G. T. Andrews overall roof. *Ken Hoole Study Centre*

Below: At Whitby engine shed in the early years of the 20th century, Class A 2-4-2Ts Nos 1579 and 35 stand in the shed yard. *Ken Hoole Collection, NYMR Archive*

Right: The main eastern portico at Whitby, photographed on 3 September 1978, still displayed the tangerine British Railways North Eastern Region 'Whitby Town' designation. The suffix 'Town' was only introduced in timetables during BR days to distinguish the station from Whitby West Cliff, although it then continued in common use for several years after West Cliff closed in 1961. *John Edgington*

Right: Lealholm station on the Esk Valley line, seen in around 1905, displays the distinctive Prosser 'crow-stepped' gables on the end walls of the station building. *National Railway Museum/Pendragon Collection*

Below: Built for an earlier phase of the Esk Valley line, Castleton displays a more conventional appearance. *National Railway Museum/Pendragon Collection*

Left: **Battersby is seen in 1955 from the Picton (western) end of the through platforms. The 12 milepost indicates the distance from Picton on the former Leeds Northern route, closed to passenger services the previous year. The single platform on the right does not appear to have seen use for some time.** *NYMR Archive*

consisted of a large goods warehouse, again designed by Andrews. A number of other buildings also developed over the years, supporting not just local traffic but also freight handled through the small harbour.

The Y&NM erected an engine shed at Whitby with the commencement of locomotive operations in 1847. The shed was extended by the NER in 1867 in order to accommodate a total of eight locomotives on two roads, the work being completed in 1868 after some modifications were made to assuage local objections over the proposed height. Originally a 42-foot turntable was provided in the shed yard, but this was replaced in 1902 by a 50-foot table at Bog Hall; supplanted in turn with one of 60-foot diameter in 1936. A steam crane replaced a hand crane for coaling, following a strike in 1910 that led to the personal intervention of Vincent Raven, the NER Chief Mechanical Engineer. Thereafter, apart from the damage suffered during the September 1940 air raid, there was little change to the shed arrangements until closure in 1959. After remaining derelict for many years there are now plans to convert the building into a museum dedicated to the life of explorer Captain James Cook.

The Esk Valley line stations were, like Goathland, built to the design of Thomas Prosser, the NER's in-house architect from 1854 to 1872. While the buildings for those at the western end were relatively modest single-storey affairs, those on the Castleton to Grosmont extension had two storeys to the same style as Goathland, being built by the same contractor.

During the preservation era, the NYMR has had to develop a number of new facilities in order to operate as a self-sufficient railway. It is not intended to cover these developments in any detail here, but the relocation of a number of wooden former NER structures is of note. At Grosmont today's booking office was previously the waiting room on the down platform at Sleights, no longer in use. Similarly some wooden buildings from Whitby and Gilling have found a new use as offices and staff facilities at Pickering. NER footbridges (formerly on Tyneside) have been installed at Goathland and Pickering, with another footbridge, from Robertsbridge in Sussex, linking Grosmont station with the NYMNP car park on the former ironworks site. Currently the NYMR's four owned stations are each restored to a different time-period: Pickering to LNER, circa 1937; Levisham to NER, circa 1912; Goathland to NER, circa 1922; and Grosmont to BR (NER), circa 1957. At Grosmont MPD a two-road running shed sits alongside the heavy repair and fabrication shop, whilst a steel-fabricated coaling tower is believed to be the only one of its kind on a heritage railway. The 1984 two-road C & W shed at Pickering has been joined in 2008 by a new shed specifically for carriage restoration work. New Bridge permanent way yard also has a two-road maintenance shed. In 2006 a locomotive compound and servicing pit was commissioned at New Bridge, in effect re-created the Pickering 'sub-shed' facility for overnight locomotive stabling.

The first phase of a major restoration scheme at Pickering was completed in 2000 with the aid of a £312,000 Heritage Lottery Fund grant, and it is hoped to undertake the second phase with a further grant over the next two years. This will include the NYMR's long-cherished ambition to restore the roof and station to its original condition. Over the years the NYMR has received a number of awards for the quality of its restoration work.

Tunnels and bridges

The first timber bridges on the W&PR were replaced during the wholesale rebuilding by the Y&NM in the 1840s. An idea of their

Below: **The northern tunnel portals at Grosmont. The original Whitby & Pickering horse train tunnel is on the left, now in use as a footpath and dwarfed by the York & North Midland double-track bore opened in 1847.** *J. W. Armstrong Trust*

Top left: The southern mouth of Grosmont new tunnel with a Sentinel steam railcar (either No 246 or 248) entering with a Goathland to Whitby service in 1932. Note the well of Grosmont turntable in the foreground. *D. Ibbotson, John Edgington Collection*

Above: In 1964 'B1' No 61337 crosses bridge 31 at Water Ark on the Grosmont deviation route with a Whitby to Malton train. *David Sutcliffe*

Left: Ruswarp Viaduct over the River Esk is crossed by 'A8' No 69852 in August 1964. *John Boyes, J. W. Armstrong Trust*

Left: **Several metal bridges on the deviation route were rebuilt by the NER in the early 1900s. A new girder is being eased into place on bridge 27 at Goathland in 1908 to accommodate a third track, which will provide a head-shunt for the goods yard. Compare this view with the photographs on pages 26 and 30.**
National Railway Museum

Right: **Larpool Viaduct viewed from the Ruswarp direction around 1900; note Foundry Siding signal box.**
Whitby Museum

appearance and construction can be seen from the George Dodgson engravings, and early paintings of Grosmont. The original tunnel at Grosmont faired rather better. Designed under George Stephenson's command, it still survives, having been retained as a footpath when the new larger tunnel was built. Constructed from locally quarried Lease Rigg stone, the tunnel is 130 yards long with a height of 14 feet and a width of 10 feet. Immediate responsibility for construction was in the hands of Stephenson's assistant, Frederick Swanwick, and the minutes of the W&PR directors' meeting take him to task for wasting money on the castellated north entrance. Today it provides pedestrian access to the NYMR's Grosmont Motive Power Depot.

Many of the replacement bridges built by the Y&NM were of timber, although some, including small viaducts, were of stone or iron construction. The new double-track tunnel at Grosmont closely paralleled the old tunnel with its design, together with the neighbouring single-span Esk river bridge, attributed to John Cass Birkenshaw. Reference is made in NER Locomotive Committee minutes in February 1857 to a Pickering Viaduct, having been converted to an embankment, and other NER records for the same period also refer to replacement bridges between Grosmont and Sleights following flooding.

The Goathland deviation required no fewer than 12 new under-bridges, five over-bridges and a small viaduct. Seven of the under-bridges (Nos 22, 23, 31, 32, 35, 38 and 39) had either stone or brick arches, stone piers and abutments, and four of the over-bridges (Nos 26, 29, 33 and 36) are also of stone. The remaining five under-bridges (Nos 24, 25, 27, 28 and 30) were of wrought iron and, together with the one cast-iron over-bridge (No 34), were supplied by Head Ashby & Co of Middlesbrough. The four-arch viaduct at Esk Valley (No 37) is of stone.

The NER embarked on a major bridge programme in 1908 along the Whitby & Pickering line. This was to include replacement of the small under-line bridges on the original line by new steel-rivet structures with timber waybeams supporting the lines of rails. On the deviation section, four of the wrought-iron bridges were also replaced or rebuilt, and the remaining one (No 30) strengthened. This involved replacing the bridge at Darnholm (No 28) with a single brick arch, while a new steel bridge at Goathland station (No 27) catered for three rather than two tracks. South of Goathland two river bridges (Nos 24 and 25) were rebuilt, partly using material from the replaced bridges 27 and 28.

As we have already seen, the 1930 and 1931 flooding resulted in the replacement of the three-arch stone bridge along the Esk Valley line near Glaisdale (No 82) with a steel girder bridge, and repair work to other bridges.

Signalling

Even the W&PR had a form of signalling with its white 'go on', red 'go slow' and blue 'stop' flags. Early signalling developed in Britain from the use of 'policemen' using hand signals to a system of fixed signals at stations linked to 'time-interval' working by which trains were not allowed to follow each other at less than a given frequency. Although little is known about the signalling arrangements immediately following the introduction of steam traction in 1847, by this date time-interval working was well established, and is likely to have been the basic system of train control.

The NER Locomotive Committee for 29 January 1858 records a number of additional signals required between Pickering and Whitby, including several Distant signals, a signalling concept only then coming into general adoption. By the 1860s there is reference in NER records to replacement of disc signals with semaphores, and it can be assumed that this policy would have covered the Malton and Esk Valley lines to Whitby. An 1875 plan of Levisham shows a double-armed 'station signal', apparently operated by a hand lever, and was no doubt typical of arrangements at other stations during the time-interval period.

The earliest signal cabin (the term 'box' developed in the 20th century) on the NYMR route appears to have been at Deviation Junction to control the junction between the new and old routes to Goathland, the latter by then truncated at Beck Hole. By 1874 the following were listed in the NER Appendix:

Above: **The NER Signal box at Rillington Junction, controlling the line to Pickering and Whitby.**
Alf Williamson Collection

Left: In 1959, after the long-closed Rillington Junction station was finally demolished, the NER signal box was replaced by a new one. Located at the west end of the station site, the box took over control of the adjoining level crossing allowing closure of the small gate box. 'B1' No 61289 passes with an up Scarborough express.
D. P. Leckonby

Rillington	Marishes Junction (not in use)
Pickering	Hungate Crossing
	Park Lane Junction (not in use)
	Pickering Bridge Crossing
	Pickering Limestone Quarry
	New Bridge Quarry
	Parkinson's Siding
Grosmont	Deviation Cabin
	Level Crossing
	Grosmont Junction
	Eskdale Siding
Whitby	Ford Crossing (thought to have been near Bog Hall)

Above: Black Bull level crossing, showing the small gate box. The crossing-keeper has been remarkably quick in restoring the crossing signal to danger as preserved 'K4' No 3442 ***The Great Marquess*** passes with the BBC filming special on 13 April 1964. *Gavin Morrison*

Right: An unusual feature of the layout at Mill Lane Junction and level crossing, just south of Pickering, was that up trains for the diverging Forge Valley route had to cross to the down line in order to access the junction. 'G5' No 67273 does just that on 13 May 1950 with a Forge Valley branch train to Scarborough. Note the G. T. Andrews Y&NM crossing-keeper's cabin on the right.
J. W. Armstrong Trust

Above: **High Mill signal box was just north of Pickering station. 'A8' No 69877 passes with a northbound Whitby train.** *J. W. Armstrong Trust*

Above right: **New Bridge signal box prior to the British Railways closure.** *Charles Allenby*

Right: **Levisham signal box.** *Nigel Trotter Collection*

Below right: **The closed signal box at Newton Dale in 1964, still remarkably intact despite having been out of use, even as a ground frame, for more than ten years.** *David Sutcliffe*

Proposals for Block Signal Stations were approved by the NER Locomotive Committee on 22 October 1874, heralding the introduction of the 'Absolute Block' system of signalling over the next two years, using needle telegraph instruments to ensure that only one train at a time was allowed into each block section. Thus 'space-interval' replaced 'time-interval'. Twelve new cottages were also built on the Whitby branch for signalmen and their families around this time. Probable examples are the NER-design cottages at Mill Lane and on the up side of the line at Farworth.

Access to the Whitby line was via a double-line junction immediately east of Rillington station. The NER signal box was replaced in 1959 by a new signal box at the west end of the old station site to control the adjacent level crossing, and this box was itself abolished upon automation of the level crossing in 1993. The next signal box was at Marishes Road, while the box at Black Bull on the Malton to Pickering road was reduced to gate box status prior to the First World War.

Pickering retained four signal boxes as block posts until closure in 1965, with the fifth, Hungate, having been converted to a gate box early in the 20th century. The southernmost, at Mill Lane, controlled the junctions with the Gilling and Forge Valley routes. Originally the branches had been double track from Mill Lane to Goslip Bridge on the Gilling line and Eastgate on the Forge Valley route, but both were singled back to Mill Lane early in the LNER period. An unusual arrangement introduced between Rillington and Mill Lane around the end of the Second World War was the decision to store wagons on the up running line, although a section remained in use as a long siding between Mill Lane and a private siding at Kirby, near Black Bull. During this period 'Staff and Ticket' working applied, with trains in both

Above: **Goathland Summit signal box in 1955. Note the signalmen's horticultural achievements.** *J. W. Armstrong Trust*

Right: **Goathland station signal box in August 1953. 'A8' No 69877 makes a rousing departure with a Whitby to Malton train.** *Kenneth Field, Rail Archive Stephenson*

Below right: **Deviation Junction signal cabin at Grosmont seen around 1900, while the box was still a block post. Note the member of staff, possibly an inspector judging by the bowler hat.** *G. W. J. Potter, John Minnis collection*

directions using the down line. The boxes at Bridge Street and High Mill latterly controlled working in the Pickering station area, with 'Permissive Block' permitted to facilitate station working. The most northerly of Pickering's boxes, New Bridge, controlled the single line to Levisham following the 1917 singling, when 'Electric Token Block' (ETB) working, with single-line 'Tyer's No 6' instruments, replaced 'Absolute Block' over this section.

Between Pickering and Grosmont there were three signal boxes remote from any station or proper road. Farworth, between New Bridge and Levisham, closed with the singling of the line in 1917. North of Levisham, Newton Dale signal box had a single crossover and a down siding. Since the First World War the box had only been open 'as required' and it was reduced to a ground frame in 1930, although not totally closed until 1952. For a time the structure was used as a fire watch post, but fell into disrepair over the years, finally being demolished in 1995 after it became unsafe. The next box, at Goathland Summit, faired slightly better, with two crossovers, a short down siding, and control of the NRCC siding at Ellerbeck via a ground frame. Locomotives assisting up trains could return down the hill from here, but many tended to detach at Goathland station where the gradient eased somewhat (an arrangement covered by instruction in the LNER Sectional Appendix). Goathland Summit box closed in 1964 and, being of timber construction, rapidly fell into disrepair and was dismantled in the early 1970s. As we have seen, Deviation signal box was converted to a ground frame in 1930, finally being taken out of use upon closure of the Beck Hole branch in 1951. In NER days a special coupling was kept here for use by banking engines to enable them to uncouple without stopping the train. The brick structure remained intact until demolished in the early preservation period to make way for the Grosmont motive power complex.

The box at Grosmont controlling the junction between the Rillington and Esk Valley routes was located on a restricted site in the apex of the two lines, necessitating a narrow tall brick base with an overhanging wooden operating cabin for the signalman.

There is something of a mystery surrounding the history of signal boxes between Grosmont and Sleights. The 1892 NER Appendix listed two boxes just to the north of Grosmont at Birtley Mines and Eskdale Siding, both shown as closed, but the small signal box at Eskdale Mines (note the different name), controlling siding facilities on the up side of the line, was shown as open in 1909. It seems to have seen little use after the First World War, however, and was no longer listed in the 1931 Working Timetable Appendix. Photographs taken shortly thereafter show the box becoming derelict, although as a structure it seems to have survived until 1947. A number of ground-frame-controlled sidings also existed on this section of line, remaining listed in the Working Timetable Appendix up to the Second World War.

There was one other intermediate box on the approach to Whitby at Hutton's Sidings, serving an iron foundry; in fact, the signal box was actually called Foundry Siding. It also came to serve the adjoining gasworks siding, but was still reduced to the status of a ground frame in 1930, having already been worked only 'as required' for many years. At Whitby the station layout was controlled by the distinctively tall Town box, with Bog Hall, just a short distance from the station, controlling the junction

Right: Grosmont Junction and its 1907 signal box are seen from a departing train on 1 September 1956. Compare with the picture on page 102. *H. C. Casserley*

Below left: The signal box diagram at Grosmont around the time of the closure of the Malton line in 1965. *John Hunt*

Below right: The signal cabin and crossing at the east end of Sleights station around 1905. *National Railway Museum*

Bottom right: 'J27' No 65883 passes Bog Hall signal box on 18 June 1951. *Alec Ford*

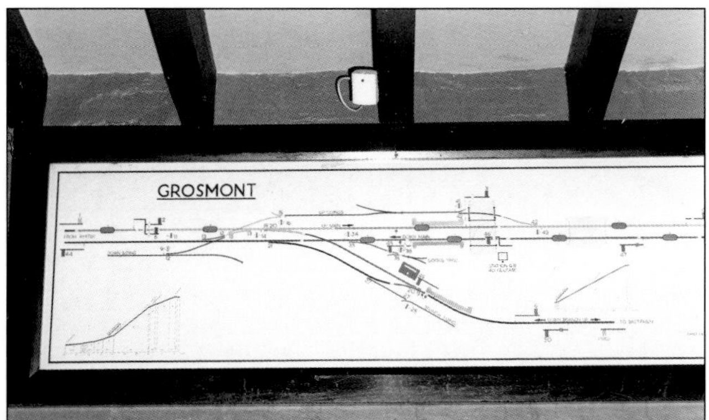

with the chord line to Prospect Hill. The wooden signal box at Prospect Hill Junction straddled the line up from Bog Hall.

By the end of the 19th century most signal boxes had been established using NER brick-built designs and equipment. NER wooden slotted-post lower-quadrant signals remained in place for many years, well into the BR period, although more modern upper-quadrants started to appear after they were adopted as the future standard by the LNER in 1926.

On the Esk Valley line ETB working applied between Battersby and Grosmont, with passing loops at Kildale, Castleton, Danby and Glaisdale, and at one time signal cabins were also listed at Commondale, Lealholm and Egton (although by 1908 the Working Timetable Appendix specifically stated that these were not block posts). Rationalisation took place in later years, with the loop at Kildale removed in 1956, and that at Danby in 1965. Since then signalling on the remaining route has been progressively reduced. The BR Grosmont signal box was closed upon singling of the line to Sleights in 1972, and a ground frame was installed to control movements between the Esk Valley line and the NYMR. Castleton loop and signal box were abolished in 1982, and the last remaining section of double track from Sleights to Whitby was singled in 1984, resulting in the closure of Sleights, Bog Hall and Whitby Town signal boxes. Finally, in 1989, Battersby and Glaisdale signal boxes were closed. This resulted from the introduction of 'No Signaller

Above: **The height of Whitby Town signal box was dictated by the need for the signalmen to see above the roof of the adjoining goods shed. Note the comparatively rare placement of two Home signal arms on the same post. Standard Class 3 2-6-2T No 82029 enters with the 16.10 service from Malton.** *Brian Rutherford*

Left: **This 1964 view shows Prospect Hill Junction signal box where the cord line from Bog Hall Junction joined the Middlesbrough to Scarborough route. The design of cabin was unusual, although not unique, as it straddles the Bog Hall route. A Metro-Cammell DMU heads for Scarborough.** *J. Clarke, Ian Allan Library*

Token Remote' working supervised by Nunthorpe signal box near Middlesbrough, a form of ETB signalling that enables train drivers to obtain the single-line key token from remotely located instruments (see also Chapter 9).

In the preservation era, the NYMR was able to take over the signal boxes at New Bridge, Levisham and Goathland, although the period out of use had taken its toll. Most of the signalling had to be installed afresh, particularly since much of the line was being converted from double to single track. One-train working applied south of Levisham for many years; however, 1986 saw the completion of track-circuiting and colour light signalling, with New Bridge signal box controlling all train operations in the Pickering area, a huge job for a largely volunteer workforce. In 1996 a new signal box was commissioned at the south end of Grosmont station to control the adjacent level crossing and station layout, now expanded to three platforms. Built to the traditional NER style of the 1870 era, the signal box incorporates original fittings from Whitby Town box and elsewhere, and is the largest signal box on the NYMR.

The line is signalled by ETB between Grosmont and Goathland using 'Tyer's No 6' tablet machines. On the two sections Goathland to Levisham and Levisham to New Bridge, however, the high cost of installing a signal cable over 14 route miles has delayed the extension of ETB operation. 'Staff & Ticket' working applies (with trains being offered and accepted verbally using a dedicated BT telephone line). Although not as flexible, the system is very safe and can handle the NYMR's standard train service pattern. NER slotted-post signals predominate at Levisham and Goathland, many retrieved from other parts of the North East. Signals at Grosmont are of late-LNER/BR upper-quadrant type with tubular or fabricated posts, while multiple-aspect colour lights predominate at New Bridge.

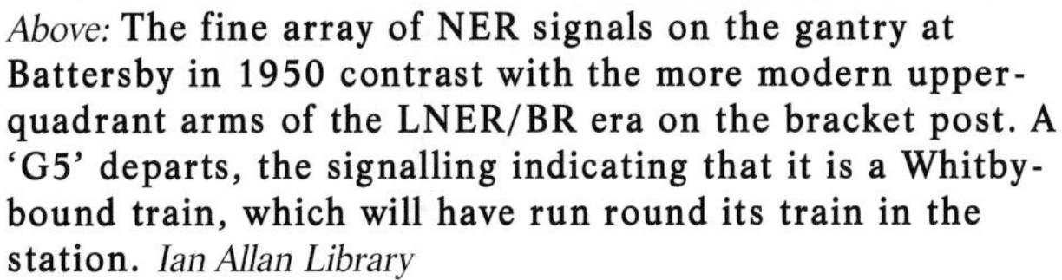

Above: The fine array of NER signals on the gantry at Battersby in 1950 contrast with the more modern upper-quadrant arms of the LNER/BR era on the bracket post. A 'G5' departs, the signalling indicating that it is a Whitby-bound train, which will have run round its train in the station. *Ian Allan Library*

Above right: This 1969 shot near Goathland shows NYMR signalling in the early days of preservation before public services began, indicating that the route into the station is set. *NYMR Archive*

Right: The signal frame in Goathland signal box, restored and in use on 14 February 1993. *NYMR Archive*

Below: The new signal box at Grosmont was commissioned by the NYMR in 1996. The 19th century Tunnel Inn, now the Station Tavern, is visible behind the box. *Author*

9

Return to Whitby

Right from the start of public services the NYMR had been talking to BR about through train operation from Whitby; remember that the opening special in 1973 had only been prevented from doing so by BR's industrial dispute. Over the years the occasional steam special had run to Whitby, and on 11 October 1987 the first through passenger train ran between Whitby and the NYMR, hauled by the National Railway Museum's 9F 2-10-0 No 92220 *Evening Star*. Over the following years several such trains ran from time to time, but they were always worked by BR staff when running on the Esk Valley line.

Privatisation radically changed the landscape of Britain's railways. The Railways Act (1993) abolished BR, and the network's track was put in the hands of a new infrastructure company, first Railtrack, then later Network Rail. Trains were run by private train operating companies (TOCs). Most passenger TOCs operated under franchises let by government, but the legislation also made provision for new operators to run trains under so called 'open access' rules. Any new operator would have to satisfy the government's regulatory authority, the Office of Rail Regulation (ORR), that they were 'a fit and proper person' to run a train service – so in theory the new structure might enable the NYMR to run to Whitby, literally under its own steam.

After privatisation, first Regional Railways North East then the 'charter' operator, the West Coast Railway Company (WCRC), were engaged by the NYMR to operate the occasional Whitby services. In 2003, however, these arrangements came to an abrupt halt when Network Rail declared the track between Sleights and Whitby too worn out to handle other than the lightweight 'Pacer' and 'Sprinter' diesel units that worked the Esk Valley local service between Middlesbrough and Whitby. It was possible to charter Christmas specials to Middlesbrough in 2003 and 2004, but for the time being Whitby was inaccessible.

Meanwhile, the government agency responsible for franchising rail services, the Strategic Rail Authority (SRA), was developing a strategy for little-used, mainly rural branch lines. Published in 2004, the Community Rail Development Strategy looked to see more regional and local responsibility for such services. The Esk Valley line was one of six routes selected to pilot the concept. There was already a Community Rail Partnership in place for the line, with the Esk Valley Railway Development Company (EVRDC) created to promote the route. Through the strenuous efforts of the local MP, Lawrie Quinn (a railwayman himself) and the EVRDC, Network Rail was persuaded to bring forward plans to renew the track into Whitby. This would allow loco-hauled train operation to recommence, including potentially a steam service for the NYMR.

The possibility of establishing a regular service to Whitby had been discussed by the NYMHRT and its members many times over the years. Although the town could be clearly seen from the

Top: On 5 May 2003 one of the shuttle trains run for the NYMR by the West Coast Railway Company waits to leave Whitby for Glaisdale, behind Standard Class 4 2-6-4T No 80135. *John Hunt*

Above: The first NYMR-operated train, a crew-training special worked by 'K1' No 62005, is seen after arrival at Whitby on 13 February 2007. From left to right are driver John Fletcher, guard Marj Hamilton, driver Stuart Whitter, Operations Manager Norman Hugill, guard John Alexander, guard Alastair Dalgleish, Footplate Standards Manager Chris Cubitt, driver Dave Gatland, and the author. *NYMR*

Left: **The Intermediate Key Token Instrument installed at Grosmont for the movement of trains to and from the Esk Valley line.** *Author*

Below left: **The special train run to celebrate the start of NYMR train operations on the Esk Valley Line is seen after arrival at Whitby on 3 April 2007 headed by 'K1' No 62005.** *Lesley Benham*

moors above Grosmont, frustratingly the NYMR's tracks finished 6 ½ miles short. As a tourist railway the chance to tap into the holiday market in Whitby seemed to make sense, but there were also very real concerns about the risks of the railway over-reaching itself. Now, with the SRA's strategy and a commitment given on the track renewals, a new impetus was provided.

The Network Rail track renewal work took place in February 2005, just in time to allow the running of a special train from Whitby through to Pickering on 6 March to commemorate the 40th anniversary of closure. The NELPG's 'K1' No 62005 hauled the train, recalling its operation on the last-day special in 1965, and one of the guests was Norman Antlett, who had been a fireman on that train. This acted as a curtain-raiser for more extensive operations. Regular through-train operation between the NYMR and Network Rail at Grosmont was impracticable due to limitations with the signalling arrangements. Instead, during the spring and summer, a limited number of steam trains were operated between Whitby and Glaisdale, with passengers changing to and from other NYMR trains at Grosmont. Locomotives and rolling stock were provided by the NYMR (locomotives were actually hired from the NELPG and Ian Riley), with WCRC again as train operator.

Research carried out among passengers and visitors during the summer showed that there was a definite market for steam trains between the NYMR and Whitby. Figures for the 22 days were encouraging, with an income of £50,000. A business case was developed, and at an Extraordinary General Meeting on 17 September 2005, following a members' ballot, the decision was made to pursue an application for an NYMR Passenger Train Licence. This was a big step that, if successful, would give the NYMR the ability to run trains between Whitby and Battersby in its own right.

Before any of this could happen, however, there were many arrangements to put in place. The granting of a train operator's Passenger Licence by the ORR would happen only when the ORR was satisfied that the NYMR had the competence to run trains safely and reliably, and could comply with a number of other licence obligations. The most significant were:

- Negotiation of contracts with Network Rail for track access;
- Negotiation with Northern Rail (the operator of Esk Valley Line services, and manager the stations) for station access;
- Approval by the SRA (later Department for Transport) of various 'consumer protection' arrangements covering third-party insurance, care of disabled passengers, complaints handling, and through ticketing with other operators;
- Acceptance by the ORR through HM Railway Inspectorate (HMRI) of a Railway Safety Case demonstrating that the NYMR could operate safely on Network Rail (HMRI would also wish Network Rail to be satisfied with the safety case).

Finally, since it was not possible for the 'heritage' rolling stock used by the NYMR to comply with modern-day standards, some exemptions would be needed. Many of these were no different from any operator of steam-hauled trains on Network Rail, but there was a particular issue with 'on-train monitoring and recording' equipment (OTMR). Equivalent to an aircraft's 'black box', all traction units were now required to have these fitted, including steam engines, but this could add up to £25,000 for every NYMR locomotive working over Network Rail. Such a cost would seriously damage the Whitby running business case, and the NYMR sought, and received, from the Rail Safety & Standards Board (RSSB) a 'derogation' from OTMR for trains operating solely between Battersby, Grosmont and Whitby.

The process took time, with most of 2006 spent in negotiations and preparation of all the documentation required. There was a great deal of goodwill shown towards the NYMR by all the parties involved, and it is pleasing to pay tribute especially to Network Rail, Northern Rail, the ORR, HMRI, the Department for Transport and the RSSB, to name but a few. The positive and constructive approach adopted by all was vital to success of the Whitby development. Meanwhile a further series of Whitby to Glaisdale shuttle trains had run, and it had proved possible to run the first train in the morning through between Pickering and Whitby, and back again in the evening. This time 50 days were operated and 15,000 passengers made the journey.

Gradually the pieces of the jigsaw fell into place, with a major milestone reached on 13 December 2006 when the NYMR's safety case for operation between Battersby and Whitby was accepted by HMRI. The aim was to start NYMR operations at Easter 2007. Before then, sufficient footplate crews and guards needed training, and route-learning trains were planned to run from Grosmont to Whitby and Battersby in February. This required the track access agreement with Network Rail to be in force (it first had to be approved by the ORR), and the issue of the NYMR's licence, and there was another deadline as the

Above: **The first public passenger services to Whitby operated by the NYMR ran on Good Friday, 6 April 2007. Driver Stuart Whitter checks Standard Class 4 4-6-0 No 75029 ready for departure from Grosmont on to the Esk Valley line with the first train, the 08.45 Pickering to Whitby.** *Author*

Right: **Steam trains pass at Glaisdale for the first time in more than 40 years. The NYMR's licence allows trains to be operated between Whitby and Battersby. During a 'Steam Gala' weekend on Sunday 30 September 2007, 'B1' No 4-6-0 No 61264, with a train from Battersby, waits to cross with 'K4' 2-6-0 No 61994 *The Great Marquess* on the 14.25 Whitby to Battersby.** *Author*

NYMR had to submit its timetable 'bid' for 2008 to Network Rail on 18 January. Without the track access agreement, this would have no contractual value. The ORR approval came through, allowing the contract with Network Rail to be signed by the author (as NYMR General Manager) in the nick of time on 17 January 2007. The NYMR's licence was issued the same day.

History was made on Tuesday 13 February 2007 when 'K1' No 62005 headed the first NYMR route-learning train from Grosmont to Whitby and Battersby. Driving under the instruction of inspector Chris Cubitt were John Fletcher, Dave Gatland and Stuart Whitter, the first volunteer drivers authorised to drive on the national railway network.

There was one other critical requirement before the NYMR's timetabled service to Whitby could begin. The market research had indicated very clearly that passengers wanted through services without the need to change trains at Grosmont. To understand why through train operation presented a problem, a brief description of the signalling on the Esk Valley line is needed. The single-track branch is operated by the 'No Signaller Token Remote' system, a form of ETB. The key tokens are contained in instruments at the ends of each single-line section, and drivers obtain authority to remotely release a key token by telephone from the supervising signal box at Nunthorpe near Middlesbrough. Grosmont is situated within the Glaisdale to Whitby block section, with the connection to the NYMR controlled by a ground frame unlocked and locked by the key token, thus ensuring it is always present as the driver's authority for any train proceeding on or off the Esk Valley line.

When installed in 1972 the connection was intended to be used only for the occasional stock transfer, and on each such occasion a token had to be brought from and returned to the token instrument at Glaisdale by road, some 3½ miles away. This was clearly not a practical procedure for the daily passenger train movements now envisaged by the NYMR. The solution was to install an 'Intermediate Key Token Instrument' into Network Rail's signalling system at Grosmont. A plan was agreed between the two companies; the NYMR would provide the key token instrument (such equipment was now scarce) and Network Rail would install it. This collaborative approach kept the cost to a minimum and, with the additional help of a European Regional Development Fund grant, the NYMR was able to fund the work. With amended electrical circuitry and additional power supplies, the Network Rail work was quite complex, but was completed on schedule and to budget in March 2007. A number of related changes to the NYMR's internal signalling were carried out by the railway's largely volunteer signalling team.

Just before Easter, on Tuesday 3 April 2007, 'K1' No 62005 hauled the first passenger train to Whitby under NYMR's operator's licence. After a short ceremony, including a speech by the Lord Lieutenant for North Yorkshire (Lord Crathorne, who proudly announced that his grandfather had been at the opening of the Stockton & Darlington Railway), the 11.00 to Pickering departed from Whitby behind the NYMR's Standard Class 4 4-6-0 No 75029, certified to run on Network Rail the previous day. That year saw around 40,000 passengers use the Whitby service, helping to lift NYMR passenger numbers to a record 321,986. The Whitby to Pickering Railway was back in business.

10

Looking Forward

So what does the future hold for George Stephenson's old Whitby & Pickering Railway? One thing is certain: whatever the crystal ball may suggest, the reality is bound to be different. Today's North Yorkshire Moors Railway has come a long way in 35 years, and is established as both a major tourist attraction in the North of England, and a significant economic generator in a region with limited industry and employment.

Over the years the question has often been asked, 'Is the NYMR going to extend south of Pickering and reopen the line back to Rillington?' With trains now running again to Whitby is this the next step? Over recent years several agencies have expressed an interest in recreating a southern link to the national rail network, including the Association of Community Rail Partnerships and Network Rail. Indeed, in 2000 North Yorkshire County Council commissioned a study that concluded that a line to Pickering could be re-laid for approximately £27m.

So will it happen, what would the implications be for the NYMR, and what stance should the railway take? Such a sum, although quite cheap for a new railway, is way beyond the means of the NYMR. A connection built for purely commercial, rather than heritage, purposes, would surely lead to demands for a modern train service continuing north from Pickering through to Whitby. What would this mean for the NYMR's essential

Shades of the 1950s created by 'B1' 4-6-0 No 61264 departing from Levisham with the 12.20 Pickering to Whitby train on 25 August 2007. *Author*

LNER Heritage: Gresley 'A4' Pacifics raise steam at Grosmont MPD on 4 April 2008 during NYMR's LNER Festival. Home-based No 60007 *Sir Nigel Gresley* is joined by visiting classmates No 60009 *Union of South Africa* and No 60019 *Bittern. Author*

heritage character? No doubt the modern and the old could live side by side – they already do at the northern end of the line – but the nature of the railway would undoubtedly change; for starters, a line speed of 25mph would hardly be acceptable.

The NYMR's current position is that, while it would co-operate with an appropriate agency wanting to establish a southern rail link to Pickering, the railway will not initiate such a proposal. The essential character of the NYMR must also be protected in any development. However, new rural railways built for purely commercial or economic reasons do not have a good track record in England (there have been none since the 1920s), and it seems unlikely that the implications of a southern link will need to be considered for some time to come.

There are, however, many other challenges ahead. As is the way with railways, track must be relayed, signalling renewed and bridges rebuilt, while the cost of keeping elderly locomotives and rolling stock serviceable rises inexorably. In the near future it is hoped to finally restore Pickering station to its original condition with reconstruction of the G. T. Andrews roof, as part of a bid for Heritage Lottery Funding to complete the development of the station as the principal gateway to the railway. If the NYMR is to fulfil this potential, the creation of additional car parking space near Pickering station is a critical priority for early attention.

Looking further ahead, one of the biggest challenges is how to increase line capacity, a vital question if traffic is to grow in the long term. Currently, running times over the 9-mile central section between Levisham to Goathland limit train frequencies to hourly. While fine for much of the year, in high summer and on some busier weekends this is already barely adequate. But the key to any capacity improvements is first to tackle the current signalling arrangements. For many years the railway has wanted to extend ETB signalling over the two block sections from Goathland to Levisham and Levisham to New Bridge. The high cost of installing a signal cable over the14 route-miles involved has always proved difficult to justify, with so many other demands on limited capital funds. But advances in signalling technology mean it is now possible for electronic messages to be passed securely over the standard telephone network without the risk of corruption, clearly an essential requirement where safety-critical communications are involved. This much cheaper solution to the signalling problem looks to be the way forward.

With block signalling in place, a major constraint will be removed, but of course this is only one element of the capacity problem. The limitations of the long stretch of single line between Levisham and Goathland still need to be tackled. An extended loop running from Goathland a few miles south to a remotely signalled double-to-single-line connection would be one option. Remote signalling would also be needed for another prime contender, a loop probably located near Newton Dale Halt. Restoration of double track over the whole route section may, however, offer a more straight forward solution. A couple of bridges renewed as single-line structures during the preservation era would need attention, but further signalling work should be minimal and maximum flexibility delivered. None of these options will come cheap, but the most cost-effective of the three must surely hold the key to future growth.

In due course some infrastructure developments may also be needed to make the most of the Whitby expansion. More flexible working at Grosmont will depend on the final phase of re-signalling to better control the north-end layout. The possibility of some changes at Whitby to simplify locomotive run-round would also be desirable, but this is Network Rail infrastructure, of course, and it remains to be seen what is both practicable and affordable.

Away from train operations, at Grosmont it is planned to establish a museum on the Bellwood Site (named in memory of the late locomotive engineer John Bellwood, who played a vital role in the railway's early days), where railway vehicles can be displayed awaiting their turn in the overhaul and restoration programme. Given the Grosmont area's rich industrial archaeology, there is more to be told about this story. Focused on the Bellwood development, is there scope to make more of the popular heritage trail footpath via Beck Hole up the old incline to Goathland, possibly with a more active railway element? More mundane, but just as important, Grosmont is also the likely location for the NYMR's first carriage stabling shed, at last giving some much-needed protection from the North Yorkshire elements.

For the foreseeable future steam locomotion can be expected to remain predominant, although heritage diesel traction also now has a definite part to play. Locomotives from all the former 'Big Four' companies have their home base at Grosmont and the ability to portray such variety in motive power is an important element in the appeal of the NYMR to visitors. But the railway is also very proud of its NER and LNER heritage. With 'A4' Pacific No 60007 *Sir Nigel Gresley*, the recently restored North Eastern 'Q6' No 63395 and other ex-LNER locomotives firmly based on the railway, the NYMR is keen to develop this connection, and there are plans to bring other LNER locomotives into the fold at Grosmont. To complement the locomotives, the NYMR's associate body, the LNER Coach Association, continues its work to restore a complete train of LNER vehicles with sufficient seating capacity to meet the heaviest traffic demands.

But does the railway have yet more to offer? With closure of the main rail route to the south in 1965, Whitby feared a slump in its holiday market. In the event the huge growth in car transport very quickly made up for the loss of the railway, and today the town is one of the country's fastest-growing resorts. But nearly half a century on there have been other changes as well. With environmental considerations now to the fore, congestion on North Yorkshire's limited road network and in her picturesque towns and villages threatens the very attractions that visitors come to see. For much of the summer, parking is a major headache, and the drive along the scenic A169 moorland road is often marred by nose-to-tail traffic.

If the railway's own car parking problem can be solved here surely is a major opportunity for the NYMR, as 'Park & Ride' gateway to North Yorkshire's moors and coastline. Conveying visitors onto the moors was a vital element in the 1973 reopening, and today the railway already keeps several hundred cars a day off the roads in the Moors National Park during spring and summer. Now those seeking a leisurely day at the coast can also go by train, while the Whitby holidaymaker has the ideal means to explore the scenery of the National Park or the market town attractions of Pickering. In this way two aims are met. The railway remains true to its roots as a living museum, here to engage, educate and entertain future generations about the steam railway of the past. But it will also be meeting a real transport need, which, after all, is what it was first built to do more than 170 years ago.

Back to where it all began: 'K4' No 61994 *The Great Marquess* heads away from Whitby with the 11.00 service to Battersby on 30 September 2007. The train is about to pass the remains of the W&PR Weigh House just visible beyond the building to the left of the line. *Author*

Bibliography

Bairstow, Martin *Railways around Whitby*, Volume 1 (Amadeus Press, 1988/89)
Railways around Whitby Volume 2 (Amadeus Press, 1996)

Beaumont, Robert *The Railway King* (Headline Book Publishing, 2002)

Belcher, Henry *The Scenery of the Whitby and Pickering Railway* (1836, re-printed by E. P. Publishing, 1976)

Blakemore, Michael *LNER in Transition* (Pendragon, 2004)
Railways of the North York Moors (Atlantic Publishers, 2001)

Bolger, Paul *BR Steam Motive Power Depots* (Ian Allan, 1984)

Brown, Alfred R. *Fair North Riding* (Country Life Ltd, 1952)

Browne, H. B. *Chapters of Whitby History, 1823-1946: the story of Whitby Literary and Philosophical Society and of Whitby Museum* (A. Brown & Sons, 1946)

Crump, Norman *By Rail to Victory*' (LNER, 1946)

Fawcett, Bill *A History of North Eastern Railway Architecture*, Volume 1 'The Pioneers' (North Eastern Railway Association, 2001)
A History of North Eastern Railway Architecture, Volume 2 'A Mature Art' (North Eastern Railway Association, 2003)

'General Appendix to the Rules & Regulations and Working Time Tables with Sectional Appendix for the North Eastern Area' (LNER)

Hall, Stanley *The History & Development of Railway Signalling in the British Isles*, Volume 1 'Broad Survey' (Friends of the National Railway Museum, 2000)

Helm, John W. E. 'The bombing of Britain's Railways: 1914-18' (*Back Track* magazine, Volume 20, No 9)

Hughes, Geoffrey *LNER* (Book Club Associates/Ian Allan, 1987)

Hunt, John *The North Yorkshire Moors Railway: A Past & Present Companion* (Past & Present Publishing, 2001)
The North Yorkshire Moors Railway: A Past & Present Companion, Volume 2 (Past & Present Publishing, 2004)

Hoole, Ken *A Regional History of the Railways of Great Britain* (3rd ed) (David & Charles, 1974)
An Illustrated History of NER Locomotives (Haynes Publishing (OPC), 1988)
North-Eastern Branch Line Termini (Haynes Publishing (OPC), 1985)
North Eastern Locomotive Sheds (David & Charles, 1972)
Railways in Cleveland (The Dalesman, 1971)

Howat, Patrick *The Railways of Ryedale* (Amadeus Press, 2004)

Jenkinson, David and Lane, Barry C. *British Railcars 1900-1950* (Atlantic Publishers, 1996)

Joy, David *Whitby & Pickering Railway* (The Dalesman, 1969)

Line Diagrams of the North Eastern Railway (North Eastern Railway Association, 2004)

Locoshed Allocations (various) (Ian Allan)

McRae, Andrew 'Camping Coaches on Britain's Railways' (*Back Track* magazine, Volume 8, Nos 2 and 4, Pendragon Publishing, 1994)

Ludlam, A. J. 'Steam Days at Whitby' (*Steam Days* magazine, September 2007, Redgauntlet Publications)

Minnis, John 'G. W. J. Potter's Whitby & Pickering Railway' (*Back Track* magazine, Volume 13, No 8, Pendragon Publishing, 1999)

Modern Railways/ Trains Illustrated magazines (Ian Allan Publishing)

Moorsline, the journal of the North Yorkshire Moors Railway Preservation Society and The North York Moors Historical Railway Trust (1969-2008)

'Mountain Railway Experiments at Goathland near Whitby, 21-22 June 1872' (Manning Wardle, 1872)

Mullay, A. J. *Railways for the People* (Pendragon, 2006)

Naylor, Tammy 'Industry in the Murk Esk Valley' (paper, 2005)

North Eastern Record, Volume 1 (Historical Model Railway Society, 1988); Volume 2 (Historical Model Railway Society, 1997); Volume 3 (Historical Model Railway Society, 2000)

North Yorkshire Moors Railway Stock Book, 6th Edition (complied by David Idle)

The Oxford Companion to British Railway History (edited by Jack Simmons & Gordon Biddle, Oxford University Press, 1996)

Servicing the North Eastern Railway's Locomotives (edited by John G. Teasdale, North Eastern Railway Association, 2007)

Stirling, David *The History & Development of Railway Signalling in the British Isles*, Volume 2 'The Telegraph & The Absolute Block, Single Line Operation' (Friends of the National Railway Museum, 2002)

Potter, G. W. J. *A History of the Whitby and Pickering Railway* (1906, reprinted by SR Publishers, 1969)

The Railway Magazine (Tothill Press)

Reussner, Graham 'North Yorkshire Moors Railway Conservation Management Plan' (NYMR, 2007)

Rutherford, Michael J. 'Railways around Whitby' (*Back Track* magazine, Volume 20, No 1, Pendragon Publishing, 2006)

'Sectional Appendix to the Working Timetable & Book of Rules & Regulations, Northern Area' (British Railways, Eastern Region)

Timetables (Public and Working) (NER, LNER, British Railways (NER), Bradshaw, National Rail)

Thompson, Alan R. and Groundwater, Ken *British Railways Past and Present No 14: Cleveland & North Yorkshire* (Part 2) (Silver Link Publishing, 1992)

Wood, P. 'Cruises of The Northern Belle' (*The Gresley Observer*, journal of The Gresley Society, No 142)

White, Andrew *An Early Railway Building: The Weighing Machine House, Whitby* (Yorkshire Archaeological Society)

Whitehouse, Patrick and Thomas, David St John *LNER 150* (Guild Publishing/David & Charles, 1989)

Yeadon, W. B. *Yeadon's Register of LNER Locomotives* (various) (Challenger Publications)

Original documents in the National Archives at Kew, and the National Railway Museum, York

Appendix 1

Key Dates

Event	Date
Whitby & Pickering Railway	
First meeting to discuss a railway to Whitby	02.03.1831
Consideration of Storey survey – subscription started	06.05.1831
George Stephenson survey report produced	05.07.1832
Meeting to consider and accept Stephenson report recommending a railway from Whitby to Pickering	12.09.1832
Whitby & Pickering Railway Bill receives Royal Assent	06.05.1833
First meeting of W&PR directors	30.05.1833
First W&PR coach *Premier* runs for directors	15.05.1835
W&PR services commence from Whitby to Grosmont	08.06.1835
Railway opens throughout between Whitby and Pickering	26.05.1836
Takeover by York & North Midland Railway receives Royal Assent	30.06.1845
York & North Midland Railway	
First Y&NM steam train to Pickering (possibly freight)	07.07.1845
Board of Trade Inspector approves opening from Pickering to Levisham for steam (one line only)	01.09.1846
First steam locomotive enters Whitby	04.06.1847
Rebuilt railway reopened throughout from Rillington to Pickering – locomotive-hauled public services begin	01.07.1847
Amalgamation to create North Eastern Railway receives Royal Assent	31.07.1854
North Eastern Railway	
Takeover of North Yorkshire & Cleveland Railway	01.01.1859
Goathland deviation and Castleton-Grosmont lines receive Royal Assent	11.07.1861
Deviation route opened and Goathland incline abandoned	01.07.1865
NY&C route completed with opening from Castleton to Grosmont	02.10.1865
Gilling to Pickering branch opened	01.04.1875
Seamer to Pickering (Forge Valley) branch opened	01.04.1882
Whitby, Redcar & Middlesbrough Union Railway opened to Whitby	03.12.1883
Scarborough & Whitby Railway opened	16.07.1885
Beck Hole 'auto-car' summer passenger service begins	01.07.1908
Beck Hole 'auto-car' service suspended upon outbreak of First World War	21.09.1914
Line between Pickering (New Bridge) and Levisham singled	31.12.1916
London & North Eastern Railway	
'Grouping' merges NER into LNER	01.01.1923
Plans to re-double line between New Bridge and Levisham abandoned	29.07.1926
Sentinel railcar allocated to Pickering for Forge Valley (No 237 *Rodney*)	23.03.1928
Flooding destroys bridge 82 (Glaisdale) and damages others	23.07.1930
Rillington (and other stations between York and Scarborough) closed	20.09.1930
First Sentinel railcar allocated to Whitby	31.12.1931

Event	Date
Introduction of Camping Coaches to North Yorkshire Moors and Whitby	Summer 1933
Emergency timetable introduced following outbreak of Second World War	02.10.1939
British Railways	
British Railways takes over from LNER upon Nationalisation	01.01.1948
Pickering to Seamer (Forge Valley) passenger service withdrawn (Pickering-Thornton Dale Quarry remains open for freight)	03.01.1950
Beck Hole branch closed (last train date)	18.09.1951
Gilling to Pickering passenger service withdrawn (closed Helmsley to Pickering)	31.01.1953
Whitby to Stockton via Picton passenger service withdrawn	14.06.1954
Whitby to Loftus line closed	03.05.1958
DMU operation introduced, Scarborough-Whitby-Middlesbrough	03.05.1958
Whitby shed closed	06.04.1959
Whitby West Cliff closed	12.06.1961
Pickering to Thornton Dale Quarry line closed	21.01.1963
Malton-Whitby passenger service withdrawn (line closed Pickering-Grosmont)	06.03.1965
Malton shed closed	13.04.1963
Scarborough (Gallows Close) to Whitby line closed	06.03.1965
Rillington to Pickering (New Bridge) line closed	01.07.1966
North Yorkshire Moors Railway	
First meeting to discuss preservation	03.06.1967
North Yorkshire Moors Railway Preservation Society inaugural meeting	18.11.1967
Arrival of first rail vehicle (railbus No W79978)	09.08.1968
First rail movement from Pickering to Grosmont (0-4-0ST *Mirvale*)	02.02.1969
Last British Rail scrap removal train departs via Rillington	02.11.1969
First NYMR Members' Day passenger trains	28.03.1970
First steam passenger train Grosmont to Pickering (for NRCC)	23.07.1971
North York Moors Historical Railway Trust incorporated	31.12.1971
Commencement of NYMR public services (Grosmont to Pickering)	22.04.1973
Official NYMR opening by HRH Duchess of Kent	01.05.1973
Public services extended into Pickering station	24.05.1975
First through train from Whitby to Pickering in preservation era	11.10.1987
40th anniversary of closure, through train Whitby to Pickering	06.03.2005
NYMR approves extension of operations to Whitby and the Esk Valley line	17.09.2005
Railway Safety Case accepted for NYMR Esk Valley line operation	13.12.2006
NYMR train operator's Passenger Licence issued and access contract with Network Rail signed	17.01.2007
First NYMR train on Network Rail (route-learning special)	13.02.2007
Commencement of NYMR passenger operations to Whitby	03.04.2007

Appendix 2

Whitby & Pickering Railway Half Year Traffic Returns 1841-45

	Passengers			Horses		Carriages		Merchandise	
	1st Class No	2nd Class No	Income (£/s/d)	No	Income (£/s/d)	No	Income (£/s/d)	Income (£/s/d)	**Total Income** (£/s/d)
1841 Jan-Jun	2716	3581	669- 0- 4	N/A	N/A	N/A	N/A	1833- 0- 0	N/A
Jul-Dec	2753	5017	771- 5- 6	0	0	22	23- 2- 0	N/A	N/A
1842 Jan-Jun	2264	3407	337-11- 0	2	1- 0- 0	17	17- 0- 0	N/A	N/A
Jul-Dec	3084	4036	762-15- 7	5	2-10- 0	37	38-17- 0	1466- 8- 1	2270-10- 8
1843 Jan-Jun	2321	2014	503- 4-11	1	10- 0	5	5- 1- 0	979- 5- 6	1488- 1- 5
Jul-Dec	3370	5855	711- 1- 1	12	6- 0- 0	27	27- 0- 0	1182-13- 3	1926-12- 4
1844 Jan-Jun	2525	3545	481- 1- 5	0	0	8	4- 0- 0	996-10- 3	1481-11- 8
Jul-Dec	4584	6213	884-10- 1	8	4- 0- 0	29	29- 0- 0	1043- 9- 9	1960-19-10
1845 Jan-Jul	2324	3901	468-12- 0	1	10- 0	12	12- 0- 0	1453- 0-11	1934- 2-11
	25941	37569	5589-1-11	29	N/A	157	N/A	N/A	N/A

Traffic figures analysis: July – December 1843

	Passenger Traffic					Goods				
	Passengers	Passenger Miles	Fare/mile	Ave Speed	Income (£/s/d)	Traffic	Trains/ Day	Ave Speed	Tons carried	Income (£/s/d)
1st Class	3370	46586	2d (inside) 1½d(outside)	9mph	451-18- 7	Stone	5	3mph	9509	330-12- 7
						Coal	5	3mph	1209	195- 8- 7
2nd Class	5855	68387	1d	7mph	259- 2- 6	Limestone	1	3mph	693	59-19- 8
	No	Miles	Fare/journey			Oak	1	3mph	287	118- 8- 4
Horses	12	288	10s		6- 0- 0	Fir	5	3mph	133	45- 1- 6
Carriages	27	648	£1		27- 0- 0	Fish	5	5mph	714	320- 6- 3
						Commercial	1	3mph	61	20- 2- 5
						Groceries	5	4mph	125	92-13-11
						TOTAL				1182-13- 3

Note: Some small traffic flows may not have been reported (eg sheep)
Source: PRO RAIL 1053/5

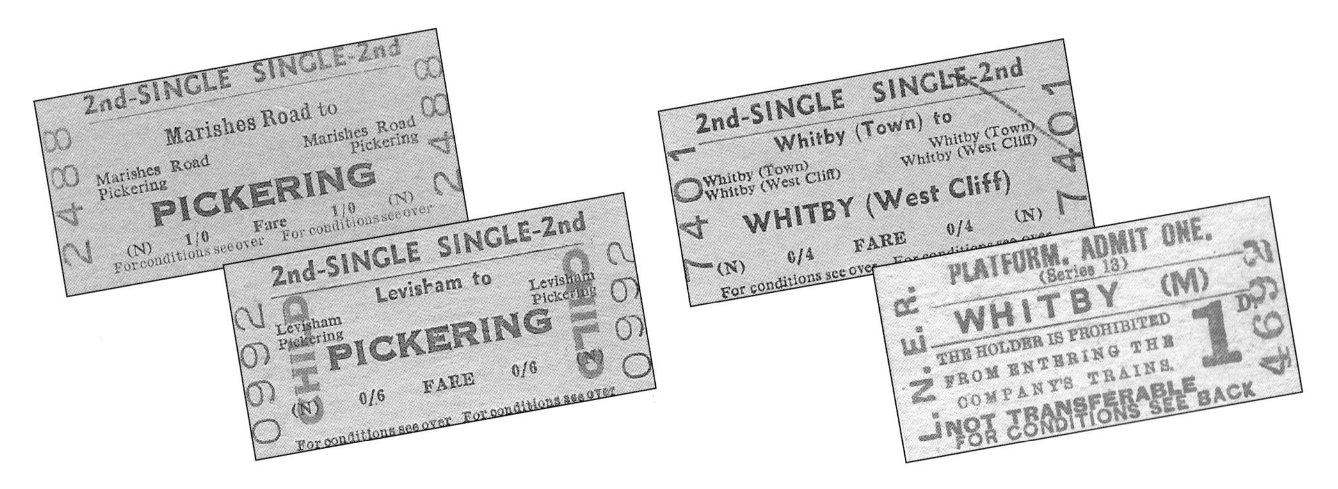

Appendix 3

NER/LNER Traffic Returns
(representative years 1902-34)

	Passenger & Parcels				Goods (Note ii)		
	Passengers	Parcels Forwarded	Parcels Received	Passenger Debit (£)	Tonnage Forwarded	Tonnage Received	Goods Debit (£)
Marishes Road							
1902	3563	113	157	157	367	1041	47
1907	2941	110	195	134	530	1148	84
1912	2560	153	275	141	474	1416	95
1917	2914	Note i		270	580	633	147
1922	3089	269	103	404	519	1055	910
1926	1763	295	132	247	400	1610	656
1930	1483	208	102	126	1323	786	515
1934	1389	105	151	96	1873	290	293
Pickering							
1902	45068	13118	12984	4692	5635	7903	2536
1907	45662	11476	15733	4815	9813	10519	3791
1912	46286	11362	16548	5018	7574	12455	4197
1917	30468	Note i		5293	10737	5741	4518
1922	40785	9066	17758	9017	17908	10311	10144
1926	29051	8772	18321	6396	41233	11355	13760
1930	18474	8458	20658	4393	16256	11494	7707
1934	16727	7577	19874	4018	10317	8460	5456
Levisham							
1902	5922	390	353	377	202	250	53
1907	6389	505	481	464	832	275	99
1912	6932	402	577	460	432	170	151
1917	4451	Note i		414	718	111	343
1922	5049	468	332	612	158	293	178
1926	4607	102	1218	369	102	1218	40
1930	3525	242	238	285	186	165	41
1934	4852	129	254	266	79	540	63
Goathland							
1902	10254	816	1810	782	6997	2248	1110
1907	11950	1456	2732	991	7387	765	909
1912	14443	1072	2971	1206	5751	1936	970
1917	10641	Note i		1491	3832	576	848
1922	15700	892	2102	2315	4518	1723	1196
1926	12543	704	2504	1570	6391	7873	1777
1930	10395	769	2846	1262	6564	1773	2399
1934	11745	614	2784	1135	4045	1330	1314

	Passenger & Parcels				Goods (Note ii)		
	Passengers	Parcels Forwarded	Parcels Received	Passenger Debit (£)	Tonnage Forwarded	Tonnage Received	Goods Debit (£)
Grosmont							
1902	21988	1742	1568	1089	42947	2147	6003
1907	24679	2106	2074	1172	44970	1582	6751
1912	24373	1659	2203	1150	47654	1308	6626
1917	19038	Note i		1576	20159	840	3842
1922	25606	1232	1861	2240	62573	1011	17236
1926	21640	1432	2323	1692	83149	2961	16369
1930	20204	1260	1981	1275	51007	1894	9127
1934	26452	947	2136	1523	Goods reported with Whitby		
Sleights							
1902	32848	1239	1369	1120	458	1798	211
1907	45616	1993	2464	1496	130	2351	304
1912	53035	2087	3109	1833	251	2125	342
1917	34694	Note i		2107	259	1180	163
1922	37996	1730	2077	2932	259	2119	454
1926	21898	1368	2250	1888	121	8114	838
1930	16039	1211	2650	1203	250	3607	333
1934	23277	1532	3625	1351	139	5445	522
Ruswarp							
1902	32191	636	683	543	1247	4314	1269
1907	36312	909	927	606	1764	4198	1323
1912	43829	1171	1376	842	1177	3444	953
1917	25755	Note i		1017	2025	3034	1242
1922	37860	725	719	1397	1906	7189	3017
1926	21188	810	1172	980	2328	7618	2298
1930	11874	691	1099	565	983	5651	2063
1934	17794	580	1186	568	870	5054	2370
Whitby Town							
1902	127253	18054	31065	13996	7847	15801	6004
1907	143507	24052	41023	11823	7248	13743	5535
1912	149272	25699	48026	15099	6827	15662	5950
1917	121115	Note i		15009	4977	8041	3513
1922	124441	18622	45877	26167	5870	14917	10505
1926	87311	20816	48763	20029	4207	23419	7686
1930	65141	18428	53630	15243	5026	17966	7051
1934	65628	17675	51780	13756	25355	12290	9290
Whitby West Cliff							
1902	Not reported				Not reported		
1907	67943	1620	1306	3267	181	1294	102
1912	70115	1781	862	3275	231	1034	105
1917	42500	Note i		2872	886	1085	425
1922	66512	1144	1075	6170	305	3874	412
1926	34230	1052	1257	3647	71	4698	496
1930	19517	1020	2040	2206	153	7842	518
1934	19971	1311	4241	2143	78	13484	588

	Passenger & Parcels				Goods (Note ii)		
	Passengers	Parcels Forwarded	Parcels Received	Passenger Debit (£)	Tonnage Forwarded	Tonnage Received	Goods Debit (£)
Glaisdale							
1902	11792	812	1228	645	2187	1252	435
1907	12581	1200	1742	651	606	1028	184
1912	12245	1500	1681	638	841	1434	271
1917	9746	Note i		843	2522	791	162
1922	14257	1086	1383	1321	14074	1287	13422
1926	11608	1099	1521	983	19429	883	17246
1930	7466	1085	1575	692	940	812	405
1934	7613	681	1080	657	7793	857	4641
Castleton							
1902	12802	2130	2215	912	15889	2730	2549
1907	11504	2923	3065	900	15272	2485	2486
1912	10902	2329	3060	867	16461	2330	2531
1917	9437	Note i		1126	23044	1272	2246
1922	11284	1448	2317	1619	7889	1661	2611
1926	7185	1932	1814	1077	7721	2156	3122
1930	4765	1570	2325	642	10784	9553	3603
1934	5290	655	1849	580	7313	3459	2860
Battersby Junction							
1902	6055	275	363	312	249	715	unclear
1907	6977	297	424	410	213	1022	79
1912	5966	614	502	362	167	1034	118
1917	6917	Note i		610	854	976	269
1922	7752	600	151	675	266	694	75
1926	5598	198	384	399	144	165	54
1930	5317	174	211	326	29	107	28
1934	5011	86	384	355	-	5	4

Notes:

(i) Parcels figures not reported during First World War

(ii) Income (Debit) figures for goods should be treated with care – it is possible that some revenue (eg large customer accounts handled centrally) may not be recorded at stations

Source: Summary of annual receipts by station 1902-35 (PRO RAIL 527/2142)

Appendix 4

Timetables (NER, LNER, BR)

1861 NER Working Timetable York-Scarborough and Whitby

10 Scarbro' & York and Whitby & Rillington Branches.

UP	Distance M.	Distance C.	1 PASSENGER.	2 PASSENGER.	3 Goods.	4 PASSENGER.	5 Goods.	6	7 Coal and Cattle. Tuesdays only.	8 Goods.	9 Cattle.	10 Cattle and Coal Empties.	11 Coal Empties.	12 PASSENGER EXPRESS	13 Market Train.	14 Driffield Goods.	15 Coal.	16 Goods.	17 PASSENGER.	18 Goods.	19	Sundays. 1 PASS.	Sundays. 2 PASS.
			a.m.	a.m.	a.m.	a.m.	a.m.		a.m	a.m.	a.m.	a.m.	p.m.	p.m.	p.m.	p.m.	p.m.	p.m.	Mail. p.m.	p.m.		a.m.	Mail p.m.
SCARBOROUGH	...	...	...	7 15	...	9 20	...	...	...	...	10 10	11 45	1 0	1 45	3 30	...	...	4 10	6 30	...	...	...	6 30
Seamer	2	70	...	7 22	...	9 28	...	...	...	...	...	11 55	1 10	1 52	3 37	...	...	4 20	6 37	...	...	...	6 37
Ganton	7	49	...	7 30	...	*	...	...	...	...	...	12 10	1 25	2 0	3 45	...	...	4 40	6 45	...	...	...	6 45
Sherburn	9	16	...	7 35	...	9 40	...	...	...	...	...	12 20	1 35	2 5	3 50	...	...	4 55	6 50	...	...	...	6 50
Heslerton	12	50	...	7 43	...	*	...	...	...	...	...	12 35	1 50	2 10	3 55	...	...	5 10	6 55	...	...	...	6 55
Knapton	14	41	...	7 48	...	*	...	...	...	...	...	12 45	...	2 15	4 0	...	...	5 20	7 0	...	...	...	7 0
RILLINGTON ......arr.	16	39	...	7 56	...	9 53	...	...	...	...	...	12 55	2 0	2 23	4 8	...	...	5 28	7 8	...	...	...	7 8
WHITBY ....dep.	...	...	...	...	...	8 10	6 30	...	...	10 0	...	...	...	12 40	...	...	...	3 0	5 25	6 0	...	7 30	5 25
Ruswarp	1	32	...	..	...	8 15	6 45	...	...	10 15	...	...	...	12 45	...	...	...		5 30	6 10	...	7 35	5 30
Sleights	2	77	...	...	...	8 20	7 0	...	...	10 30	...	...	...	12 50	...	...	...	...	5 35	6 20	...	7 40	5 35
Grosmont	6	28	...	...	...	8 30	7 15	...	...	10 45	...	...	...	1 0	...	...	...	3 30	5 45	6 35	...	7 50	5 45
Beck Holes	8	43	...	...	...	...	7 30	...	...	11 0	...	...	...	...	...	...	...	3 50	...	6 45	...	8 0	...
Goathland	9	21	...	...	...	8 50	10 5	...	...	...	...	...	...	1 20	...	...	2 0	4 10	6 5	7 30	...	...	6 5
Levisham	11	3	...	...	...	9 15	10 55	...	...	...	...	...	...	1 42	...	...	2 30	...	6 30	8 5	...	...	6 30
PICKERING...... arr.	...	...	...	...	...	9 28	11 15	...	...	...	...	...	...	1 55	...	...	2 50	...	6 43	8 30	..		6 43
PICKERING...... dep.	23	74	6 45	...	7 45	9 30	12 15	...	...	...	...	...	...	1 57	...	...	3 15	4 55	6 45	8 45	...	6 45	6 45
Kirby	25	53	...	...	...	...	12 25	...	...	...	...	...	...	...	...	...	...	...	...	8 55	...	...	...
Marishes Road	27	32	6 55	...	...	9 40	12 35	...	...	...	...	...	...	...	...	...	...	...	6 55	9 5	...	6 55	6 55
RILLINGTON ......arr.	30	42	7 5	...	...	9 50	12 45	...	...	...	...	...	...	2 16	...	...	...	5 20	7 5	...	...	7 5	7 5
Dep. for York	...	...	...	7 58	...	9 55	...	...	...	...	...	1 0	2 5	2 25	4 10	...	3 35	5 30	7 10	9 15	...	...	7 10
MALTON ....dep.	20	72	...	8 8	8 45	10 10	1 0	...	10 35	...	...	1 30	2 40	2 35	4 20	3 30	4 0	6 0	7 20	9 45	...	...	7 20
Hutton	23	52	...	8 17		...		...	...	...	...	1 35	...	†	On Thursdays Only.	3 45	...	...	7 28	...	...	...	7 28
Castle Howard	26	19	...	8 23	...	†	...	...	...	...	...	1 45	...	†		4 0	...	...	7 35	...	...	...	7 35
Kirkham	26	79	...	8 26	...	†	...	...	...	...	...	1 50	...	2 53		4 10	...	...	7 38	...	...	...	7 38
Barton Hill	30	44	...	8 36	...	10 25	...	...	...	...	...	2 10	...	3 3		4 25	...	...	7 48	...	...	...	7 48
Flaxton	32	60	...	8 43	...	10 32	...	...	...	...	...	2 25	...	3 10		4 40	...	...	7 55	..	...	...	7 55
Strensall	35	33	...	8 51	...	...	...	...	...	...	...	2 35	...	3 18		4 55	...	...	8 3	...	...	...	8 3
Haxby	37	62	...	8 59	...	...	...	...	...	...	...	2 45	...	3 25		5 10	...	...	8 10	...	...	...	8 10
YORK	42	50	...	9 20	...	11 0	...		11 35	...	1 0	3 0	3 50	3 45		5 30	5 20	7 15	8 25	11 0	...	...	8 25

† No. 4 stops at Castle Howard and Kirkham when Passengers require, and 12 stops at Hutton and Castle Howard when passengers require.
* On Saturdays No. 4 train stops at Ganton, Heslerton, and Knapton. No. 9 runs on every Tuesday and every alternate Wednesday previous to York Fortnight Fair, calling at all Stations. No. 11 stops at Stations between Malton and York for Empty Wagons when required. When No. 14 is unable to clear the Stations between York and Malton, No. 16 may be stopped for that purpose. When No. 18 is unable to clear all the Goods away from Gothland at one Trip he must take a load to Levisham, and return for the remainder. On Saturdays a Market Train leaves Whitby for Goathland about 2-55 p.m., arriving at Goathland about 3-40 p.m.

DOWN	Distance M.	Distance C.	1 Cattle.	2 Coal and Cattle.	3 Goods.	4 PASSENGER.	5 Coal.	6 Driffield Goods.	7 Coal.	8 PASSENGER.	9 Coal.	10 Goods.	11 Goods.	12 Goods.	13 EXPRESS.	14 Goods.	15 PASSENGER.	16	17	18	SUNDAY 1 PASS.	SUNDAY 2 PASS.	SUNDAY 3
			a.m.	a.m.	a.m.	Mail. a.m.	a.m.	a.m.	a.m.	a.m.	a.m	noon	p.m.	p.m.	p.m.	p.m.	p.m.				Mail. a.m.	p.m.	
YORK	...	...	4 0	4 45	...	6 0	6 50	7 5	7 30	9 40	10 0	12 0	...	1 30	3 0	...	6 30	...	...	...	6 0	...	...
Haxby	4	68	...	...	...	6 11	...	7 26	7 50	9 51	...	*	...	1 45	...	...	6 41	...	...	...	6 11	...	...
Strensall	7	17	...	...	...	6 18	...	7 37	8 0	9 58	...	*	...	1 55	3 10	...	6 48	...	...	...	6 18	...	...
Flaxton	9	70	...	...	...	6 25	...	7 48	8 10	10 5	...	*	...	2 5	3 21	...	6 55	...	...	...	6 25	...	...
Barton Hill	12	6	...	...	...	6 32	...	7 59	8 20	10 12	...	*	...	2 15	3 28	...	7 2	...	...	...	6 32	...	...
Kirkham	15	51	...	...	...	6 41	...	8 10	8 30	10 21	...	*	...	2 30	3 35	...	7 11	...	...	...	6 41	...	...
Castle Howard	16	31	...	...	...	6 44	...	8 16	8 35	10 24	...	*	...	2 35	...	...	7 14	...	...	...	6 44	...	...
Hutton	18	78	...	...	...	6 50	..	8 27	8 45	10 30	...	*	...	2 45	...	...	7 20	...	..	...	6 50	...	...
MALTON ....dep.	21	58	...	6 0	...	7 0	8 10	9 5	9 0	10 40	10 20	1 15	1 30	3 20	3 50	...	7 33	...	...	...	7 0	...	...
RILLINGTON ......arr.	26	11	...	...	...	7 9	8 25	...	9 13	10 49	...	1 37	...	...	4 0	...	7 44	...	...	...	7 9	...	...
Dep. for Whitby	...	...	...	On Tuesdays only.	...	7 25	...	9 20	...	10 55	11 35	...	...	3 40	4 5	5 45	7 55	...	...	...	7 18	7 15	...
Marishes Road	3	10	...		...	7 30	...	9 30	...	11 0	...	...	...	...	4 10	...	8 0	...	...	...	7 25	7 25	...
Kirby	4	69	...		...	...	...	...	...	...	...	...	...	...	...	...	...	...	...	...	...	...	...
PICKERING ... arr.	...	...	...		...	7 40	...	9 50	...	11 13	12 0	...	2 20	4 0	4 20	6 20	8 10	...	...	...	7 33	7 35	...
PICKERING ... dep.	6	48	...		...	7 42	...	10 10	...	11 15	12 30	...	...	4 40	4 22	...	8 12	...	...	...	7 35	...	...
Levisham	12	39	...		...	7 57	...	10 40	...	11 30	12 53	...	...	5 10	4 3	...	8 27	...	...	...	7 50	...	...
Goathland	21	21	...		...	8 20	...	11 20	...	11 57	1 30	...	...	6 0	5 0	...	8 50	...	...	...	8 13		...
Beck Holes	21	74	...		9 0	8 28	...	1 30	...	12 5	...	...	...	7 0	5 8	...	8 58	...	...	...	8 26	6 5	...
Grosmont	24	19	...		9 15	8 34	...	1 45	...	12 13	...	...	...	7 10	5 14	...	9 4	...	...	...	8 34	6 15	...
Sleights	27	45	...		9 45	8 44	...	2 5	...	12 22	...	...	...	7 20	5 24	...	9 14	...	...	...	8 44	6 25	...
Ruswarp	29	10	...		9 50	8 54	...	2 20	...	12 28	...	..	...	7 30	5 30	...	9 19	...	...	...	8 54	6 30	...
WHITBY ....arr.	30	42	...		10 0	9 0	...	2 30	...	12 35	...	...	...	7 45	5 40	...	9 30	...	...	...	9 0	6 35	...
Dep. for Scarborough ...	...	...	...	...	...	7 11	8 35	...	9 20	10 51	...	1 45	...	...	4 2	...	7 46	...	...	...	7 11	...	...
Knapton	28	9	...	...	...	7 18	8 45	...	9 35	10 58	...	1 55	...	...	...	...	7 53	...	...	...	7 18	...	...
Heslerton	30	0	...	...	...	7 24	9 0	...	9 50	11 4	...	2 5	...	...	...	...	7 59	...	..	...	7 24	...	...
Sherburn	33	34	...	...	...	7 33	9 20	...	10 10	11 13	...	2 20	...	...	4 17	...	8 7	...	...	...	7 33	...	...
Ganton	35	1	...	...	...	7 39	9 40	...	10 30	11 19	...	2 35	...	...	...	...	8 13	...	...	...	7 39	...	...
Seamer	39	60	...	...	...	7 49	10 0	...	10 5	11 29	...	3 5	...	...	4 30	...	8 24	...	...	...	7 49	...	...
SCARBOROUGH	42	50	7 30	...	...	8 0	10 20	...	11 10	11 40	...	3 20	...	...	4 45	...	8 35	...	...	...	8 0	...	...

No. 1 runs every Tuesday, and on the Wednesday previous to York Thursday Fortnight Fair, calling at all Stations.
No. 10 stops at all Stations marked thus * for Goods beyond Malton. When No. 12 is unable to take its whole load from Levisham to Goathland, a portion of the load must be left in Levisham Siding, and the Engine must return from Goathland for it. On Saturdays No. 13 train stops at all intermediate Stations.

1865 NER Working Timetable York-Scarborough and Whitby

York, Scarbro', and Whitby Lines.

UP	1	2	3	4	5	6	7	8	9	10	11	12	13	14	15	16	17	18	19	20	21	22	23	24	25	26	27	28			SUN. 1	SUN. 2
	PASSR.	Goods.	EXPRESS.	Goods, &c.	PASSR.		Cattle.	EXPRESS.	Goods.	Coal Empties.	Goods, &c.	Goods and Em[illegible]	Cattle & Coal Empties.	PASSR.	Goods & Empties.	EXPRESS.	Goods.	Fish when required.	Driffield Goods.	Goods.	Goods.	PASSR.	PASSR.	Fish when required.	PASSR. Mail.	Goods.	Coke.		Market Train.	Market Train.	Passr.	Mail.
					a		b			c				a			o															
	a.m.	a.m.	a.m.	a.m.	a.m.		a.m.	a.m.	a.m.	p.m.	a.m.	a.m.	a.m.	p.m.	a.m.	p.m.	p.m.	p.m.	p.m.	p.m.	p.m.	p.m.	p.m.	p.m.	p.m.	p.m.	a.m.		p.m.	p.m.	am.	p.m.
WHITBY ......dep.	5 20	6 30	8 0	...	8 25	...	...	...	10 0	...	...	...	...	1 0	...	...	3 0	3 15	...	...	4 0	...	4 45	...	6 5	6 10	...	...	2 55	...	...	5 50
Ruswarp	5 25	6 40	...	...	8 30	...	...	...	10 10	...	...	...	...	1 5	...	...	...	...	...	...	4 10	...	...	...	6 10	...	...	...	3 0	...	...	5 55
Sleights	5 30	6 50	...	...	8 35	...	...	...	10 20	...	...	...	...	1 10	...	...	...	...	...	...	4 20	...	...	...	6 15	...	...	...	3 5	...	...	6 0
Grosmont	5 39	7 10	...	8 50	8 44	...	...	...	11 15	10 45	11 0	11 10	...	1 20	1 25	...	3 25	...	...	3 35	4 40	...	...	...	6 24	6 35	...	...	3 15	...	...	6 10
Goathland Mill	5 48	7 20	...	...	8 53	...	...	...	11 25	11 0	...	...	...	1 30	1 40	...	3 40	...	...	3 50	5 10	...	...	...	6 33	6 50	...	...	3 25	...	...	6 20
Levisham	6 8	...	...	9 35	9 14	...	...	...	12 0	11 20	11 50	...	...	1 51	...	...	...	...	...	...	5 40	...	...	...	6 54	...	...	...	...	...	...	6 41
PICKERING arr.	6 20	8 20	...	...	9 28	...	...	...	12 30	11 50	...	12 20	...	2 8	2 30	...	4 30	4 50	...	4 50	6 10	...	...	...	7 8	7 50	...	...	...	...	...	6 58
PICKERING dep.	6 22	...	8 50	...	9 30	...	...	...	12 50	12 5	...	...	...	2 10	2 55	...	4 40	5 0	...	5 10	6 40	...	5 35	...	7 10	8 0	...	...	...	...	6 45	7 0
Marishes Road	6 30	...	...	...	9 40	...	...	...	1 5	12 15	...	...	...	a	...	...	...	...	...	...	6 55	...	...	...	7 20	...	...	...	...	...	6 55	7 10
Rillington	6 40	...	...	...	9 50	...	...	...	1 20	12 25	...	...	...	2 28	...	...	...	...	...	...	7 5	...	...	...	7 30	...	...	...	...	...	7 5	7 17
MALTON ....arr.	6 50	...	...	...	10 0	...	...	...	1 35	12 40	...	...	...	2 40	3 30	...	5 10	5 35	...	5 45	7 20	...	...	...	7 40	8 35	...	...	...	...	...	...
Seamer ar. f. Whitby	...	...	...	...	...	...	...	...	...	...	...	...	...	...	...	...	...	...	...	...	...	...	6 8	...	...	...	...	...	...	...	...	...
Scarbro' "	...	...	9 30	...	...	...	...	...	...	...	...	...	...	...	...	...	...	...	...	...	...	...	6 15	...	...	...	...	...	...	...	...	...
SCARBOROUGH ...	6 40	...	8 20	...	9 15	...	9 25	10 10	...	...	...	...	1 0	1 55	...	2 35	4 10	...	...	...	...	4 30	...	5 0	7 0	7 20	...	...	...	3 10	...	6 45
Seamer	6 47	...	...	...	9 23	...	...	...	...	...	...	...	1 15	2 2	...	...	4 20	...	...	...	...	4 37	...	5 10	...	...	...	...	...	3 17	...	6 52
Ganton	6 55	...	...	...	9 33	...	...	...	...	...	...	...	1 30	a	...	...	4 40	...	...	...	...	4 45	...	...	7 15	...	...	...	...	3 25	...	7 0
Sherburn	7 0	...	...	...	9 40	...	...	...	...	...	...	...	1 40	a	...	...	4 55	...	...	...	...	4 50	...	...	7 20	...	...	...	...	3 30	...	7 5
Heslerton	7 8	...	...	...	9 47	...	...	...	...	...	...	...	1 55	a	...	...	5 10	...	...	...	...	4 58	...	...	7 27	...	...	...	...	3 35	...	7 13
Knapton	7 13	...	...	...	9 50	...	...	...	...	...	...	...	2 5	a	...	...	5 20	...	...	...	...	5 3	...	...	...	...	...	...	...	3 40	...	7 18
RILLINGTON arr.	7 21	...	...	...	g	...	...	...	...	...	...	...	2 15	g	...	...	5 28	...	...	...	...	5 11	...	...	...	...	...	...	...	3 48	..	7 22
RILLINGTON dep.	7 23	...	...	...	...	...	...	...	...	...	...	...	2 20	...	...	...	5 30	...	...	...	...	5 13	...	...	...	...	...	...		3 50	...	7 24
MALTON ... arr.	7 30	...	...	...	10 5	...	...	...	...	...	...	...	2 30	2 45	...	...	...	...	...	...	...	5 20	...	6 10	7 45	8 40	...	...		4 0	...	7 31
MALTON ... dep.	7 33	...	8 50	...	10 10	...	...	10 42	...	12 55	...	...	3 5	2 48	...	...	6 0	5 50	3 30	...	...	5 23	...	6 20	7 52	9 0	8 40	...		...	...	7 38
Hutton	7 41	...	...	...	...	...	...	...	...	...	...	...	3 10	a	...	...	...	...	3 45	...	...	5 31	...	...	r	...	...	...			...	7 46
Castle Howard	7 48	...	...	...	a	...	...	...	...	...	...	...	3 20	a	...	...	...	...	4 0	...	...	5 38	...	...	r	...	...	...			...	7 53
Kirkham	7 51	...	...	...	10 23	...	...	...	...	...	...	...	3 25	a	...	...	...	...	4 10	...	...	5 41	...	...	8 7	...	...	...	On Saturdays only.	On Thursdays Only.	...	7 56
Barton Hill	8 1	...	...	...	10 31	...	...	...	...	...	...	...	3 35	3 6	...	...	...	...	4 25	...	...	5 51	...	...	r	...	...	...			...	8 6
Flaxton	8 8	...	...	...	10 37	...	...	...	...	...	...	...	3 45	a	...	...	...	...	4 40	...	...	5 58	...	...	8 19	...	...	...			...	8 13
Strensall	8 16	...	...	...	...	...	...	...	...	...	...	...	3 55	3 20	...	...	...	...	4 55	...	...	6 6	...	...	8 27	...	...	...			...	8 21
Haxby	8 24	...	...	...	...	...	...	...	...	...	...	...	4 5	...	...	...	...	...	5 10	...	...	6 14	...	...	r	...	...	...			...	8 28
YORK	8 40	...	9 30	...	11 5	...	12 30	11 30	...	2 10	...	...	4 20	3 50	...	3 55	7 15	7 5	5 30	...	...	6 30	...	7 25	8 45	10 0	9 55	...			...	8 45

a No. 5 Train stops at Castle Howard, and No. 14 at Stations marked thus (a) when Passengers require.
b No. 7 runs on every Tuesday and alternate Wednesday, calling at all Stations.
c No. 10 stops at Stations between Malton and York for Empty Wagons when required.
g Nos. 5 and 14 only stop at Rillington to set down passengers booked for that place.
* Runs from Grosmont to Beckholes and back before starting for Goathland.
o No. 17 Train starting from Whitby runs through to York only when required
r Stops at Stations marked thus (r) to set down Passengers arriving at Malton by the Driffield and Whitby Trains.
No. 21 must Shunt at Grosmont deviation for the 4-45 p.m. Express to pass, and clear the Road Stations, take all Coke, Coal, and Limestone Wagons from Grosmont, and if there are more Wagons than the Engine can take, those left must be so placed at Goathland or Pickering that No. 26 can attach them without any shunting.
All Goods and Mineral Engines must make a double run between Grosmont and Goathland when required.

York, Scarbro', and Whitby Lines.

DOWN	1	2	3	4	5	6	7	8	9	10	11	12	13	14	15	16	17	18	19	20	21	22	23	24	25	26	27	28	SUNDAYS. 1	2	3	4
	MAIL.	Coke		Cattle.	PASSR. Mail.	Fish when required.	Fish when required.	Coal.	Driffield Goods.	Coal.	Goo's.	Goods.	Limestone, &c.	PASSR.	PASSR.	Coke.	Goods.	Limestone.	Goods.	Limestone.	EXPRESS.	EXPRESS.	PASSR.	EXPRESS		Coke.	PASSR.	Market Train.	Mail.	Mail.		
				a													d					e	e									
	a.m.	a.m.		a.m.	a.m.	a.m.	a.m.	a m.	a.m.	a.m.	a.m.	a.m	a.m.	a.m.	a.m.	p.m.	a.m.	noon.	p.m.	p.m.	p.m.	p.m.	p.m.	p.m.		p.m.	p.m.	p.m.	a.m.	a.m.	p.m.	p.m.
YORK	3 44	...	...	4 0	6 0	6 5	6 20	6 30	7 5	7 30	...	...	...	9 45	...	...	10 0	...	1 0	...	2 30	3 0	4 30	5 40	...	6 15	7 0	3 30	3 44	6 0	...	...
Haxby	...	...	...	...	6 11	...	...	...	7 26	7 50	...	...	...	9 56	...	...	*	...	...	...	...	...	...	...	...	...	7 11	3 41	...	6 11	—	...
Strensall	...	...	...	...	6 18	...	...	...	7 37	8 0	...	...	...	10 3	...	...	*	...	...	—	...	...	...	...	...	...	7 18	3 48	...	6 18	...	...
Flaxton	...	...	...	...	6 25	...	...	...	7 48	8 10	...	...	...	10 11	...	...	*	...	...	...	...	e	4 50	...	...	...	7 24	3 55	...	6 25	...	..
Barton Hill	...	...	...	..	6 32	...	...	...	7 59	8 20	..	...	...	10 18	...	...	*	...	...	...	...	e	4 57	...	...	...	7 30	4 2	...	6 32	...	...
Kirkham	...	...	...	...	6 41	...	...	...	8 10	8 30	...	...	...	10 28	...	...	*	...	...	...	...	...	5 6	...	...	...	7 39	4 11	...	6 41	...	...
Castle Howard	...	...	...	...	6 44	...	...	...	8 16	8 35	...	...	...	10 31	...	...	*	...	...	...	..	...	e	...	...	...	7 42	4 14	...	6 44	—	...
Hutton	...	...	...	...	6 50	...	...	...	8 27	8 45	...	...	...	10 37	...	...	*	...	...	...	...	...	...	..	...	...	7 48	4 20	...	6 50	...	...
MALTON ... arr.	4 25	...	...	...	6 55	7 20	7 35	7 45	8 35	...	...	...	...	10 45	...	...	...	...	2 10	...	...	3 40	5 19	...	...	7 30	7 55	4 25	4 25	6 55	...	...
MALTON ... dep.	4 28	...	...	...	7 0	...	7 45	..	...	9 0	...	...	...	10 50	...	...	11 15	...	2 25	...	...	3 45	5 21	...	...	...	8 0	4 33	4 28	7 0	...	...
RILLINGTON arr.	...	...	...	...	7 9	...	...	..	Stop	9 13	...	...	...	g	...	...	11 37	...	2 35	...	...	g	g	...	...	...	g	4 42	...	7 9	...	...
Dep. for Scarbro'	...	...	...	...	7 11	...	...	...	...	9 20	...	...	...	...	...	...	11 45	...	2 35	...	...	...	...	...	...	...	...	4 44	...	7 11	...	...
Knapton	...	...	...	...	7 18	...	...	...	...	9 35	...	...	...	11 5	...	...	11 55	...	...	...	...	...	e	...	...	...	8 18	4 51	...	7 18	...	...
Heslerton	...	...	...	...	7 24	...	...	...	...	9 50	...	...	...	11 10	...	...	12 5	...	...	...	...	...	e	...	...	...	8 24	4 57	...	7 24	...	...
Sherburn	...	...	...	...	7 33	...	...	..	...	10 10	...	...	...	11 20	.	...	12 20	...	...	...	...	e	e	...	...	...	8 31	5 6	...	7 33	...	...
Ganton	...	...	...	...	7 39	...	...	...	...	10 30	...	...	...	11 24	...	...	12 35	...	...	...	...	e	5 46	...	...	...	8 39	5 12	...	7 39	...	—
Seamer	...	...	...	...	7 49	...	...	...	...	10 50	...	...	...	11 34	...	...	1 5	...	...	...	...	4 20	5 57	...	...	...	8 49	5 22	...	7 49	...	...
SCARBOROUGH ...	5 10	...	...	7 30	8 0	...	8 50	...	...	11 10	...	...	...	11 45	...	...	1 20	...	3 30	...	3 45	4 30	6 10	6 55	...	...	9 0	5 35	5 10	8 0	...	...
Scarbro' d. f. Whitby	...	...	...	...	...	...	...	...	...	...	...	...	...	...	9 50	...	...	...		...	...	...	...	6 40	...	...	...	On Saturdays only.	...	...	...	...
Malton dp. f Whitby	4 33	6 0	...	...	7 5	7 30	...	8 0	...	...	8 30	9 0	...	10 55	...	...	...	...	2 30	...	...	3 50	5 30	...	...	...	8 10		4 33	...	...	...
Rillington	...	...	...	...	7 25	...	...	8 15	...	...	...	9 15	...	11 5	...	...	...	...	2 40	...	...	4 0	5 40	...	...	...	8 20		...	7 18	...	7 25
Marishes Road	...	...	...	...	7 30	...	...	8 25	...	...	...	9 25	...	11 10	...	...	...	...	2 55	...	...	...	5 45	...	...	...	8 25		...	7 25	...	7 35
PICKERING arr.	...	6 40	...	...	7 40	8 5	...	8 40	...	...	9 5	9 40	...	11 20	...	...	...	...	3 10	...	...	4 13	5 58	...	...	...	8 35		...	7 33	...	7 45
PICKERING dep.	...	6 50	...	...	7 42	8 15	...	9 0	...	...	12 0	10 0	9 5	11 22	10 30	...	...	...	4 20	1 30	...	4 15	6 0	7 20	...	...	8 37		...	7 35	...	...
Levisham	...	...	...	...	7 57	...	...	9 30	...	...	12 40	10 30	9 25	11 37	...	9 50	...	12 0	5 0	...	...	...	6 15	...	...	...	8 52		...	7 50	...	...
Goathland Mill	...	...	...	...	8 18	..	...	10 0	...	...	1 20	11 10	...	11 58	...	...	...	...	5 30	...	...	...	6 36	...	...	...	9 13		...	8 11	...	...
Grosmont	...	8 5	...	...	8 28	...	..	10 15	...	...	1 45	11 30	10 30	12 8	...	10 50	...	1 0	5 40	3 0	...	5 0	6 46	...	...	...	9 23	...	...	8 21	...	...
Sleights	...	...	...	...	8 37	...	..	...	...	...	2 0	11 45	..	12 17	...	...	...	...	...	...	...	5 9	6 55	...	...	...	9 32	...	...	8 30	...	...
Ruswarp	...	...	...	...	8 42	...	..	...	...	...	2 15	11 55	...	12 23	...	...	...	...	...	...	...	5 15	7 0	...	...	...	9 37	...	...	8 35	...	...
WHITBY ......arr.	5 35	...	...	...	8 50	10 15	..	...	...	...	2 30	12 15	...	12 30	11 20	...	...	...	6 20	...	...	5 25	7 10	8 10	...	...	9 45	...	5 35	8 45	...	..

a—No. 4 runs every Tuesday and alternate Wednesday, calling at all Stations.
d—No. 17 stops at all Stations marked thus * for Goods beyond Malton. e—Nos. 22 & 23 stop at Stations marked thus (e) when 1st class Passengers require.
g—Only stops at Rillington when passengers are booked at that place.
The Engine of No. 11 must assist No. 12 up the bank if required before starting at noon for Whitby.

Trains shewn in italics do not run daily throughout the period for which this time table is issued.

102 WHITBY AND STOCKTON

A For other trains between Whitby and Grosmont, see below. e Via Darlington, pages 34-40. SO Saturdays only. † a.m.

MALTON AND WHITBY

A For other trains between Grosmont and Whitby, see above. B Through carriage between King's Cross and Whitby. c Stops when required. d 12.24 a.m. on Mondays. • Stops when required to take up for York or beyond. f Stops when required to set down from York or beyond.

L·N·E·R 214

Table 110 MALTON and WHITBY

For OTHER TRAINS between York and Pickering, see Table 118—Grosmont and Whitby, Table 131.

Table 111 MALTON and DRIFFIELD

Table 112 SCARBOROUGH and PICKERING—(One class only)

For OTHER TRAINS between Scarborough and Seamer, see Tables 105 and 109

Above: 1920 NER Summer Timetable (Malton-Whitby and Stockton-Whitby)

Above Right: 1939 LNER Summer Timetable (July-September) (Malton-Whitby)

Below: 1939 LNER Wartime Emergency Timetable (Malton-Whitby, Town-West Cliff)

Right: 1947 LNER Summer Timetable (Malton-Whitby)

Table 108 WHITBY and WHITBY WEST CLIFF (One class only)

Table 109 YORK and SCARBOROUGH

NOTES

A Through Train between Leeds and Scarborough
a Mrn
B Dep. 12 55 aft. on Saturdays
D Via Scarborough
E or E Except Saturdays
N Night time
S or S Saturdays only
s Saturday night

For OTHER TRAINS between Seamer and Scarborough, see Tables 105 and 112

Table 110 MALTON and WHITBY

For OTHER TRAINS between York and Pickering, see Table 118—Grosmont and Whitby, Table 131.

213-4 L·N·E·R

970 L·N·E·R

Table 110 MALTON and WHITBY

Miles from Malton	Week Days only	a.m	a.m	a.m. C	a.m. S	p.m C	p.m	
	103 NEWCASTLE .... dep	2 1	..	8 15	10 0	1F 4	2V30	..
	116 LEEDS (City) ... "	3 0	..	9A10	12P 5	1R50	4 0	..
	109 YORK .... "	4 30	..	10J15	1 20	3K 5	5 8	..
—	Malton .... dep	5 20	..	11 5	2 3	4 0	6 0	..
7½	Marishes Road	..	..	11 17	..	4 12	6 12	..
11	Pickering	5B46	..	11 27	2 20	4 20	6 19	..
17	Levisham	5 57	..	11 38	2 31	4 31	6 30	..
25½	Goathland	6 14	8 25	11 55	2 48	4 48	6 47	..
29	Grosmont	6 26	8 32	12 2	3 56	4 55	6 54	..
32½	Sleights	..	8 41	12 11	3 5	5 4	7 3	..
33¾	Ruswarp	Aa	8 46	12 16	3 10	5 9	7 8	..
35¼	Whitby .... arr	6 40	8 50	12 21	3 14	5 13	7 12	..

Miles	Week Days only	a.m C	a.m	a.m. C	a.m S	p.m	pm	p.m.	
—	Whitby .... dep	7 5	7 48	9 30	1145	3 20	..	6 45	..
1½	Ruswarp	7 10	7 53	9 35	1150	3 25	..	6 51	..
3	Sleights	7 14	7 57	9 39	1154	3 29	..	6 55	..
6¼	Grosmont	7 23	8 6	9 48	12 3	3 39	..	7 4	..
9¾	Goathland	7 33	8 16	9 58	1213	3 49	..	7 14	..
18¼	Levisham	7 50	..	10 15	1230	4 6	..	7 31	..
24¼	Pickering	8 5	..	10 29	1242	4 20	725	7 45	..
27¾	Marishes Road	8 11	..	..	1248	..	..	7 51	..
35¼	Malton .... arr	8 22	..	10 44	1259	4 35	745	8 2	..
56¼	109 YORK .... arr	9L 9	..	11N35	1 54	5 25	825	9 6	..
81¾	116 LEEDS (City) ... "	9 55	..	12 30	2U24	6 37	949	10 0	..
136¾	103 NEWCASTLE .... "	1215	..	2 31	5 6	9X 5	..	11 11	..

A Dep. 9 20 a.m. on Saturdays. Aa Calls when required to set down from York. B Arr. 5 36 a.m.
C Through train between York and Whitby on Mondays and Saturdays. F Dep. 1 15 p.m. on Saturdays.
J Dep. 10 25 a.m. on Mondays and Saturdays. K Dep. 3 10 p.m. on Mondays and Saturdays. L Arr. 8 55 a.m. on Mondays and Saturdays. N Arr. 11 17 a.m. on Mondays and Saturdays. P Dep. 11 30 a.m. commencing 20th September. p p.m. R Dep. 2 0 p.m. on Saturdays until 27th September inclusive. S Saturdays only.
U Arr. 2 45 p.m. on 4th October. V Dep. 2 38 p.m. on Saturdays 28th June to 30th August inclusive.
X Arr. 8 45 p.m. on Fridays.

For OTHER TRAINS between York and Pickering, see Table 118—Grosmont and Whitby, Table 131.

Table 111 MALTON and DRIFFIELD

Miles	Week Days only	a.m		Saturdays only a.m.		p.m		
—	Malton .... dep	7 0	..	11 10	..	5 55	..	..
3½	Settrington	7 8	..	11 18	..	6 3	..	..
4¾	North Grimston	7 11	..	11 21	..	6 6	..	..
6¾	Wharram	7 16	..	11 26	..	6 11	..	..
9	Burdale	7 21	..	11 31	..	6 16	..	..
11½	Sledmere and Fimber.	7 26	..	11 36	..	6 21	..	..
13½	Wetwang	7 30	..	11 40	..	6 25	..	..
16¾	Garton	7 36	..	11 46	..	6 31	..	..
20	Driffield .... arr	7 42	..	11 55	..	6 37	..	..

Miles	Week Days only	a.m		Saturdays only p.m.		p.m	
—	Driffield .... dep	8 56	..	12 25	..	7 30	..
3¼	Garton	9 3	..	12 32	..	7 37	..
6½	Wetwang	9 9	..	12 38	..	7 43	..
8½	Sledmere and Fimber..	9 14	..	12 43	..	7 48	..
11	Burdale	9 20	..	12 49	..	7 54	..
13¼	Wharram	9 25	..	12 54	..	7 59	..
15½	North Grimston	9 29	..	12 58	..	8 3	..
16½	Settrington	9 32	..	1 1	..	8 6	..
20	Malton .... arr	9 39	..	1 8	..	8 15	..

Table 112 SCARBOROUGH and PICKERING (One class only)

Miles	Week Days only	a.m		p.m		p.m	
—	Scarborough (Cen.). dep	8 40	..	2 50	..	6 30	..
3	Seamer	8 47	..	2 57	..	6 37	..
6½	Forge Valley	8 55	..	3 5	..	6 46	..
8	Wykeham	9 0	..	3 9	..	6 50	..
9¾	Sawdon	9 5	..	3 14	..	6 56	..
11½	Snainton	9 10	..	3 19	..	7 1	..
14	Ebberston	9 16	..	3 25	..	7 7	..
16¾	Thornton Dale	9 22	..	3 31	..	7 13	..
19¾	Pickering .... arr	9 30	..	3 38	..	7 20	..

Miles	Week Days only	a.m		a.m.		p.m			
—	Pickering .... dep	7 0	..	9 43	..	5 10	..	..	..
3	Thornton Dale	7 7	..	9 51	..	5 17	..	..	..
5¾	Ebberston	7 13	..	9 57	..	5 23	..	..	..
8¼	Snainton	7 19	..	10 3	..	5 31	..	..	..
10	Sawdon	7 24	..	10 8	..	5 36	..	..	..
11¾	Wykeham	7 30	..	10 13	..	5 41	..	..	..
13¼	Forge Valley	7 35	..	10 17	..	5 45	..	..	..
16¾	Seamer	7 44	..	10 26	..	5 53	..	..	..
19¾	Scarborough (Cen.). arr	7 50	..	10 32	..	5 59	..	..	..

For OTHER TRAINS between Scarborough & Seamer, see Tables 105 and 109

1955 BR North Eastern Region Summer Timetable (Malton-Whitby)

Table 40 — **MALTON and WHITBY**

Miles from Malton	Week Days	a.m	a.m O	a.m S (TC York to Whitby)	a.m	a.m J	p.m	p.m C	p.m L	p.m	Sundays a.m T (TC Selby (dep. 9 50 a.m.) to Whitby)	Sundays a.m (TC Leeds to Whitby)
—	23 Leeds (City) .. dep	3 0	8 12	9 15	..	9 22	..	12 25	2 10	4 25	9 10	9 48
—	23 York .... "	4 30	9 [illegible]	9 55	..	10 15	..	1 35	3 5	5 8	1023	1040
—	Malton .... dep	5 20	9 53	1025	..	11 0	..	2 15	4 0	5 50	1050	1110
7¼	Marishes Road	..	..	..	..	11 12	..	[illegible]	4 12	[illegible]	..	..
11	Pickering	5 44	1016	..	..	11 21	..	[illegible]	4 20	[illegible]	11 8	1129
17	Levisham	5 55	..	..	..	11 33	..	[illegible]	4 31	[illegible]	..	..
25½	Goathland	6 12	1044	..	8 15	11 49	1 20	[illegible]	4 48	6 37	1138	1156
29	Grosmont	6 23	..	..	8 23	11 56	1 27	[illegible]	4 55	6 44	1144	12 6
32¼	Sleights	6 32	..	..	8 31	12 5	1 33	3 15	5 4	6 53	1153	1215
33½	Ruswarp	Aa	..	..	8 36	12 10	1 41	3 21	5 9	6 58	..	..
35¼	Whitby (Town) .. arr	6 39	11 5	1125	8 41	12 14	1 45	3 28	5 13	7 2	12 0	1224

Miles	Week Days	a.m F	a.m	a.m SN (TC Whitby to York)	a.m D	a.m K (TC Whitby to York)	a.m E	a.m S (TC Whitby to York)	p.m	p.m S (TC Whitby to Leeds)	p.m	p.m O (TC Whitby to York)	p.m M	Sundays a.m U (TC Whitby to London (King's C.) arr. 3 45 p.m.)	Sundays p.m T (TC Whitby to Selby arr. 9 4 p.m.)	Sundays p.m (TC Whitby to Leeds)
—	Whitby (Town) .. dep	7 2	7 38	9 0	9 20	1025	1127	1136	1235	2 10	3 15	6 10	6 57	9 30	7 0	7 12
1¾	Ruswarp	7 7	7 43	..	9 25	..	1132	1141	1240	2 15	3 20	..	7 [illegible]	..	..	..
3	Sleights	7 11	7 47	..	9 [illegible]	..	1138	1145	1244	2 19	3 24	..	7 7	..	..	7 19
6¼	Grosmont	7 20	7 55	9 15	9 [illegible]	1040	1145	1154	1250	2 [illegible]	3 33	..	7 16	9 45	..	7 28
9¾	Goathland	7 33	8 6	9 35	9 45	1050	1155	12 5	1 3	2 [illegible]	3 4[illegible]	..	7 29	9 55	7 21	7 38
18¼	Levisham	7 47	—	..	10 5	11 7	1212	1221	..	2 55	4 0	..	7 43	..	..	..
24¼	Pickering	8 0	—	9 53	10 15	1120	1224	1233	..	3 8	4 15	..	7 57	1025	7 52	8 10
27½	Marishes Road	8 6	—	..	..	..	1230	1238	..	..	..	..	8 3	..	..	..
35¼	Malton .... arr	8 17	..	1010	10K33	1137	1241	1250	..	3 22	4 35	7 17	8 17	1042	..	8 26
56½	23 York .... arr	9F 3	..	1040	11J[illegible]	12 7	1 28	1 21	..	3 54	5 18	7 50	9Y 4	1137	8 31	8 57
82	23 Leeds (City) "	9 47	..	1135	12 4	1 12	2 47	2 47	..	4 44	6 22	8 49	10 9	1237	..	9 49

A Dep 9 50 am on Saturdays
Aa Calls when required to set down
B From 18th July to 2nd September, also on Mondays 4th, 11th July, 5th September and on Saturdays dep 10 28 am
C Through Train York to Whitby on Saturdays
c Arr. 4 11 p.m.
D Through Train Whitby to York on Saturdays; also on Fridays 29th July to 26th August
d Arr. 5 36 a.m.
E Except Saturdays
F or f Through Train Whitby to York (arr 8 48 am) daily from 18th July to 3rd September, also on Saturdays until 16th July and 10th and 17th September; and Mondays 4th, 11th July and 5th September
H Dep Leeds 2 2 pm on Saturdays and York 3 25 pm on Saturdays; also on Fridays 29th July to 26th August
J Through Train Leeds to Whitby on Saturdays. York to Whitby (except Saturdays) 18th July to 2nd September; also on Mondays 4th, 11th July and 5th September
j Arr 11 10 am on Saturdays; also on Fridays 29th July to 26th August
K Saturdays only. Runs 2nd July to 10th September inclusive
k 5 minutes later on Saturdays
L Through Train from York to Whitby on Saturdays; also on Fridays 29th July to 26th August. Through Carriages from London (King's Cross) dep 11 20 am to Whitby on Saturdays until 10th September; also on Fridays 29th July to 26th August inclusive
M Through Train Whitby to York 18th July to 3rd September inclusive
N Through Train Whitby to London (King's Cross) (arr 2 58 pm)
n Dep 1 45 pm on Saturdays
O Except Saturdays. Runs 18th July to 26th August inclusive
S Saturdays only
T Runs 17th July to 21st August inclusive
TC Through Carriages
U Commences 17th July
Y Arr 8 43 pm from 18th July to 3rd September inclusive

For OTHER TRAINS between Grosmont and Whitby, see Table 51.

1962 BR North Eastern Region Winter Timetable (Malton-Whitby)

Table 33

MALTON and WHITBY

WEEKDAYS ONLY

Miles		am	D am	D am (Through Train—York (dep 10.28 am) (Table 32) to Whitby)	D pm	D pm	pm	D pm (Through Train—York (dep 6.0 pm) (Table 32) to Whitby)
—	MALTON ...... dep	5 20	....	11 0	....	2 20	4 0	6 30
7½	Marishes Road .. "	..	..	..	..	..	4 12	6 42
11	Pickering .... "	5B44	....	11 19	....	2 37	4 20	6 51
17	Levisham .. .. "	5 55	..	11 30	..	2 48	4 31	7 3
25½	Goathland ...... "	6 12	8 7	11 47	1 20	3 5	4 48	7 21
29	Grosmont.. .. "	6 23	8 14	11 54	1 27	3 12	4 55	7 31
32¼	Sleights .... "	6 32	8 22	12 2	1 35	3 20	5 4	7 39
33¾	Ruswarp .. .. "	C	8 26	12 6	1 39	3 24	5 9	7 43
35¼	WHITBY (Town) arr	6 39	8 29	12 9	1 42	3 27	5 13	7 46

WEEKDAYS ONLY

Miles		D am (Through Train—Whitby to York (arr 8.40 am) (Table 32))	D am	am	D am	D pm	D pm (Through Train—Whitby to York (arr 4.50 pm) (Table 32))	pm
—	WHITBY (Town) dep	7 2	7 38	8 55	11 37	12 35	3 12	6 54
1½	Ruswarp .. .. "	7 5	7 41	9 0	11 40	12 38	3 15	7 0
3	Sleights .... "	7 9	7 45	9 4	11 44	12 42	3 19	7 5
6¼	Grosmont.. .. "	7 17	7 53	9 13	11 52	12 50	3 27	7 13
9¾	Goathland ...... "	7 26	8 2	9 23	12 1	12 59	3 36	7 23
18¼	Levisham .. .. "	7 41	—	9 40	12 16	—	3 51	7 40
24¼	Pickering .. .. "	7 53	....	9 52	12 28	....	4 4	7 54
27¾	Marishes Road .. "	7 59	..	..	..	..	..	..
35¼	MALTON ...... arr	8 10	....	10 7	12 43	....	4 19	8 9

For other trains between Whitby (Town) and Grosmont, see Table 34.

D—Diesel Train. | B—Arrives Pickering 5.36 am. | C—Calls when required to set down.

187

2008 National Rail Winter-Spring Timetable (Middlesbrough and Pickering-Whitby)

Table 45 — **Middlesbrough and Pickering → Whitby** — Mondays to Fridays — Network Diagram - see first page of Table 44

Miles		NT	NT A	NT	NY ThFO B	NY MFO C	NY MFX D	NT	NY ThFO B	NY MFO C	NY MFX D	NT	NT E	NY ThFO B	NY MFO C	NY MFX D	NT E	NT	NT E	NT E
—	Newcastle 44 d	06b00	07 00	07 30				09b12				12b40	13 30				15 30	16b06	16 30	18 30
—	Darlington 44 d	06 36	07 48	08 10				09 53				13 30	14 08				15 57	16 59	17 15	18 33
0	Middlesbrough d	07 08	08 13	08 49				10 38				14 16	14 49				16 47	17 40	17 54	19 49
3	Marton d	07 13	08 18	08 54				10 43				14 21	14 54				16 52	17 45	17 59	19 54
4	Gypsy Lane d	07 16	08 21	08 58				10 46				14 24	14 57				16 55	17 48	18 02	19 57
4½	Nunthorpe d	07 19	08a26	09a01				10 49				14 27	15a03				16a59	17 51	18a05	20a03
8½	Great Ayton d	07 25						10 55				14 33						17 57		
11	Battersby a	07 31						11 01				14 39						18 03		
—	Battersby d	07 39						11 05				14 43						18 07		
12½	Kildale d	07 44						11 10				14 48						18 12		
16½	Commondale d	07 51						11 17				14 55						18 19		
18½	Castleton Moor d	07 55						11 20				14 58						18 22		
20	Danby d	07 58						11 23				15 01						18 25		
23½	Lealholm d	08 05						11 30				15 08						18 32		
25½	Glaisdale a	08 10						11 34				15 12						18 36		
—	Glaisdale d	08 12						11 37				15 15						18 39		
27½	Egton d	08 16						11 40				15 18						18 42		
—	Pickering § d				08 45	09 00	09 00			12 00	12 00				16 00	16 00				
—	Goathland § d				09 42	09 50	09 50		12 30	12 50	12 50			16 25	16 50	16 50				
28½	Grosmont d	08 20			10 00	10 10	10 10	11 44	13 10	13 10	13 10	15 22		16 45	17 10	17 10		18 46		
32	Sleights d	08 29						11 53				15 31						18 55		
33½	Ruswarp d	08 34						11 58				15 36						19 00		
35	Whitby a	08 41			10 20	10 35	10 35	12 05	13 30	13 35	13 35	15 43		17 10	17 35	17 35		19 07		

Saturdays

	NT	NT	NT	NY G	NY H	NT	NT E	NY G	NY H	NT	NT E	NY G	NY H	NT E	NT	NT E	NT E
Newcastle 44 d	06b00	07 00	07 30			09b12	10 30			12b40	13 30			15 30	16b20	16 30	18 30
Darlington 44 d	06 36	07 38	08 10			09 51	10 47			13 31	13 53			16 00	17 04	.	18 30
Middlesbrough d	07 06	08 04	08 49			10 38	11 49			14 12	14 49			16 47	17 38	17 50	19 48
Marton d	07 11	08 09	08 54			10 43	11 54			14 17	14 54			16 52	17 43	17 55	19 53
Gypsy Lane d	07 14	08 12	08 58			10 46	11 57			14 20	14 57			16 55	17 46	17 58	19 56
Nunthorpe d	07 17	08a18	09a01			10 49	12a01			14 23	15a01			16a59	17 49	18a01	20a01
Great Ayton d	07 23					10 55				14 29					17 55		
Battersby a	07 29					11 01				14 35					18 01		
Battersby d	07 33					11 05				14 39					18 05		
Kildale d	07 38					11 10				14 44					18 10		
Commondale d	07 45					11 17				14 51					18 17		
Castleton Moor d	07 49					11 20				14 54					18 20		
Danby d	07 52					11 23				14 57					18 23		
Lealholm d	07 59					11 30				15 04					18 30		
Glaisdale a	08 04					11 34				15 08					18 34		
Glaisdale d	08 06					11 37				15 11					18 37		
Egton d	08 10					11 40				15 14					18 40		
Pickering § d				08 45	09 00				12 00				16 00				
Goathland § d				09 42	09 50			12 30	12 50			16 25	16 50				
Grosmont d	08 14			10 00	10 10	11 44		13 10	13 10	15 18		16 45	17 10		18 44		
Sleights d	08 23					11 53				15 27					18 53		
Ruswarp d	08 28					11 58				15 32					18 58		
Whitby a	08 35			10 20	10 35	12 05		13 30	13 35	15 39		17 10	17 35		19 05		

For general notes see front of timetable
For details of catering facilities see Directory of Train Operators
§ North Yorkshire Moors Railway. For full service between Pickering, Goathland and Grosmont, please refer to separate publicity.

A From Bishop Auckland (Table 44)
B 27 and 28 December
C 21 to 28 March and 4 May
D From 25 March
E From Hexham (Table 48)
G 29 December
H 22 March to 5 April, 19 April and from 3 May
b Change at Darlington and Middlesbrough

Appendix 5

Whitby Train Departures (Summer Saturdays 1939 and 1955)

July 1939

Town	W Cliff	Destination
06.45	06.56	Scarborough
06.54		Middlesbrough (via EVL)
07.07		Malton
07.15	07.23	Middlesbrough
07.25		Glaisdale
08.00		Malton
	08.24	Scarborough
09.15		West Cliff
09.20		Goathland
	09.31	Scarborough
	09.35	Middlesbrough
	09.37	Town
09.40		London Kings' X (Restaurant Car Train)
09.54		West Cliff
10.00		Malton
	10.07	Scarborough
10.10		West Hartlepool (via EVL)
	10.12	Town
10.30		West Cliff
10.35		Goathland
	10.49	Middlesbrough
	10.50	Scarborough
	10.55	Town
11.15		Malton
	11.21	Scarborough
11.25		West Cliff
	11.33	Town
	11.42	Scarborough
11.45		Leeds
	11.46	Town
	11.58	Town
	12.16	Scarborough
12.10		Leeds
12.23		West Cliff
12.30	12.44	Scarborough
12.40		Glaisdale
12.50		Goathland
	12.56	Middlesbrough
	12.58	Town
13.15		West Cliff
13.20		Stockton (via EVL)
	13.28	Scarborough
13.32		Malton
	13.32	Town
	13.54	Scarborough
14.08		West Cliff
14.15		Goathland
	14.20	Scarborough
	14.32	Thornaby
	14.33	Town
14.45		Malton

July 1955

Town	W Cliff	Destination
06.47		Middlesbrough (via EVL)
06.52	07.00	Middlesbrough
07.02		York
07.38		Goathland
	08.10	Scarborough
09.00		York & London Kings' X
09.05		West Cliff
09.20		York
	09.24	Scarborough
	09.24	Middlesbrough
	09.29	Town
	09.55	Scarborough
10.12		West Cliff
	10.24	Scarborough
10.26		York
	10.30	Town
10.45		West Cliff
	10.54	Town
	11.11	Scarborough
	11.25	Town
11.36		York
	11.53	Scarborough
	11.57	Town
12.00		Middlesbrough (via EVL)
	12.17	Scarborough
12.30		West Cliff
12.35		Goathland
	12.46	Scarborough
	12.56	Middlesbrough
	13.01	Town
	13.41	Scarborough
13.55	14.06	Scarborough
14.10		Leeds
	14.16	Middlesbrough
	15.02	Town
15.15		Malton
	15.35	Town
	16.03	Middlesbrough
16.05		Battersby
16.20	16.31	Scarborough
	17.10	Middlesbrough
17.35		Middlesbrough (via EVL)
	17.45	Middlesbrough
17.58		West Cliff
	18.19	Scarborough
	18.28	Town
18.33	18.41	Middlesbrough
18.57		York
	18.58	West Hartlepool
19.13		West Cliff
	19.30	Stockton

July 1939			July 1955		
Town	W Cliff	Destination	Town	W Cliff	Destination
15.05		West Cliff	19.30	1941	Scarborough
	15.24	Scarborough	19.35		Middlesbrough (via EVL)
	15.35	Middlesbrough		19.45	Town
	15.36	Town	20.05		West Cliff
15.38		Castleton		20.19	Darlington
15.44		West Cliff		20.22	Town
15.53		Malton	20.33		Middlesbrough (via EVL)
16.07		West Cliff		21.04	Stockton/West Hartlepool
	16.23	Scarborough		21.26	Town
16.25		Goathland			
	16.27	Town			
	17.02	Town			
17.15		West Cliff			
	17.32	Middlesbrough			
	17.33	Town			
17.47		Stockton (via EVL)			
18.02		West Cliff			
18.05		Leeds			
	18.21	Scarborough			
	18.20	West Hartlepool			
18.25		Glaisdale			
	18.25	Town			
	18.59	Middlesbrough			
19.00		Malton			
19.10	19.19	West Hartlepool			
19.25		West Cliff			
	19.49	Stockton (via Middlesbrough)			
	19.51	Scarborough			
	19.55	Town			
19.57		Middlesbrough (via EVL)			
20.12		Stockton (via EVL)			
	20.27	Stockton (via Middlesbrough)			
	20.57	Stockton (via Middlesbrough)			
	20.58	Town			
20.40		West Cliff			
21.05		Goathland			
21.25		Middlesbrough (via EVL)			
	21.27	Stockton (via Middlesbrough)			
21.38		West Cliff			
	21.58	West Hartlepool			
	22.00	Scarborough			
	22.04	Town			
22.20	22.36	Scarborough			
	22.38	Stockton (via Middlesbrough)			
	23.57	Town			
	00.44	Town			

Appendix 6

Locomotive Shed Allocations (1920-1963) — Malton, Pickering and Whitby

	Malton								Pickering (ii)						Whitby				
Loco Class (i)	1920	1923	1933	1939	1950	1955	1959	1963 (vi)	1933	1939	1950	1955	1920	1923	1933	1939	1950	1955	1959 (v)
A6 (W) 4-6-2T													692	686 689 691 692 695	686 688 689 691 692 695	686 688 691 692 695			
A7 (Y) 4-6-2T			1136																
A8 4-6-2T						69877	69861 69886									1523 1527 2155	69858 69860 69861 69864 69865 69888 69890	69860 69861 69864 69865 69888 68890	
38 4-4-0	126																		
D20 (R) 4-4-0																201 (iii)			
D23 (G) 4-4-0		214																	
D49 4-4-0											62774								
F4 (GE) 2-4-2T					67155														
F8 (A) 2-4-2T	419 1580	201 419 1580 1581	262 1580										201 205 537 1579	490 537 1577 1579 1583					
G5 (O) 0-4-4T	394 2088	394 505	394 505	381 394 505 1886 1888	67273 67275 67330 67332 67349	67289 67293 67319 67332			1888			67308	1334 1739 1914	1319 1739 1914	1319 1739 1865 1914	1319 1739 1865	67302 67335	67240 67302	
G6 (BTP) 0-4-4T	28 297 466 604																		

Loco Class (i)	Malton								Pickering (ii)						Whitby				
	1920	1923	1933	1939	1950	1955	1959	1963 (vi)	1933	1939	1950	1955	1920	1923	1933	1939	1950	1955	1959 (v)
398 0-6-0	90 327 636	616																	
1001 0-6-0	1275																		
J21 (C) 0-6-0																			
J22 (59) 0-6-0	682	235 440 506 508 812 1106											142 192 208 1489	142 208 1489					
J23 (H&B) 0-6-0			2447 2454 2455 2470 2515						2453						2440 2459 2476 2522				
J24(P) 0-6-0			1896	1821 1844 2892 1951 1958	65600 65631 65636 65640 65642 65644									1952	1947 1958	1850 1947	65621 65624 65627 65628		
J25(P1) 0-6-0													2060	2060				65647 65663 65685	
J26(P2) 0-0-0			(1)	831 1159															
J27(P3) 0-6-0						65827 65844 65848 65849	65827 65844 65848 65849	65844 65849 65888								1231			
J39 0-6-0						64928 64938 64947 64867	64928 64938												
N8 (B) 0-6-2T	860	860	860																
N9 (N) 0-6-2T										1645									
Q5 (T) 0-8-0				647															

Loco Class (i)	Malton								Pickering (ii)						Whitby				
	1920	1923	1933	1939	1950	1955	1959	1963 (vi)	1933	1939	1950	1955	1920	1923	1933	1939	1950	1955	1959 (v)
Y1 0-4-0T			171	171	68147 68150														
Y3 0-4-0T									81	192	68157								
LMR 4MT 2-6-4T																			42083 42084 42085
LMR 2MT 2-6-0								46413 46473											
LMR 2MT 2-6-2T							41251 41265	41251											
BR Std 3MT 2-6-0																			77004 77013
BR Std 4MT 2-6-4T																		80116 80117 (iv)	
BR Std 3MT 2-6-2T							82027 82029	82027 92028 82029											
Sentinel (2cyl)			2236	2236															
Sentinel (6cyl)															2136 2257	2219 246 248			
	15	15	15	15	14	13	12	9	3	2	2	1	13	18	18	18	13	13	5

Notes:

i) NER Classification in brackets

ii) Pickering was a sub-shed of Whitby, followed by Malton (locos in later days supplied by Malton)

iii)Allocated 01.07 to 11.09.39 only

iv) Followed by 80118/119/120

v) Allocation at date of closure (06.04.1959)

vi) Malton allocation at closure (13.04.1963)

Source: Yeadon's Register of LNER Locomotives; North Eastern Locomotive Sheds (K Hoole); Ian Allan Locoshed records (Yeadon preferred where discrepancies occur between sources)

Appendix 7

List of Signal Boxes and Stations, Rillington-Whitby (post-1900)

Location	Mileage		Comment
	Miles	Yards	
Rillington Junction SB	0	5	Replaced by new box 07.06.59; New box closed and Automatic Half Barrier Crossing commissioned 31.10.93
MARISHES ROAD STATION	3	143	Closed 06.03.65
Marishes Road SB	3	215	Closed 06.03.65 (i)
Black Bull	4	1750	Converted to Gate Box by 1914; closed 06.03.65 (i)
Mill Lane Junction	6	357	Closed 06.03.65 (i)
Hungate	6	806	Converted to Gate Box c 1900; closed 06.03.65 (i)
Bridge Street	6	960	Closed 06.03.65 (i)
PICKERING STATION	6	1096	Closed 06.03.65; re-opened 24.05.75
High Mill	6	1377	Closed 06.03.65 (i)
HIGH MILL STATION	7	0	Opened 22.04.73; closed 24.05.75
New Bridge	7	815	Closed 06.03.65; fully re-commissioned 1986 (i)
Farworth	19	1297	Closed 31.12.16
LEVISHAM STATION	12	944	Closed 06.03.65; re-opened 21.04.73
Leivisham SB	12	988	Closed 06.03.65; re-commissioned 10.05.75
Newton Dale	15	437	Converted to Ground Frame1930; closed 1952
NEWTON DALE HALT	15	1330	Opened 23.04.81
Goathland Summit	19	58	Closed 1964
Goathland SB	21	164	Closed 06.03.65; re-opened 21.04.73 (ii)
GOATHLAND STATION	21	200	Opened 01.07.1865; closed 06.03.65; re-opened 21.04.73 (ii)
Deviation Junction	24	346	Converted to Ground Frame 1930; closed 1951
Grosmont LC/signal cabin	24	752	Gate Box re-opened as block post 21.04.73; closed 1996 (ii)
Grosmont Crossing SB (New)	24	780	Opened 1996
GROSMONT STATION	24	830	
Grosmont Station SB (junction)	24	882	Closed 1972
Birtley Mines	25	280	Closed by 1908
Eskdale Mines	25	401	Closed by 1931 (demolished 1947)
SLEIGHTS STATION	27	1380	
Sleights SB	27	1454	Closed 09.1984
Ruswarp SB	29	645	Converted to Gate Box; Converted to Automatic Barrier
Crossing and de-staffed 1986			
RUSWARP STATION	29	652	
Foundry Siding	29	1567	Converted to Ground Frame 1930
Bog Hall Junction	30	894	Closed 1984
Whitby Town SB	30	894	Closed 1984
WHITBY TOWN STATION	30	1374	Closed 1984

Notes:

i) Marishes Rd, Black Bull, Mill Lane, Hungate, High Mill, New Bridge LCs manually operated 06.03.65 to 01.07.66

ii) The re-opening date shown is that for commencement of public services; in use for NYMR members passenger trains from 28.03.70

iii) Ground Frames serving sidings were located at various times at:

Black Bull Siding (Up line)	(4 miles 1388 yds)	
Raindale Siding (Down line)	(13 miles 887 yds)	
Ellerbeck Siding (Up line)	(18 miles 924 yds)	(from 1926 – controlled by Goathland Summit SB)
Dorsley Bank Siding (Down line)	(25 miles 1048 yds) (iv)	
Newbiggin Siding (Down line)	(25 miles 1584 yds)	
Gantry Siding (Up line)	(26 miles 278 yds)	
Woodlands Siding (Down line)	(26 miles 1210 yds) (iv)	
Sneaton Siding (Up line)	(29 miles 275 yds)	

iv) Some records suggest that Dorsley Bank Siding and Woodlands Siding may at one time have been classed as Signal Cabins.

v) Other ground frames may have existed to serve sidings in the 19th Century.

vi) Level crossings and solely Gate Boxes with no point controls not shown

Appendix 8

NYMR Principal Owned and Home-Based Locomotives, as at 01.01.2008

No	Name	Type	Owner
Owned or in long-term custody of NYMR			
Steam			
5		Robert Stephenson 0-6-2T	
29		Kitson 0-6-2T	
3672	Dame Vera Lynn	WD Class 2-10-0	
2253		USA Class S160 2-8-0	
30926	Repton	SR Schools 4-4-0	
34101	Hartland	SR Rebuilt West Country 4-6-2	
45428	Eric Treacy	LMS Class 5MT 4-6-0	
75029		BR Standard Class 4MT 4-6-0	
80135		BR Standard Class 4MT 2-6-4T	
3180	Antwerp	WD 0-6-0ST (On loan from National Mining Museum) *	
Diesel			
D2207		BR Drewery Class 04 shunter	
12139	Neil Barker	English Electric Class 11 350hp shunter	
08556		English Electric Class 08 BR 350hp shunter	
08850		English Electric Class 08 BR 350hp shunter	
D5032	Helen Turner	BR Sulzer Class 24	
D5061		BR Sulzer Class 24	
D7541		BR Sulzer Class 25 *	
D7628	Sybilla	BR Sulzer Class 25	
101105		Metro-Cammell Class 101 3 car DMU	
205208		BR Class 205 Diesel Electric MU *	
Home-based steam locomotives and others subject to long term hire agreements			**Owner**
825		SR S15 Class 4-6-0	Essex Locomotive Society
5224		GWR 42xx Class 2-8-0T	Peter Waterman
6619		GWR 56xx Class 0-6-2T	Kevin Gould/Peter Proud
45212		LMS Class 5MT 4-6-0	Keighley & Worth Valley Railway
44767	George Stephenson	LMS Class 5MT 4-6-0	Ian Storey
49395		LNWR Class G2 0-8-0	National Railway Museum
60007	Sir Nigel Gresley	LNER A4 Class 4-6-2	Sir Nigel Gresley Locomotive Preservation Trust
61264		LNER B1 Class 4-6-0	Thompson B1 Locomotive Society
62005		LNER (BR built) K1 Class 2-6-0	NELPG
63395		NER T2 Class 0-8-0	NELPG
65894		NER P3 Class 0-6-0	NELPG
69023	Joem	NER E1 design (BR built) J72 Class 0-6-0T	NELPG

* Possible transfer/sale pending

Appendix 9

Gradient Profile and Signal Box Diagrams

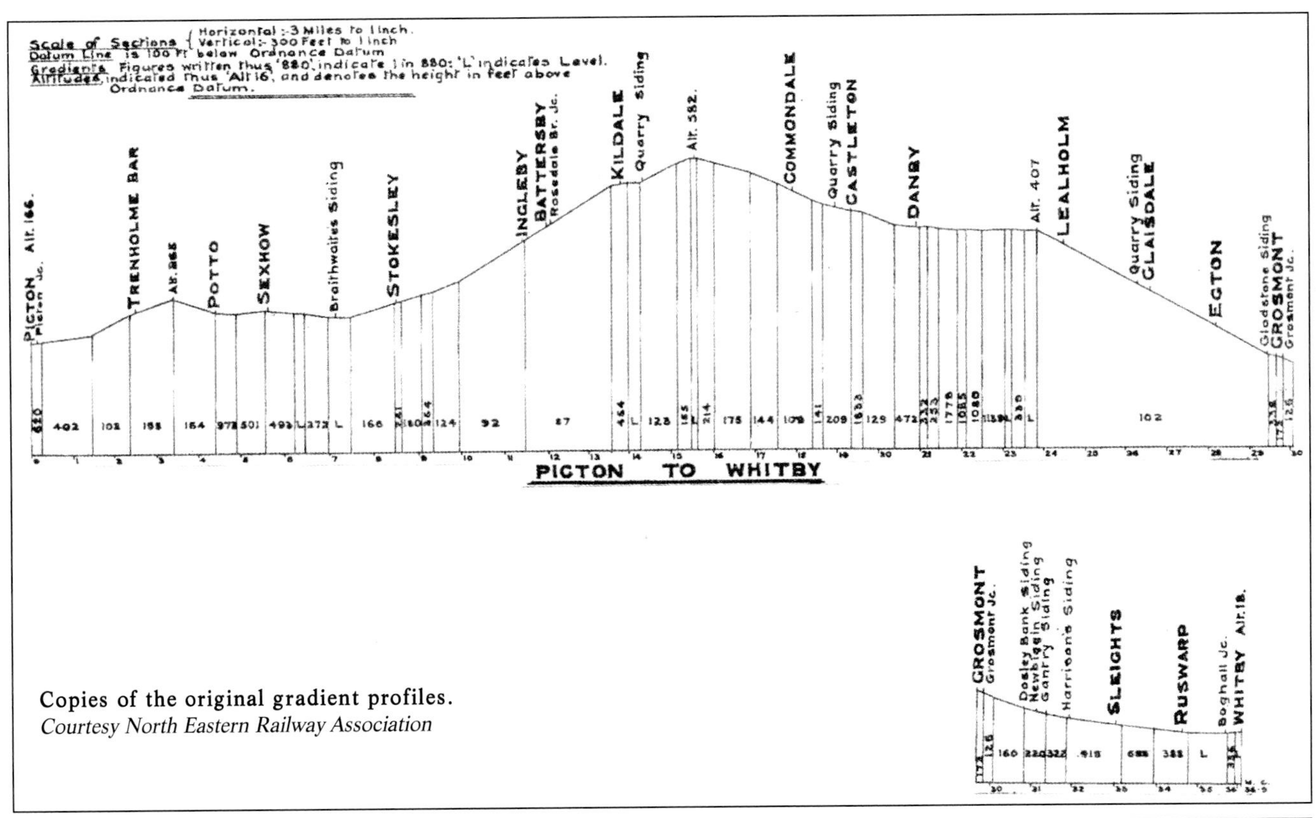

Copies of the original gradient profiles.
Courtesy North Eastern Railway Association

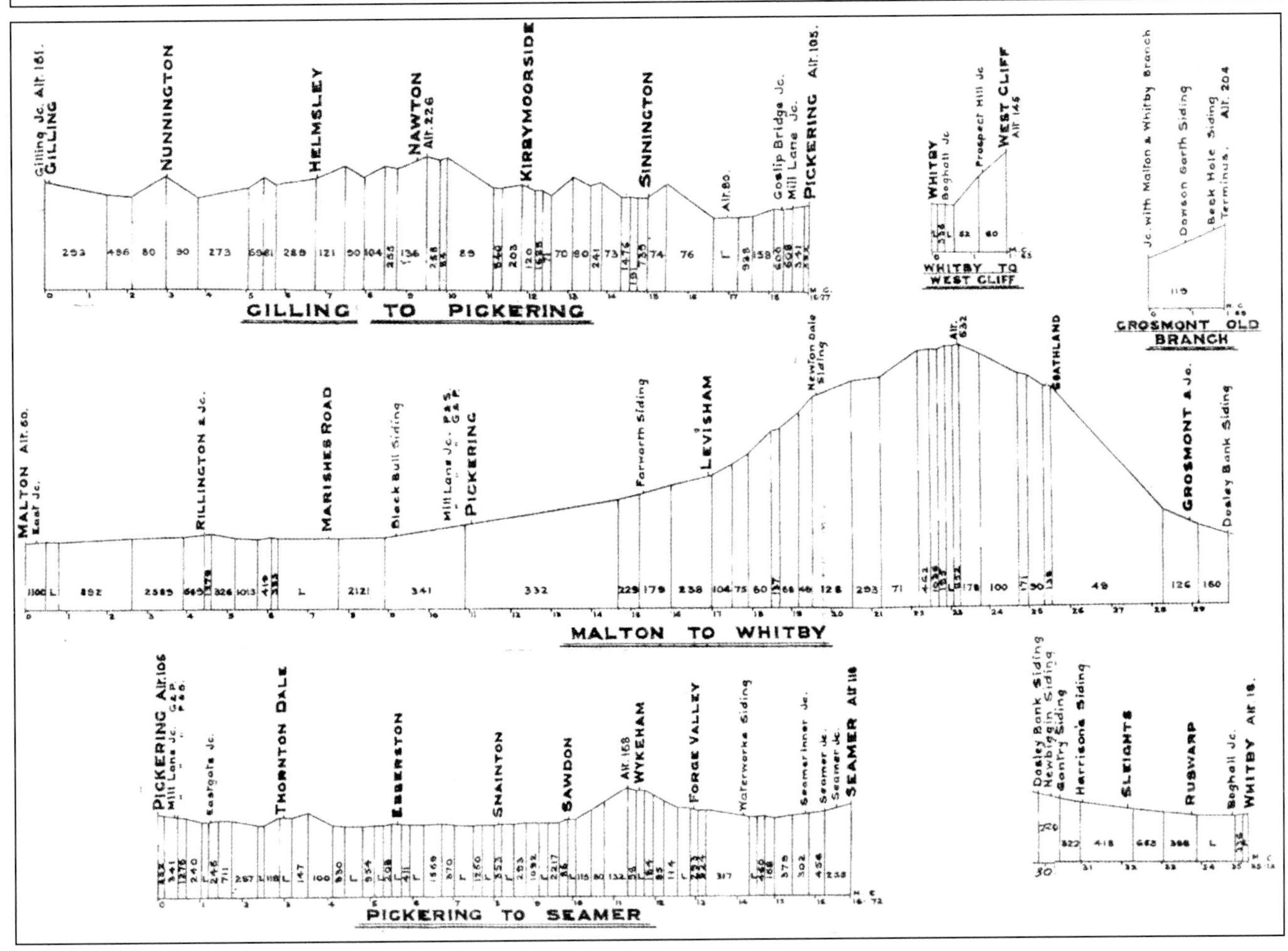

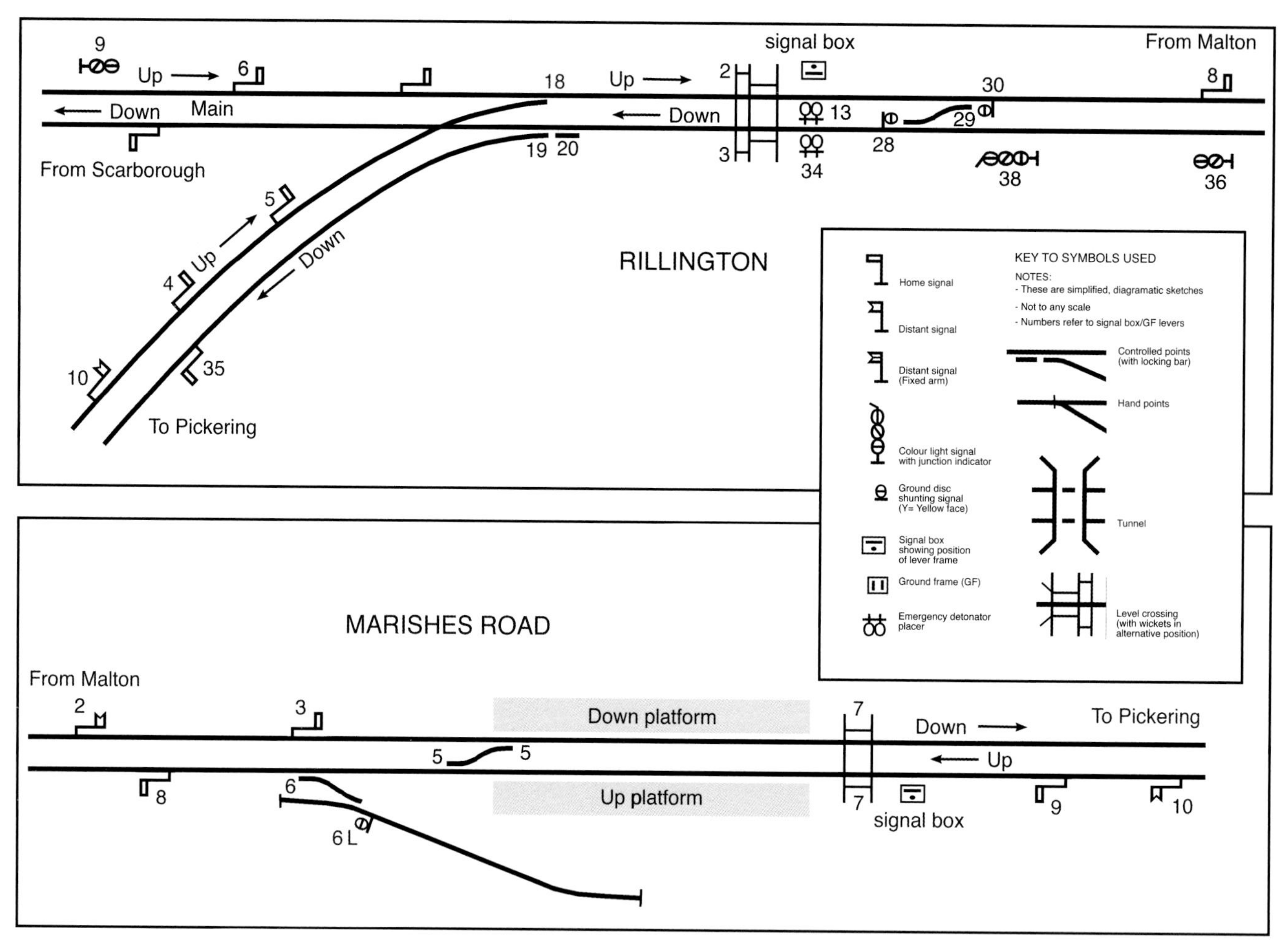
RILLINGTON
signal box
From Malton
Up
Down
Main
From Scarborough
To Pickering
KEY TO SYMBOLS USED
NOTES:
- These are simplified, diagramatic sketches
- Not to any scale
- Numbers refer to signal box/GF levers
Home signal
Distant signal
Distant signal (Fixed arm)
Colour light signal with junction indicator
Ground disc shunting signal (Y= Yellow face)
Signal box showing position of lever frame
Ground frame (GF)
Emergency detonator placer
Controlled points (with locking bar)
Hand points
Tunnel
Level crossing (with wickets in alternative position)
MARISHES ROAD
From Malton
Down platform
Up platform
To Pickering
signal box

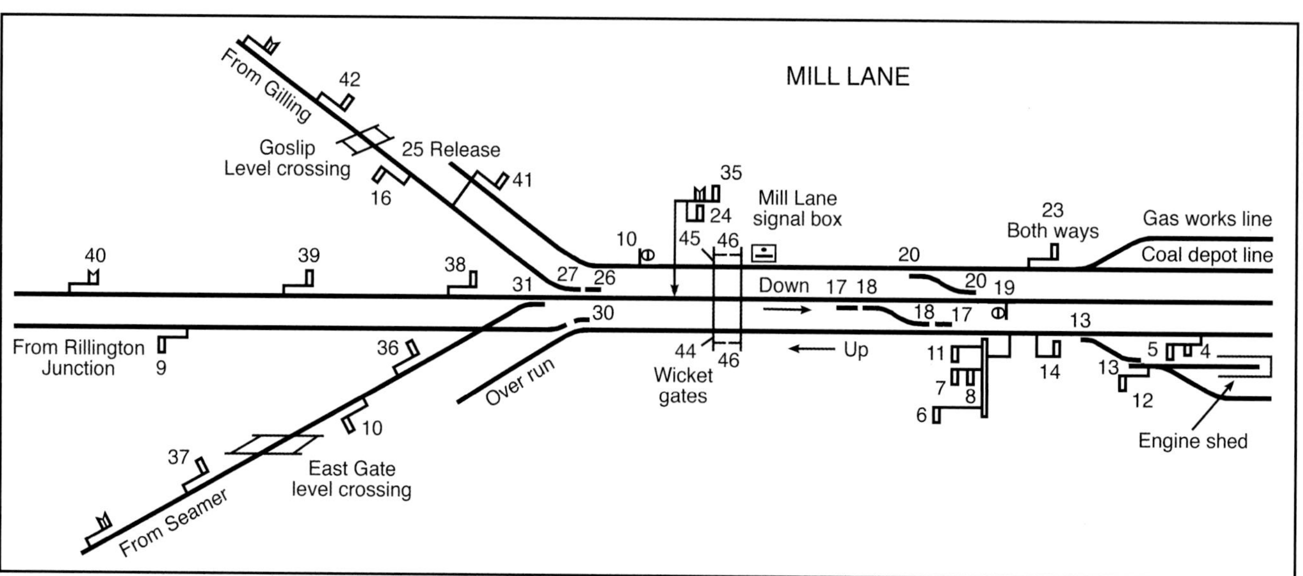
MILL LANE
From Gilling
Goslip Level crossing
25 Release
Mill Lane signal box
23 Both ways
Gas works line
Coal depot line
From Rillington Junction
Over run
Wicket gates
Engine shed
East Gate level crossing
From Seamer

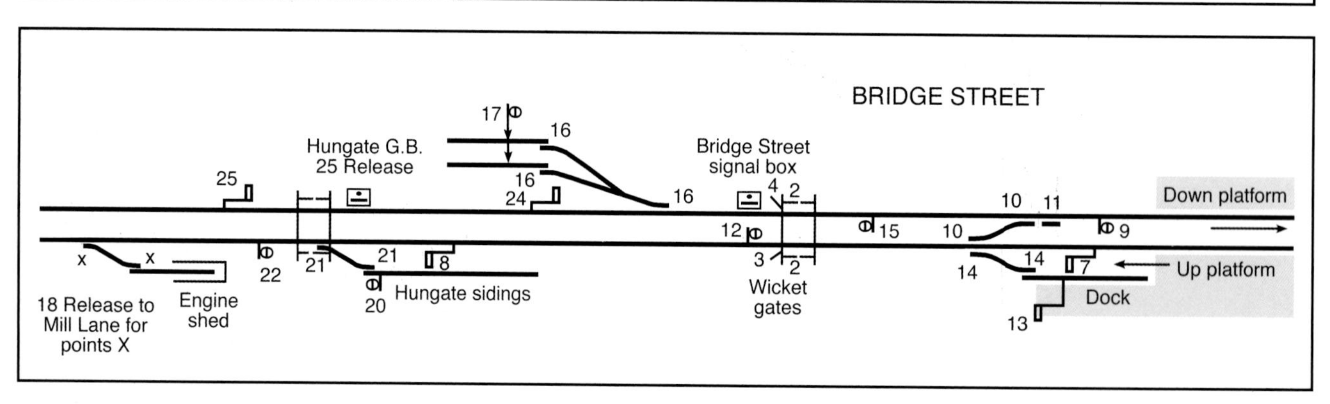
BRIDGE STREET
Hungate G.B. 25 Release
Bridge Street signal box
Down platform
Up platform
Dock
Wicket gates
Hungate sidings
Engine shed
18 Release to Mill Lane for points X

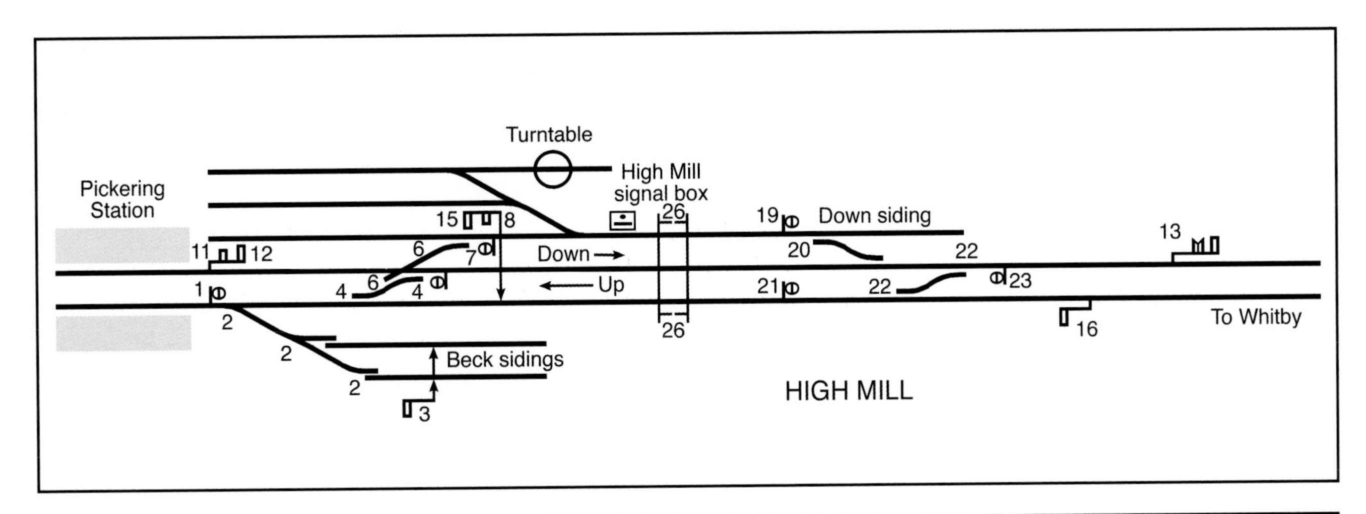
Turntable
High Mill
signal box
Pickering
Station
Down siding
Down
Up
Beck sidings
To Whitby
HIGH MILL

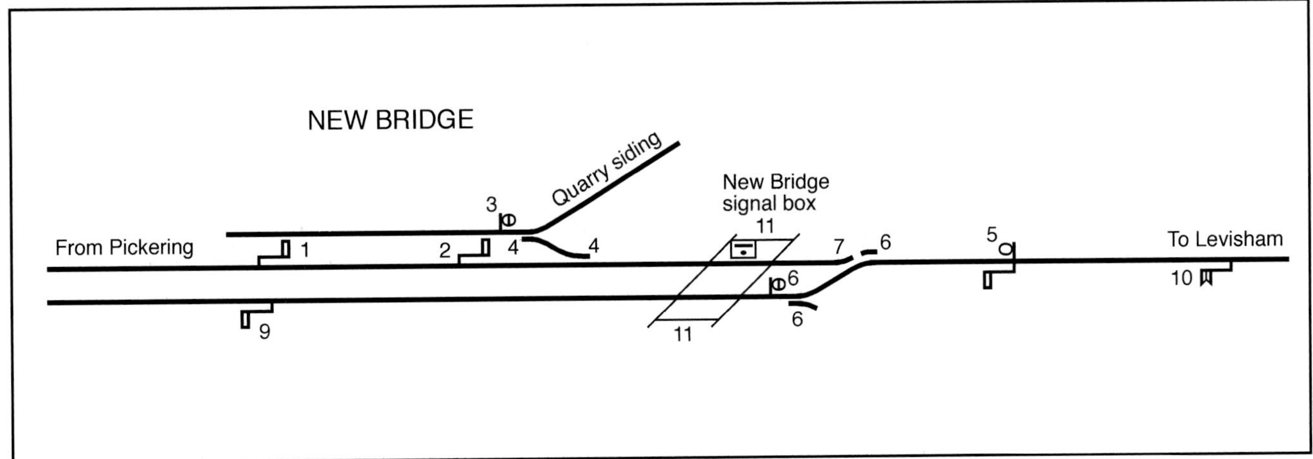
NEW BRIDGE
Quarry siding
New Bridge
signal box
From Pickering
To Levisham

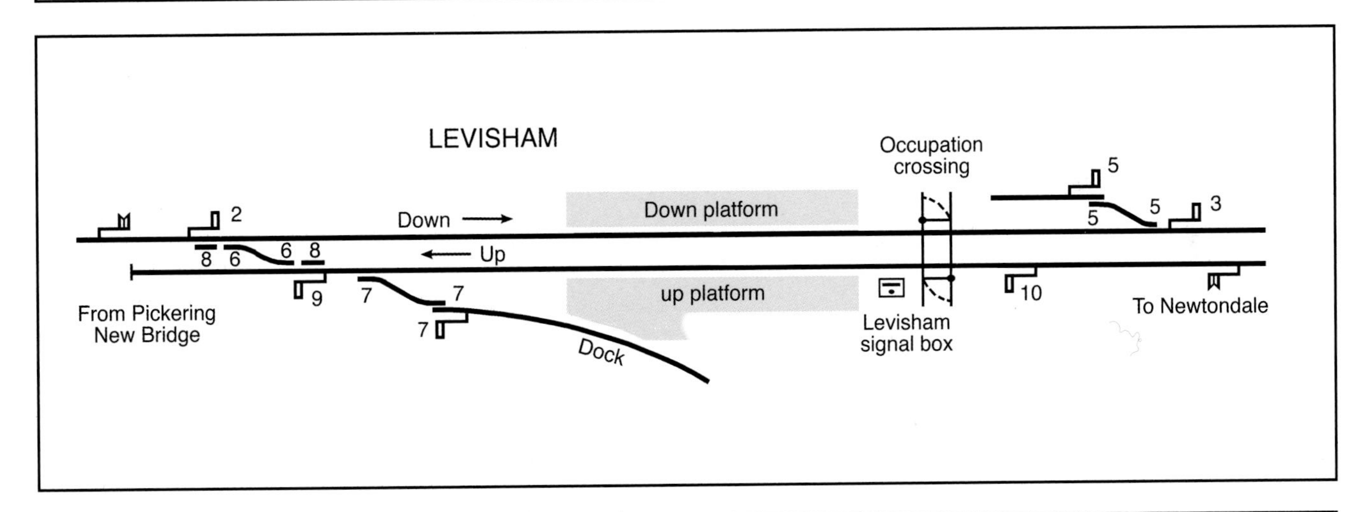
LEVISHAM
Occupation
crossing
Down
Down platform
Up
up platform
From Pickering
New Bridge
Dock
Levisham
signal box
To Newtondale

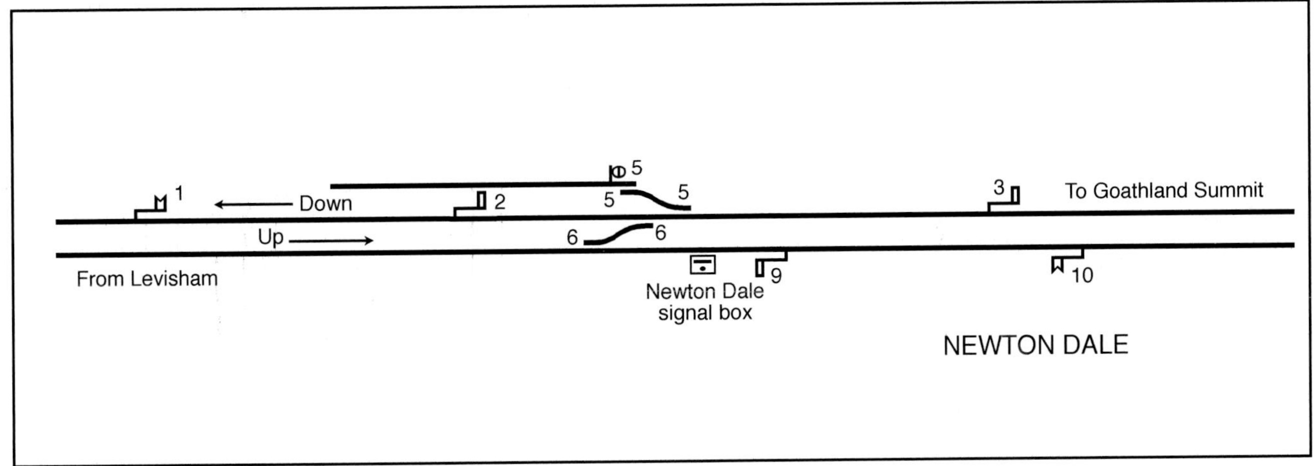
Down
Up
To Goathland Summit
From Levisham
Newton Dale
signal box
NEWTON DALE

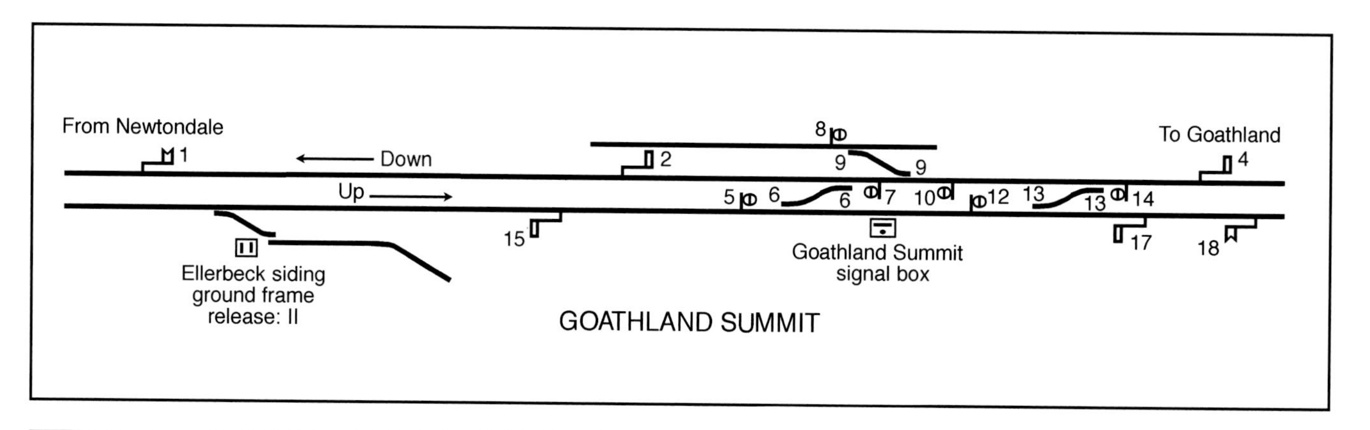
From Newtondale
Down
Up
To Goathland
Ellerbeck siding ground frame release: II
Goathland Summit signal box
GOATHLAND SUMMIT

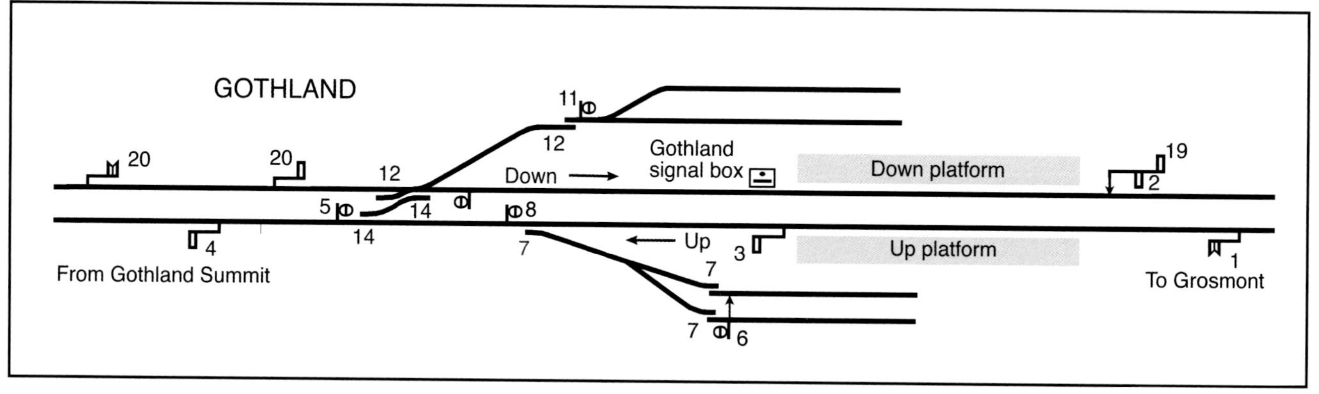
GOTHLAND
Down
Gothland signal box
Down platform
Up
Up platform
From Gothland Summit
To Grosmont

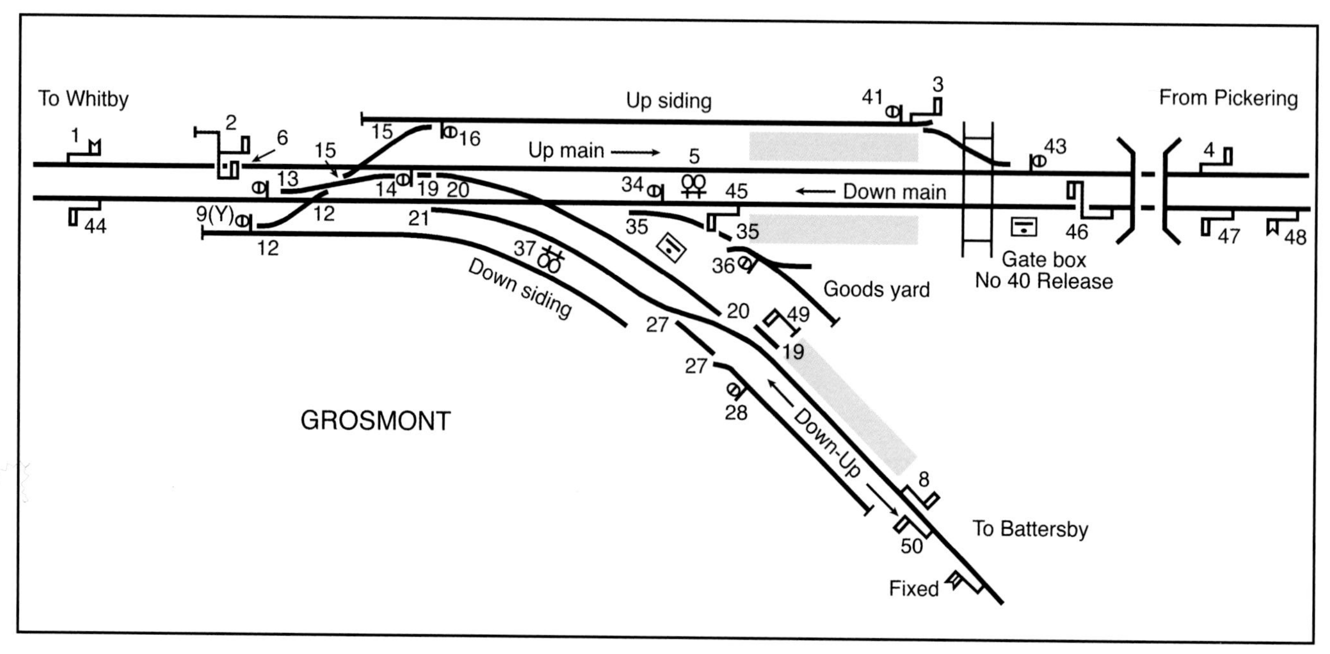
To Whitby
Up siding
From Pickering
Up main
Down main
Gate box
No 40 Release
Goods yard
Down siding
Down-Up
To Battersby
Fixed
GROSMONT

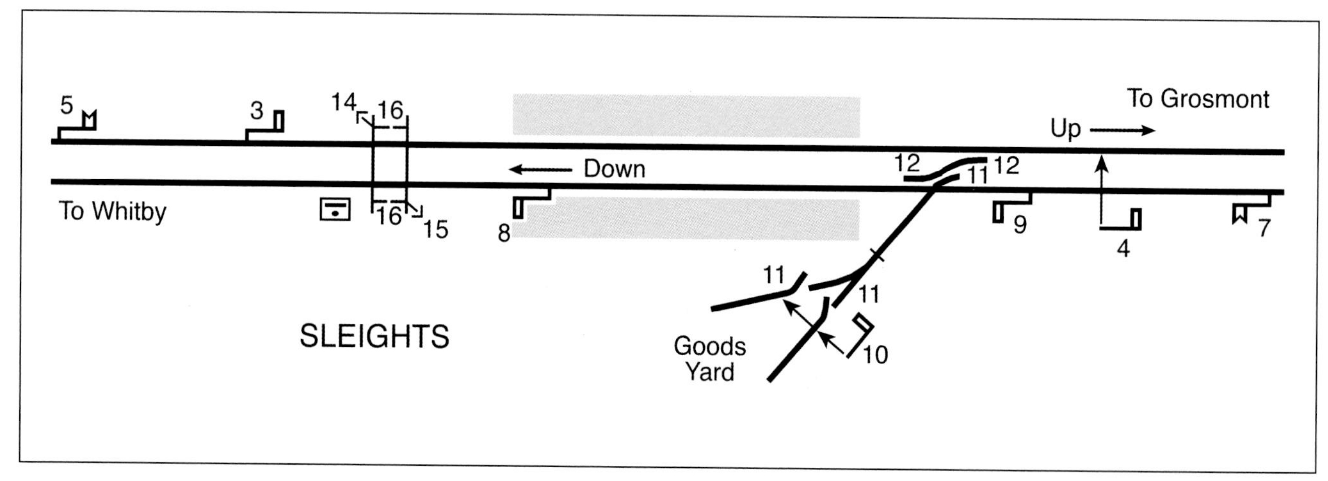
To Grosmont
Up
Down
To Whitby
Goods Yard
SLEIGHTS

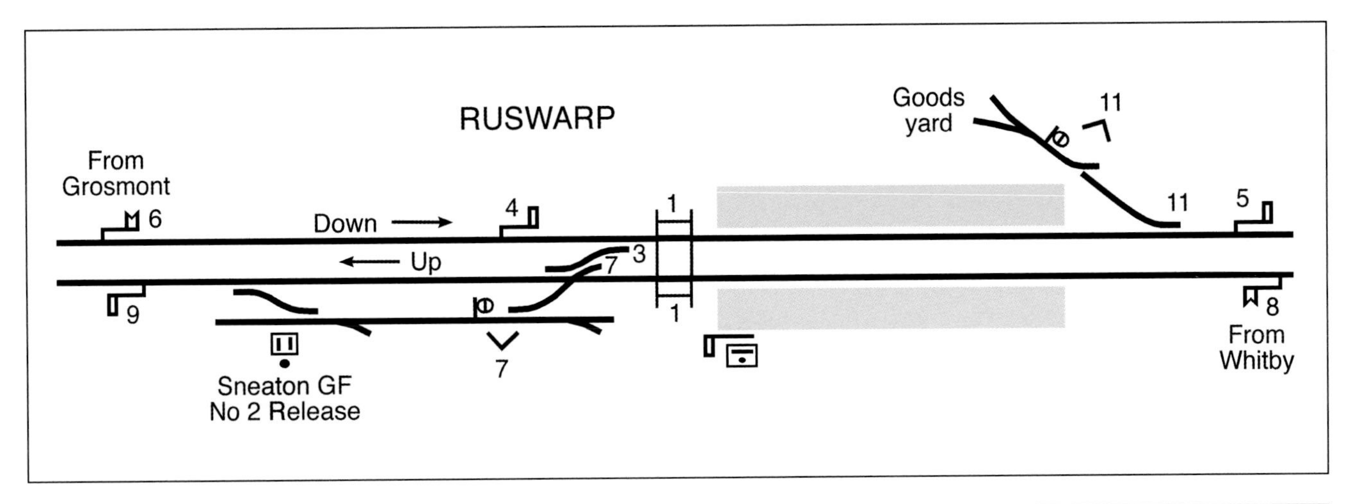

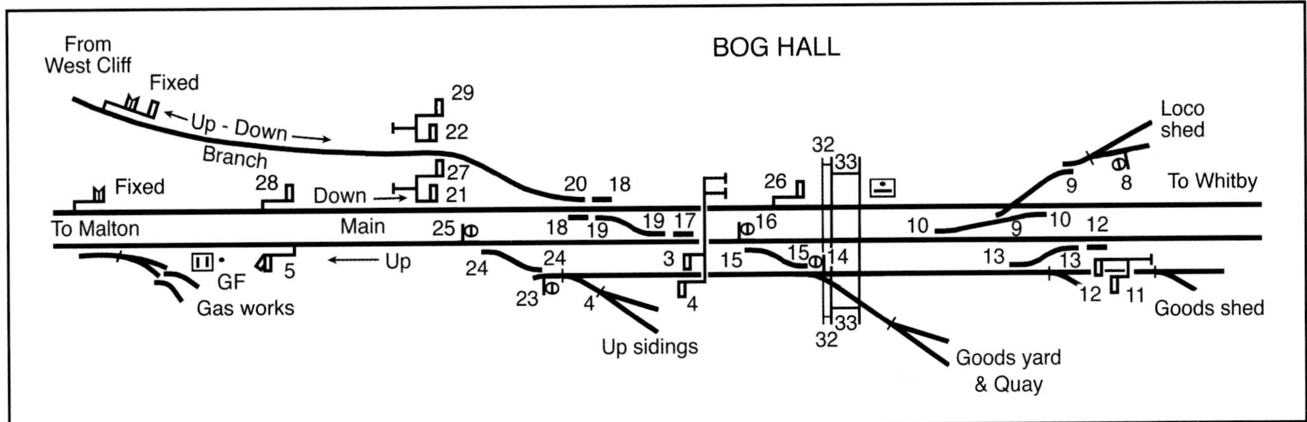

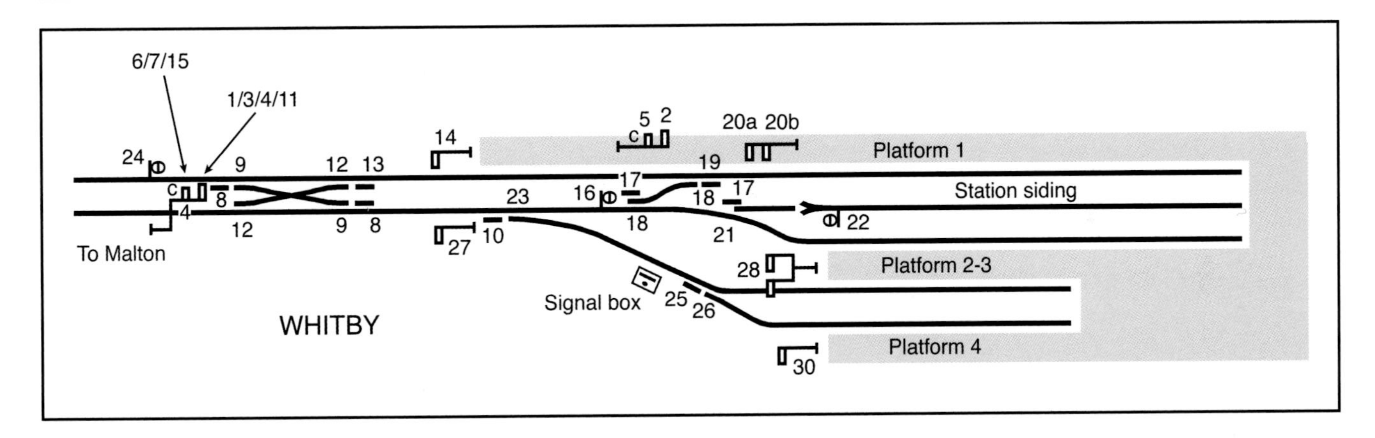

Appendix 10

NYMR Heritage and Other Awards

Wooden waiting room/booking office, relocated from Sleights to extended down platform at Grosmont: Commendation in *Railway World* category, 1990 Ian Allan Railway Heritage Awards

Renovation/rebuilding of Levisham waiting and ladies' room, including provision of completely new 'period' interior: Ian Allan Publishing Award, 1999 National Railway Heritage Awards

Renovation of goods shed (including conversion into café) and coal and lime cells at Goathland: Ian Allan Publishing Award, 2000 National Railway Heritage Awards

New 'NER' signal box at Grosmont: Westinghouse Signalling Award, 2001 National Railway Heritage Awards

Disabled toilet at Goathland in box railvan: London Transport Mobility Award, 2007 National Railway Heritage Awards

Large Railway of the Year Award, Heritage Railway Association, 2007

Visitor Attraction of the Year (50,000 and over), Yorkshire Moors & Coast Tourism Partnership, 2007

Index